PENGUIN CLASSICS

LIVES OF ROMAN CHRISTIAN WOMEN

CAROLINNE WHITE was born in London and read Classics and Modern Languages at St Hugh's College, Oxford. She wrote a doctoral thesis on Christian ideas of friendship in the fourth century, published in 1992. After two years spent teaching Latin at the University of South Africa in Pretoria, she returned to Oxford where she worked on the supplement to the Liddell and Scott Greek Lexicon and taught Patristic and Medieval Latin. She now divides her time between work as an assistant editor on the *Dictionary of Medieval Latin from British Sources*, translation from Latin and her four children. Her publications include a translation of the correspondence between Jerome and Augustine (1990), *Early Christian Lives* (Penguin, 1998), an anthology of *Early Christian Latin Poets* in translation (2000) and *The Rule of Benedict* (Penguin, 2008).

Lives of Roman Christian Women

Translated and edited with an Introduction and Notes by CAROLINNE WHITE

PENGUIN BOOKS

PENGUIN CLASSICS

Published by the Penguin Group
Penguin Books Ltd, 80 Strand, London WC2R ORL, England
Penguin Group (USA) Inc., 375 Hudson Street, New York, New York 10014, USA
Penguin Group (Canada), 90 Eglinton Avenue East, Suite 700, Toronto, Ontario, Canada M4P 2Y3
(a division of Pearson Penguin Canada Inc.)
Penguin Ireland, 25 St Stephen's Green, Dublin 2, Ireland (a division of Penguin Books Ltd)
Penguin Group (Australia), 250 Camberwell Road, Camberwell, Victoria 3124, Australia
(a division of Pearson Australia Group Pty Ltd)
Penguin Books India Pvt Ltd, 11 Community Centre, Panchsheel Park, New Delhi – 110 017, India
Penguin Group (NZ), 67 Apollo Drive, Rosedale, North Shore 0632, New Zealand
(a division of Pearson New Zealand Ltd)
Penguin Books (South Africa) (Pty) Ltd, 24 Sturdee Avenue, Rosebank, Johannesburg 2196, South Africa

Penguin Books Ltd, Registered Offices: 80 Strand, London WC2R ORL, England

www.penguin.com

This selection and translation first published 2010

1

Translation and editorial material copyright © Carolinne White, 2010
All rights reserved

The moral right of the translator and editor has been asserted

Set in 10.25/12.25 pt Postscript Adobe Sabon
Typeset by Palimpsest Book Production Limited,
Grangemouth, Stirlingshire
Printed in England by Clays Ltd, St Ives plc

ISBN: 978-0-141-44193-1

www.greenpenguin.co.uk

Contents

Chronology

(Some birth or death dates are approximate)

203 deaths of Perpetua and Felicitas in Carthage
251–356 Antony of Egypt
254 death of Origen

313 Emperor Constantine decrees religious tolerance throughout the Roman Empire
325 Council of Nicaea
325–380 Macrina
325–410 Marcella
331–385 Gregory of Nyssa
340 birth of Melania the elder
347 births of Paula the elder and of Jerome

364 Valens, supporter of Arian Christians, becomes emperor
368–431 Palladius
around 368 birth of Eustochium
379 Melania the elder settles in Jerusalem; Council of Antioch
380 The Emperors Theodosius and Gratian decree Christianity
   to be official religion of the Roman Empire
383 birth of Melania the younger
386 Jerome, Paula the elder and Eustochium settle in Bethlehem

around 400 birth of Paula the younger
404 death of Paula the elder
410 Sack of Rome by Alaric and the Visigoths; Melania the

younger and her husband Pinianus flee to North Africa;
death of Melania the elder
417 Melania the younger and Pinianus settle in Jerusalem
419 deaths of Eustochium and (before 419) Laeta
420 death of Jerome
436 Melania the younger visits Constantinople
439 death of Melania the younger

Introduction

In case anyone should think to criticize me for praising a woman, I would say that one should not refer to her [Melania] as a woman but as a man because she behaved like a man.[1]

What wonderful passion and courage! It is hard to believe that these virtues could be found in a woman.[2]

If indeed she [Macrina] was a woman, for I am not sure it is right to refer to someone by their sex when she had transcended her sex.[3]

The sceptical reader may perhaps laugh at me for wasting so much time in praise of mere women. But if he remembers those holy women, the companions of our Lord and Saviour, who took care of him using their own possessions, and the three women called Mary who stood before the cross . . . he will see that he is guilty of arrogance rather than I of foolishness.[4]

What a woman Melania is, if one can call so virile a Christian a woman! She . . . is a soldier for Christ with the virtues of St Martin, though she is of the weaker sex.[5]

Perpetua and Felicitas overcame the natural weakness of women, allowing a manly spirit to achieve great things in them.[6]

These quotations referring to women whose lives are described in this volume provide us with some indication of the general attitude to women in the Roman Empire during late antiquity, the period when the classical age was being transformed into the medieval with the added ingredient of Christianity, when paganism was starting to decline and the Roman Empire was experiencing the first shocks of barbarian invasions. In the course of this book we move from Perpetua and Felicitas in North Africa at the beginning of the third century, to Macrina and her influential family in Turkey during the fifty years after 325, to a network of friends and relations around the Roman aristocratic women Marcella, Melania and Paula in Rome, North Africa and the Holy Land during the period between 350 and 450: most of the writings are biographical and written by men but there is also some much rarer, autobiographical material composed by one woman and a letter written by two women to their friend. The writers of these mini-biographies of women who had chosen martyrdom or a life of asceticism, in other words, of austerity and self-discipline, expected to be mocked or criticized for writing in such laudatory terms about women. However, they justify their decision on the grounds that these women had shed those characteristics thought to be typical of the female sex and become like men in their courage, determination and discipline. Although St Paul had written 'there is no longer male and female, for all of you are one in Christ Jesus',[7] the nature of everyday Roman society meant that Christians of this time found it no less difficult than people of any era to disregard gender differences, but at least some of them believed that if women rejected their reproductive purpose or their familial responsibilities, they could equal men in strength of moral and spiritual commitment; by giving up sex they would slide along the gender scale in the direction of the masculine. As Jerome says in his commentary on Paul's letter to the Ephesians, 'If a woman chooses to serve Christ rather than this world, she will cease to be a woman and be called a man.'[8]

Not that such rejection came easily – indeed it is clear from these accounts that much suffering and sorrow were involved, particularly for those who already had children. It is interesting that Perpetua and Felicitas, who displayed great strength of mind as they faced death in the arena at Carthage in 203, when Christians were still subject to persecution by the non-Christian authorities for refusing to sacrifice to the emperor and the pagan gods, are those whose sufferings as women are perhaps most clearly portrayed. Perpetua chose to die rather than deny that she was a Christian, even though this meant being separated from her baby son whom she had kept with her in prison until she could wean him. Felicitas, Perpetua's servant girl, was glad to give birth in prison so that her pregnancy would not disqualify her from martyrdom: she handed over her daughter to her sister as soon as the baby was born so that she could go from the pain of childbirth to the pain of public death by the sword. The vividness of their sufferings, as they worry about the well-being of their babies, is no doubt partly due to the fact that most of this text is apparently autobiographical, written by Perpetua in the days leading up to their martyrdom. Here we have an account, largely told by a woman, involving imminent death by gruesome and humiliating means, while the other narratives in this volume are written by men about women who, after the official acceptance of Christianity in 313 when Constantine was emperor, chose to prove their commitment to Christ by dying to the world, renouncing the high status and wealth into which they had been born in order to live a life of poverty, chastity and self-discipline. This is true of Macrina, as we see in the description of her life by her brother Gregory of Nyssa; of Paula the elder and Marcella, as we see from what their friend Jerome wrote about them; and of Melania the elder and her granddaughter Melania the younger, as recorded by Palladius and by Gerontius. Two other texts deal with two young girls who Jerome hoped would dedicate their lives to these Christian ideals, which were enjoying a great vogue at the end of the fourth century: he writes to Laeta to try and persuade her to bring up her baby daughter Paula in accordance with them, and to the teenager Eustochium to strengthen her in her resolve to adopt this way of life. We hear of the pain suffered by Paula the elder when she leaves her children in Italy as she sails for the Holy Land: 'she denied that she was a mother to prove herself God's servant. She suffered profound torment and felt that she was being torn limb from limb as she fought against the pain'; we are told of the self-discipline needed when she hears of her beloved youngest child's serious illness far away in Rome; we hear of the sorrow of Macrina's mother Emmelia when her son, who is living a life of ascetic solitude, dies suddenly, and Mela-nia the younger's grief when her remaining child dies. In order to emphasize the strength of these women in putting the ascetic life before their families, their biographers are not afraid to show their feminine characteristics which did not disappear so much as become redirected towards different objects, such as the material well-being of those outside their own family and the spiritual welfare of others.

Rejection of family ties was one way in which to demon-strate self-discipline; the other principal way was by rejection of inherited wealth so as to follow Christ in poverty. The majority of the few women about whom we have detailed knowledge through biographies and letters came from some of the highest-ranking Roman families. Their rejection of the luxurious way of life into which they were born was regarded by most of their Christian contemporaries as highly impressive – or as unsettling rebelliousness by others who were more criti-cal of the ascetic life. Many of the women would nowadays be described as having lived the life of billionaires, surrounded by all sorts of luxuries, owning huge estates around the Mediter-ranean and hundreds of slaves, as well as plenty of liquid assets. Melania the younger, for example, possessed, among all her other properties, a beautiful estate with a spa complex and an outdoor pool, on one side of which lay the sea and on the other extensive woodland containing a variety of animals, so that when she went swimming she could see ships sailing by as well as animals running past. One can just imagine photos of all this appearing in a celebrity magazine! And yet Melania said that she found the hardest thing about adopting chastity and pov-erty was the struggle it involved not against physical tempta-tion and a desire for the life of luxury to which she was accustomed but against her family and the expectations and criticisms of society.

If these Christian women could be said to have deviated from society's norm it may be useful to clarify what the expec-tations were for Roman women of late antiquity. The over-whelming expectation was for women, both Christian and non-Christian, to marry (often in their early teens) and produce children, particularly male heirs: those who were unmarried or childless were restricted by law as to the amount they could inherit or bequeath. Society needed a supply of new citizens: the lower classes needed children as social security and the upper classes needed children who might ensure continuity of the family and inherit the family property, but freeborn women who had three children, or a freedwoman who had four, were rewarded by being granted greater rights of inheritance and more independence. It would seem that there were fewer women than men among the Roman population which would explain the pressure women were under to marry, pressures that are glimpsed in the writings here: Melania the younger was forced to marry at about fourteen and when she and her husband decided to live a life of poverty and chastity, her father reacted badly: she had to bribe her servants to lie to her father, concealing her self-imposed austerity.

On the other hand those who did not want to relinquish their wealth could use their responsibility to their families as a pretext. In his *Lausiac History*, Palladius tells of a wealthy unmarried woman in Alexandria who refused to give anything away to charity despite pressure from the church: instead she adopted her niece as her heir so as to safeguard her wealth, having been deceived by the devil into putting riches before salvation.[9] Such a woman would have had little understanding for Paula who, when criticized for using her children's inheritance to help the poor, retorted that she was leaving her children something far more valuable, namely Christ's mercy. But even if women did marry it was common for them to be widowed early, and then pressure would be put on them to remarry, either for their own security or that of their children or so as to bear more children. Marcella's mother was keen for her young widowed daughter to remarry so that she would have a wealthy man to protect her, but Marcella refused, saying, 'If I wished to marry . . . , I would be looking for a husband, not an inheritance.' Even among Christians there was the feeling that at least one child should take on the family responsibilities.

Jerome's writings provide numerous glimpses of married women in Roman society, often slightly exaggerated to suit his polemical purpose. In *Letter* 22 we see wealthy women who take pride in their husbands' high-ranking positions and in being surrounded by slaves, deriving enjoyment from expensive clothes and entertaining on a lavish scale; women who are only interested in their own appearance and in how much money they have. In his work written to argue against Helvidius' denial of the perpetual virginity of Mary, Jerome gives a picture of the harassed housewife who has no time for the spiritual life:[10] she has to find time to put on make-up so that her husband will think she is more beautiful than she really is; the toddlers are chattering, the servants making a noise, the older children demanding affection and attention, the bills need paying – and then her husband turns up with his business colleagues, expecting to be entertained!

Such was the life of the majority of upper-class women. The women portrayed in this book were considered by those Christians who advocated poverty and chastity as having been granted the grace to reject marriage. Though not unique (there were many holy women whose lives were not recorded by their contemporaries or whose existence is only glimpsed in such writings as the *Lausiac History*), they were regarded as extreme. It was, after all, perfectly possible for a woman to be a Christian within the normal family structure, even married to a pagan husband. Many women were the wives of priests and bishops – married priests were the norm within the church at this period. We know about married Christian women from, for example, the admiring – if also occasionally exasperated – description of Monica by her son Augustine in his *Confessions*; from Gregory of Nazianzus' funeral eulogy on his married sister Gorgonia, and from what he says of his mother Nonna; and from the picture we get of the mother of Gregory of Nyssa and Macrina in Gregory's biography of his sister. Even those writers who are concerned to sing the praises of virginity and widowhood admit that one of the positive things about marriage is that it can bring about the conversion of other family members – indeed, had not St Paul said, 'The unbelieving husband is made holy through his wife'? – as well as producing children who can be dedicated to the ascetic life.[11] Indeed the many women who continued to lead Christian lives within marriage could defend their choice by citing St Paul who, although he does consider the unmarried life superior, says that it is not wrong to marry, and advises younger widows to remarry, bear children and manage their households.[12] In fact the practicalities and demands of everyday life meant that many Christians, as today, were able to turn a deaf ear to Christ's more radical injunctions, some of which seemed decidedly anti-familial and could be interpreted as being in favour of the unmarried life, as for example: 'Whoever comes to me and does not hate father and mother, wife and children . . . and even life itself, cannot be my disciple', and 'Those who belong to this age marry and are given in marriage but those who are considered worthy of a place in that age and in the resurrection from the dead neither marry nor are given in marriage. Indeed they cannot die any more because they are like angels and are children of God.'[13]

So why did some women choose martyrdom or an extreme ascetic life? Both were ways of proving a firm commitment to Christ. In the case of martyrdom, during those times when Christians were persecuted and before Christianity became an officially accepted religion, Christians could be thrown into prison and forced to choose whether to make the required sacrifice to the Roman emperor and deny their commitment to Christ: this would allow them to avoid public execution in the arena. The description of the martyrdom of Perpetua and Felicitas, one of a number of such accounts still in existence from the second and third centuries, reveals how Perpetua refused to give in even to her father's emotional pleading despite the pity she felt for him, asserting that her Christian faith was the very essence of her being. She drew strength from her Christian fellow prisoners, as well as from the series of fascinating dream visions granted to her. When Felicitas goes into premature labour, one of the prison guards taunts her with the fact that her pain and suffering at the present is nothing compared with what she will suffer in the arena in a few days, to which she replies with similarly calm determination and fearlessness that she will in fact find that easier to bear because then Christ will be suffering for her and she for him.

With regard to the ascetic life, those who opted for it were under no compulsion from the state. Their choice, as young virgin, as wife or as widow, was freely made and it was not the state authorities to whom they had to stand up but rather their own family members, especially their fathers or husbands, who did not want the woman to cast off her responsibilities to her family. The ascetic life, a commitment to the family of Christ rather than to the Roman family, did not demand political sub-version as was involved in martyrdom but it did demand a similar spirit of single-minded obstinacy, unless it was chosen on your behalf, as in the case of the infant Paula or Melania the younger's baby daughter, 'consecrated . . . to the life of a virgin' as soon as she was born, but who died in infancy. Admittedly rebellion against the status quo was more difficult for women from an aristocratic background. They had most to rebel against and most to lose in their rejection of wealth and status: these were women who, because of their wealth, were celebri-ties whose lives would be lived in the public domain.

If girls were frequently married at the age of twelve, they had to get their rebellion in early. Ambrose tells of a girl who, when her family wanted her to marry, fled to a church and put the altar cloth over her head, claiming this as a more appropriate bridal veil for one who wanted to remain a virgin. When a member of her family, in pursuit, demanded, 'If your father were alive would he allow you to remain unmarried?' the girl replies coolly, 'Perhaps he died so that there should be no one to stop me.'[14] Macrina, as we learn from her brother, was engaged at a very young age by her parents but her young fiancé died soon after and they tried to find a replacement. But the teenager announced that she would not allow another husband to be found for her, arguing that her engagement had been tan-tamount to a marriage. She ingeniously used the Christian belief in the resurrection to argue that since her fiancé would come back to life, he was not really dead but only absent and therefore she could not marry (again) without being unfaithful to him. Here the focus is on the rejection of marriage and a determination to lead a primarily spiritual life in the family home with her mother as her close companion.

However, what some regarded as praiseworthy renunciation could also be interpreted as a form of escapism – from the problems that marriage brings or from life in degrading poverty or as a servant. Admittedly, some of the men who write in favour of chastity are not afraid to talk as if the difficulties inherent in marriage and childbearing provide a sufficiently good motivation for refusing marriage but these are not reasons any of these women gives for her actions, though Melania the younger does tell the women who live with her, having chosen the ascetic life, that they should be really grateful to God for saving them from having to experience labour pains, and in general women may have been attracted by a life which allowed them greater independence. While Jerome tries to render virginity more attractive by painting an unattractive picture of marriage, Augustine criticizes those who avoid marriage in order to make their lives more pleasant: if you avoid marriage it should be because your rewards in heaven will be greater.[15]

When it came to women of the lower classes, of whom we hear less in the writings that survive, their situation might well be improved by rejecting family responsibilities and joining a community of ascetic women. Jerome and Augustine express their concern that non-aristocratic women might be tempted to adopt the ascetic life because it meant they could be on equal terms with women of a higher social standing, and it is clear that Paula, for example, was aware of potential problems in her monastery arising from class distinctions. However, the aim of the monastic life was to bring all the participants to the same level, by having everyone take part in every aspect of this life, whether manual and domestic work, prayer or study, thereby removing class distinctions, as in the case of Macrina and her mother who performed the same tasks as the girls who had been employed as servants in their home, ate at the same table and slept on the same simple style of bed.

In fact, from what we can gather, these women seem to have adopted the ascetic life for a variety of reasons. First, one must remember that there was a tradition of virginity in the Christian church from its beginnings, although it is an ideal that is not made explicit in the Bible and one which always was treated

with a degree of ambivalence. Those who put forward virginity
as the best way of life could cite the examples of Christ himself,
of his mother Mary (whose humility and calm seriousness were
also revered), as well as early saints such as Thecla who refused
to marry, dressed as a man, was commissioned by St Paul to
teach, and who also faced violent death with fortitude (though
she was miraculously saved from it on two occasions), thus
becoming a model for virgins and martyrs alike.[16] From an
early stage there had been groups of people, both men and
women, whose lives of dedication to God involved chastity and
an austere lifestyle, such as the Encratites (a sect originating in
the second century whose name derived from the Greek word
for self-control and who abstained from sex, meat and alcohol), although later writers emphasized that chastity had to be
a matter of free choice – rather than a condition for member-
ship – for it to be valuable. Similarly, if a husband or wife tried
to persuade his or her partner to abstain from sex, the chastity
had to be consensual to be praiseworthy. And as Augustine
emphasizes, it is not physical purity in itself that is important,
but the fact that it is dedicated to God, thereby providing 'a
foretaste in the corruptible flesh of perpetual incorruption'.[17]
Secondly, there had been the growth of the desert movement,
with many men and some women withdrawing from society
into areas of wilderness, particularly in Egypt, Palestine and
Syria, to live a life of extreme simplicity in solitude and silence
or in ordered communities: Antony of Egypt, for example,
withdrew further and further into the desert on his own after
placing his sister, for whom he was responsible after their parents' death, with a group of women committed to a life without
marriage.[18] Such desert dwellers, with their stunningly radical
view of life, made an enormous impact on the Christians of the
fourth century and most of the women depicted in these pages
were inspired by hearing about them or by actually visiting
them in the desert; later generations would be inspired by reading about them in collections of sayings and biographical snip-
pets, or by works of spiritual training written as a result of
contact with them, such as the *Conferences* and *Institutes* by
John Cassian, all compiled or composed during this crucial

period. In this way, the ideal of an austere, unmarried life, filled with calm wisdom and based on a rejection of the values of mainstream society, would be carried into the early Middle Ages and enshrined, in western Europe, in the monastic *Rule of St Benedict* which provided the seedbed out of which many aspects of medieval and therefore modern culture were to grow.

Why, one might ask, did so many of the writings on virginity discuss the subject as if it were the particular preserve of women? It is not as if men did not adopt the ascetic life – we have many accounts of men rejecting their social and familial obligations and either becoming priests while remaining unmarried or withdrawing to a life of austere solitude or an ordered life of poverty, obedience and chastity in a community: such men, like many of their female counterparts, were much admired by their local communities and by visitors who came to consult their spiritual wisdom, wisdom that is still of value. Maybe it was felt that men did not need to be persuaded in the same way because it was easier for them than for women to opt for renunciation, and that consequently male renunciation was not regarded as quite so remarkable. But despite the lack of works addressed specifically to men, there were of course such works as Athanasius' *Life of Antony* and Sulpicius Severus' *Life of Martin* which presented slightly different approaches to the ideal of the male ascetic. It was the *Life of Antony* which persuaded Augustine, as he tells us in his *Confessions*, to reject the idea of marriage and give up his glittering career, thus going much further in his Christian commitment than even his mother envisaged, she who had long nagged him to settle down and make a good Christian marriage. On a more theological level, Jerome explains in his letter to Eustochium that the gift of virginity was bestowed more abundantly on women because it started with a woman, namely the Virgin Mary; before the birth of Christ it was, according to him, more usual for men, not women, to choose the unmarried life, as we see from the Old Testament.

Those who write in positive terms about the monastic life at this period bring out different facets depending on their own background and point of view. Certainly all would admit that virginity is a symbol of purity and beauty that does not fade, but they also would agree that marriage was good. As Augustine writes, 'It is good to marry since it is good to have children and to be the mother of a family, but it is better for human society not to need marriage.'[19] But, one may object, what if everybody were to reject marriage? The fourth-century writers in favour of the ascetic life would agree with Augustine when he says, rather radically but in perfect accordance with his beliefs: 'If no one married, the city of God would be filled more quickly which would be a good thing',[20] in other words, why not welcome the end of the world through the dying out of the human race? It is clear that it was not easy to maintain a balanced view – to value marriage while maintaining that chastity was better, at least for a minority – and to walk a fine line between the heretical sects, such as the Gnostics and Manichees, that disparaged the body and sex, and those who held that marriage was superior to virginity: such people might be accused of undervaluing a powerful element in the teaching of Christ and St Paul and apparently selling out to secular society. This was an area of Christian teaching that would continue to be open to different interpretations in the following centuries.

But although the women whose lives and/or deaths are described in these pages all shared a common cultural background, there were also individual factors influencing their lives. In the case of Macrina, her mother felt already during pregnancy that this unborn child would be special and so Macrina was brought up in a strictly Christian form of home education until it was time for her to be engaged on reaching puberty. It was when her fiancé died prematurely that her own determination to rebel against her parents' plans became evident, thereby showing that she was indeed special, chosen by God for a holy life. Melania the younger was actually married at an equally young age, but within a couple of years she had apparently decided that she wanted to reject the life she had been brought up for, inspired by such biblical texts as 'Love your neighbour as yourself' and 'If you wish to be perfect, sell your possessions and give the money to the poor and you will have treasure in heaven; then come and follow me.'[21] After a time she overcame her young husband's qualms, persuading him to adopt this life too, once she had given birth to two children who died in infancy: this fact enabled her to argue that she was not intended for family life. It is likely that she was also inspired by her grandmother, Melania the elder, who returned to Italy from the monastery she was running in Jerusalem to give her grand-daughter moral support when she had made her decision to reject family expectations. Melania the elder, Marcella and Paula were all widowed and all determined not to remarry but to withdraw from aristocratic society, and – in the case of Melania and Paula – to travel to the Holy Land and settle there, after selling their possessions and making financial provision for their surviving children. In the case of Eustochium and Paula the younger (Paula's daughter and granddaughter) we have the example of a teenager and a baby who Jerome hopes will adopt the life of the virgin and ascetic. He tries to persuade Eusto-chium directly, in his famous *Letter* 22, not to marry but to regard herself as the bride of Christ, leading a life of simplicity, prayer and seclusion in her family home: in fact she heeded his advice and in time accompanied her mother and Jerome him-self to Bethlehem. Regarding little Paula, Jerome addresses her mother Laeta, giving her advice on how to bring up the baby in a Christian manner so that she may live a life at home similar to that of those who, in centuries to come, would live in monas-tic communities. So it would seem that these women's motiva-tions were variously influenced by their own inner determination, the example and arguments of others, and their taking to heart of certain passages of Scripture.

Indeed, the way of life they adopted, whether in their own home or in a foreign environment, in the city, at a country retreat or in the desert, whether in solitude or community, could be seen not only as a form of rebellion against the expectations of family and society, but even as a turning upside down of the norms, in accordance with the paradox of Christ's words: 'Those who try to make their life secure will lose it but those who lose their life will keep it.'[22] We have already seen how such women were considered to have divested themselves of some aspects of their femininity and to have become like men. In a letter to Sulpicius Severus, the author of the famous life of

St Martin, Paulinus of Nola describes the life of Melania the elder in a manner that brings out the rather shocking nature of her chosen existence – and this from a man who had himself shocked the establishment by giving up huge wealth and a government career to live a simple Christian life in a small town outside Naples, renouncing sexual relations with his wife after the death in infancy of their only child. He writes of the tough and fearless Melania: 'Here was a woman of high rank who for love of Christ had sublimely lowered herself to practise humility, so that as a strong member of the weak sex she might show up idle men . . . She loved her son by neglecting him and kept him by abandoning him.'[23] Jerome describes Paula: 'Paula outdoes the virtues and powers of all by her humility . . . By trying to escape admiration she won admiration . . . [and] abandoning those who seek it she sought those who despise it', and when she left Italy and her children, 'she denied that she was a mother to prove herself Christ's servant'.

The works included in this volume provide a clear and surprisingly consistent picture of the kind of life adopted by these women for whom martyrdom was no longer an option. Our contemporaries may make much of the sexual renunciation which was to be a primary characteristic of the monastic life in the centuries to come, but in fact the aspects that are most prominent in these accounts are the financial generosity, the rejection of all that implies elegance and comfort, the fasting, the sleep deprivation, and the effort put into attaining spiritual virtues by overcoming pride, anger or covetousness. If Jerome's satirical remarks sprinkled through his writings bear any relation to the truth, there were many women who pretended to live an ascetic life because it was fashionable, but who were incapable of attaining the spiritual virtue of a Macrina, a Melania, a Paula or a Marcella, every minute of whose lives was marked by self-discipline and concern for others. In the *Lausiac History* Palladius tells us of a woman who practised asceticism out of ostentation rather than love of God, and therefore did not have the strength to resist falling in love with the man who brought food to her cell.[24] Paulinus summarizes the way of life of Melania the elder: 'There is such divine strength in that weak woman's body that she finds refreshment in fasting, repose in prayer, bread in the Word, clothing in rags. Her hard bed (for she lies on the ground on a cloak and quilt) becomes soft as she studies, for her enjoyment of reading reduces the hardship of that uncomfortable bed.'[25] Of Paula Jerome writes that she never took a bath unless she was ill and she would rest on the hard ground on a bristly mat: in her we see a woman who exchanged the life of a wealthy, high-ranking wife and mother in Rome for a life of poverty in Bethlehem, her body ravaged by her austere lifestyle, in charge of a community of women from different backgrounds who spent their time in prayer and manual work, inspired by her kindness and good example. Melania the younger is also praised for her ability to look after others while also being awarded full marks for poverty, abstinence, shabby clothes and self-discipline. And yet she and Paula came under criticism from friends and strangers. Paula is told by well-meaning friends that some people think she is insane to impose such austerity on herself, and Gerontius tells how Melania wanted to have a coffin-like box made for herself in which to spend time, so small that she could not stand up in it or turn round, but when her friends refused to allow her to do this, she accepted this for she saw that it might have made her proud as well as uncomfortable.

It was in fact within a community of like-minded people, all devoted to leading a rigorous life as followers of Christ, that most of these women lived once they had made their radical change of lifestyle. We have seen Macrina at home with her mother, and later in charge of women whom she had brought in when she found them suffering from the famine afflicting her region. Melania the elder set up a monastery in Jerusalem in the company of her friend Rufinus, while her granddaughter founded and made financial provision for several monasteries in North Africa, to be inhabited largely by the slaves she had set free. She then went to live on the Mount of Olives outside Jerusalem in a monastic community she organized there. Paula, accompanied by Jerome, set up one monastery for men and one for women in Bethlehem which she was in charge of until her death and which is described by Jerome in *Letter* 108. So large

was it – filled with women of every class and from many different countries – that she had to divide it into three sections: the
women, all dressed alike, worked and ate their meals separately
but came together at times of communal worship. Here we gain
an insight into the beginnings of the regulated monastic life
which was to develop more formally over the following centuries, as others followed these women's example and as rules for
such a life were written by Augustine and others.

While no one, not even its greatest admirers, would under-
estimate the self-discipline and physical discomfort involved in
these lives, these writings reveal many positive aspects enrich-
ing such an existence. On the personal level, one interesting
characteristic common to many is the strong relationship
between daughter and mother, as, for example, Macrina and
her mother Emmelia, Eustochium and Paula, Melania the
younger and Albina, who tried to ease her daughter's austere
life and persuade her not to be too extreme. It is a bond that
Jerome is willing to break in the case of Laeta and her baby
Paula, apparently for the good of them both, when he advises
Laeta to send the child to Bethlehem to be brought up by her
grandmother Paula and aunt Eustochium, thus relieving Laeta
of the stressful responsibility of educating a virgin dedicated to
God. There are also many instances of friendship between
women, as in Paula's circle, between Marcella and the younger
Principia who lived together on Marcella's estate on the edge of
Rome for many years, and between Melania the younger and
the Empress Eudocia, or between a woman and a man, as
between Paula and Jerome, Melania the elder and Rufinus, and
Melania the younger and Gerontius, who was her companion
in the Holy Land and, after her death, her biographer. Such
friendships between men and women, based on a shared commitment to Christ, are likely to have been impossible if the
woman had remained within the familial context. Women who
choose the ascetic life not only avoid the inconveniences of
marriage[26] and the pain of childbirth, but are also freed to
devote time to study, to travel and to use their education and
wealth to benefit many. We find Jerome giving unusually tender
advice on the earliest stages of learning when he writes to Laeta

about her baby's Christian development. We see Paula determined to study Hebrew and plaguing Jerome with questions about language and biblical interpretation, Marcella taking over as a kind of scriptural consultant once Jerome leaves Rome, and Melania the elder reading a huge amount of theology, much of it translated into Latin by her friend Rufinus. With regard to travel, Melania the younger spent time in North Africa, Egypt and the Holy Land, as well as visiting Constantinople, while her grandmother Melania spent six months travelling around Egypt visiting desert monks, before settling in Jerusalem, and going back and forth between Rome and the Holy Land. Paula seemed to specialize in spiritual and biblical tourism, not only visiting desert monks in Egypt, but also making a pilgrimage to many places associated with events recorded in both Old and New Testaments. Also included in this volume is one letter which is apparently written not only about women but by women, namely from Paula and Eustochium (admittedly in a style that is very similar to that of their teacher Jerome) in Bethlehem to their friend Marcella in Rome, urging her to travel to Jerusalem and visit them. It is clear that such women, noted for their self-discipline and learning, were much admired and often had great influence over their male contemporaries, both within their own families as in the case of Macrina's influence on her brothers, and Melania the younger's on her pagan uncle, and on men in high positions in the church or in government. One suspects that some of these men could not help being in awe of the noble birth these women had rejected. Indeed, it is notable that it was the men who had adopted a life of extreme simplicity in the desert, totally rejecting society's values, who were immune to these women's imperious, if generous, dealings with them. These women may have been largely successful in adopting an attitude of humility but occasionally they would revert to behaviour more typical of their aristocratic roots.[27]

There were, of course, not only the benefits which a modern woman might value. Beyond travel, education and an important position in a slightly alternative society, there were also positive features of a more spiritual nature. By means of self-discipline and detachment these women could enjoy a peace and stability unlikely to be attained by a married woman. By imitating the humility and gentleness of Mary, mother of Christ, these women could attain a spiritual purity which was repeatedly likened to that of the angels in heaven and indeed they are often said to have attained the life of the angels already in this life. And by imitating Mary Magdalene's passionate commitment to Christ, as Marcella is said to have done, they could draw ever closer to Christ.

However, it is not only about the particular lives – and in some cases, the approach to death – of these unusual women that we learn. These short works furnish the reader with many incidental details about the world of late antiquity in several areas around the Mediterranean. We get an idea of attitudes to the body and to sex and childbirth and of the use of contraception and abortion. We get touching glimpses of Roman family life. We meet the mother-in-law and wife of two Roman emperors. We hear of the everyday life of aristocratic Romans and people's experiences of the dramatic events of 410 when Rome itself was invaded, for the first time in eight hundred years. We find examples of the ways in which the Bible was interpreted. We find, in Jerome's letter about Paula, the elements of the Christmas story drawn from different Gospels with which we are so familiar: 'the baby wrapped in swaddling bands and crying in the manger, and the Magi worshipping God, and the star shining above them, as well as the virgin mother, the attentive foster-father, the shepherds arriving at night to see the Word that was made'. And we come across fascinating details concerning the religious conditions when paganism was being transformed or suppressed and Christian leaders were having to decide what exactly constituted the true doctrines of their faith, regarding such questions as the nature of Christ as both God and man, the relation between the persons of the Trinity, and to what extent man's will was free and how far grace was necessary. With hindsight one can label certain doctrines heretical but at this period it was frequently unclear which set of doctrines was going to triumph and be accepted as correct. In these writings we see, incidentally as it were, individuals dealing with the hot issues of the day: Macrina's brothers Basil and

Gregory are caught up in the struggle against the Arian Christians, especially during the persecutions by the Emperor Valens in the 370s; at the same time Melania the elder is helping victims of the persecutions in Palestine. She studies Origen, supports her friend Rufinus in his translations of Origen's theological works which had become suspect around 400, and intervenes in the resulting schism which involved four hundred monks, while Marcella supports Jerome in his attacks on Origen. Melania the elder, Marcella and Paula are all personally involved with the protagonists of the schism centred on the rival bishops of Antioch, Paulinus and Meletius. Melania the elder converts her cousin's pagan husband and her granddaughter Melania the younger succeeds in converting her uncle from paganism in the late 430s.

The writings included in this book all provide insights into the lives and deaths of Roman Christian women and most of them can be termed biographical, whether they come in the form of a letter or a monograph dedicated to giving an account of one person's life in order to provide a record or model of saintliness to later generations. All are written by someone who knew the subject intimately and over a long period, and who is therefore likely to be providing accurate information, even with regard to the few miracles recorded.[28] Among these, the accounts of the lives of Macrina and of Melania the younger stand out as masterpieces, both containing lengthy and moving death scenes: in the description of Melania, in particular, the subject comes across in a wonderfully realistic and sympathetic manner, as a woman of great self-discipline but also of great warmth, sharpness and often maddening obstinacy. Others, such as Jerome's letters to Eustochium and Laeta, take the form of direct advice to the addressee. We also find elements of autobiography, not only in the central section of the martyrdom account of Perpetua and Felicitas, but also in the writings by Jerome and Gregory of Nyssa. But despite differences of form, there are similarities of style and content, not only with regard to the ideal of total commitment to Christ. For example, dreams or visions play a part in a number of the narratives, including the famous occasion when Jerome is humiliated by being

accused of being more devoted to Cicero's writings than to
Christ. Certain themes such as those of pilgrimage and teenage
rebellion recur. But from a stylistic point of view, the principal
constant is the use of the Bible: all the texts are more or less
studded with biblical quotations and allusions, for the authors
could assume that their readers would be familiar with this text
which provided historical continuity with the past as well as a
moral framework for the present and an idea of the future on
which Christians should focus. For Jerome, the effect is of an
extremely complex pattern of allusion and imagery woven into
the texture, evidence of his amazing familiarity with the whole
text of the Bible, derived from all his textual and translation
work over many years. One example of this is the opening of his
letter to Eustochium in which he blends many quotations from
the Old and New Testaments, using them to exhort the young
girl to renounce her family and be united with Christ, her spiritual bridegroom: the high-flown language together with the
moral weight of Scripture combine to powerful effect. Other
writers put biblical phrases into the mouths of their subjects
which justify the women's actions, describe their subjects in biblical terms, quote the Bible to persuade their addressees to adopt
an ascetic life, or provide spiritual interpretations of Old Testament events to make them relevant to the Christian life. The
range of biblical quotation is very wide, but perhaps the most
popular texts drawn on by these writers, apart from the ethical
teachings of Christ and St Paul, are Psalm 45 and the Song of
Songs from the Old Testament. Jerome, in particular, makes
ample use of these texts in his letter to Eustochium, interpreting
them in such a way as to persuade her that she has been chosen
by Christ as his royal bride and concluding his highly rhetorical
finale with words from the Song of Songs: 'Many waters cannot
quench love, neither can floods drown it.'[29]

NOTES

1. *Life of Melania the Younger*, prologue.
2. Jerome, *Letter* 108.14, on Paula.
3. Gregory of Nyssa, *Life of Macrina*, prologue.
4. Jerome, *Letter* 127.5, on Marcella.
5. Paulinus of Nola, *Letter* 29.6, on Melania the elder.
6. Augustine, *Sermon* 281.1.
7. Galatians 3:28.
8. Jerome in *PL* 26.533. Cf. Jesus's words in the apocryphal Gospel of Thomas: 'for every woman who will make herself male will enter the kingdom of heaven'. For *PL*, see p. 235.
9. Palladius, *Lausiac History* 6.
10. Jerome, *Against Helvidius*, in *PL* 23.209, section 20.
11. 1 Corinthians 7:13; Ambrose, *Concerning Virginity*, I 7.35.
12. 1 Timothy 5:14.
13. Luke 14:26, 20:34–6.
14. Ambrose, *Concerning Virginity*, I 11.65–6.
15. Augustine, *Holy Virginity* 13.
16. Thecla is mentioned, for example, in the *Life of Macrina*, in Jerome's *Letter* 22.41 and by Ambrose, *Concerning Virginity*, II 3:19–20. She is supposed to have lived in the first century: her life is described in the apocryphal *Acts of Saints Paul and Thecla*.
17. Augustine, *Holy Virginity* 13.
18. Athanasius, *Life of Antony* 3 in *ECL*. For *ECL*, see p. 235.
19. Augustine, *On the Good of Marriage* 9. Jerome claims that he does approve of marriage but prefers virginity which is the offspring of marriage, adding: 'Will silver cease to be silver if gold is more precious than silver?' (*Against Jovinian* I 3: *PL* 23.213).
20. Augustine, *On the Good of Marriage* 10.
21. Matthew 19:19 and 19:21.
22. Luke 17:33.
23. Paulinus of Nola, *Letter* 29.7 and 9.
24. Palladius, *Lausiac History* 28.
25. Paulinus, *Letter* 29.13.
26. Ambrose, *Concerning Virginity*, I 10.56.
27. That visits from eager women were not always welcome is clear from the account of how Arsenius refused to receive a rich virgin who had come from Rome but she insisted, only to meet with rebuke from the desert ascetic: 'Why have you dared to

come all this way across the sea; you are a woman and ought not to be going about at all. Have you done this so that you can go back to Rome and say to the other women, "I have seen Arsenius"? In that way you will turn the sea into a highway with women coming to see me' (*The Desert Fathers*, p. 9).

28.   Miracles are reported in the *Life of Macrina* and in the *Life of Melania the Younger*.

29.   Song of Songs 8:7.

Further Reading

Works from Late Antiquity in translation

Acts of Saints Paul and Thecla, in *The Apocryphal New Testament* ed. J. K. Elliott (Oxford: Oxford University Press, 1993), pp. 364–80

Ambrose, *Concerning Virginity*, in *The Nun's Ideal*, trans. James Shiel (Chicago: Scepter Press, 1963), pp. 77–125

Augustine, *On the Good of Marriage* and *Holy Virginity*, in *Treatises on Marriage and Other Subjects*, ed. Roy Deferrari, The Fathers of the Church, 27 (New York, 1955)

John Cassian, *The Conferences*, trans. Boniface Ramsey, Ancient Christian Writers, 57 (New York/Mahwah, NJ: Newman Press, 1997)

—, *The Institutes*, trans. Boniface Ramsey, Ancient Christian Writers, 58 (New York/Mahwah, NJ: Newman Press, 2000)

John Chrysostom, *On Virginity, Against Remarriage*, trans. S. R. Shore (New York: Edwin Mellen Press, 1983)

Egeria's Travels, trans. John Wilkinson (Warminster: Aris and Phillips, 1999)

Life of Olympias, trans. Elizabeth A. Clark, in *Jerome, Chrysostom and Friends: Essays and Translations* (New York: Edwin Mellen Press, 1979)

Palladius, *The Lausiac History*, trans. R. T. Meyer, Ancient Christian Writers, 34 (Westminster, MD: Newman Press/London: Longman, 1965)

The Rule of Benedict, trans. Carolinne White (London: Penguin Books 2008)

*

The Desert Fathers: Sayings of the Early Christian Monks, trans. Benedicta Ward (London: Penguin Books, 2003)

Early Christian Lives, trans. Carolinne White (London: Penguin Books, 1998). Includes the lives of Antony, Paul of Thebes, Hilarion, Malchus, Martin of Tours and Benedict (referred to as *ECL*)

The Lives of the Desert Fathers, trans. Norman Russell (London: Mowbray/Kalamazoo, MI: Cistercian Publications, 1981). This is a translation of a Latin work usually known as the *History of the Monks in Egypt*, translated from the Greek by Melania the elder's friend Rufinus

Women in Early Christianity: Translations from Greek Texts, ed. P. Cox Miller (Washington DC: Catholic University of America Press, 2005)

Modern works

Brown, Peter, *The Body and Society: Men, Women and Sexual Renunciation in Early Christianity* (London: Faber and Faber, 1989)

Clark, Elizabeth A., *Reading Renunciation: Asceticism and Scripture in Early Christianity* (Princeton: Princeton University Press, 1999)

—, *Ascetic Piety and Women's Faith: Essays on Late Ancient Christianity* (New York: Edwin Mellen Press, 1986)

Clark, Gillian, *Women in Late Antiquity: Pagan and Christian Lifestyles* (Oxford: Clarendon Press, 1993)

Cloke, Gillian, *This Female Man of God: Women and Spiritual Power in the Patristic Age, AD 350–450* (London: Routledge, 1995)

Elm, Susanna, *'Virgins of God': The Making of Asceticism in Late Antiquity* (Oxford: Clarendon Press, 1994)

Kraemer, Ross Shepard, *Women's Religions in the Greco-Roman World: A Sourcebook* (Oxford: Oxford University Press, 2004)

Rousseau, Philip, *The Early Christian Centuries* (London: Longman, 2002)

Salisbury, Joyce E., *Perpetua's Passion: The Death and Memory of a Young Roman Woman* (New York/London: Routledge, 1997)

Swan, Laura, *The Forgotten Desert Mothers: Sayings, Lives and Stories of Early Christian Women* (New York/Mahwah, NJ: Paulist Press, 2001)

Williams, Rowan, *Silence and Honeycakes: The Wisdom of the Desert* (Oxford: Lion Publishing, 2004)

Note on the Texts

The Latin and Greek texts on which the translations in this volume are based are found in the following editions:

Perpetua and Felicitas: from the Latin text of 'The Martyrdom of Saints Perpetua and Felicitas', in *The Acts of the Christian Martyrs*, ed. H. Musurillo (Oxford: Clarendon Press, 1972)

Macrina: from the Greek text by Gregory of Nyssa, in Grégoire de Nysse, *Vie de sainte Macrine*, ed. P. Maraval (Paris: Sources Chrétiennes 178, 1971)

Melania the elder: from the Greek text of chapters 46, 54 and 55 of Palladius, *Lausiac History*, in Palladio, *La storia Lausiaca*, ed. G. J. M. Bartelink (Rome: Mondadori, 1974)

Marcella: from the Latin text of Jerome, *Letter* 127; Paula: from the Latin text of Jerome, *Letter* 108; Eustochium: from the Latin text of Jerome, *Letter* 22; Laeta: from the Latin text of Jerome, *Letter* 107; letter from Paula and Eustochium to Marcella, from the Latin text, collected as Jerome, *Letter* 46, in Corpus Scriptorum Ecclesiasticorum Latinorum edition (vols. 54–6), ed. I. Hilberg (reprinted Vienna, 1996), vols. 1–3

Melania the younger: from the Latin text of Gerontius, *La Vie Latine de Sainte Melanie*, ed. P. Laurence (Jerusalem: Franciscan Printing Press, 2002); and from the Greek text of chapter 61 of Palladius, *Lausiac History,* in Palladio, *La storia Lausiaca*, ed. Bartelink; *The Life of Melania the Younger*, trans. Elizabeth A. Clark, is taken from the Greek version (New York: Edwin Mellen Press, 1983)

The style of the original texts varies considerably, ranging from the stark and rather unsophisticated Latin of *The Martyrdom of Perpetua and Felicitas* and Gerontius' *Life of Melania the Younger*, through the elegant Greek of Gregory of Nyssa, to the rhetorically charged Latin of Jerome, greatly influenced by the Bible.

The biblical quotations are my translations of the texts as they are found in these writings. Because of the slight variations in the versions of the Bible at the time, the quotations may differ from modern translations; any major difference is marked in the notes. In the editorial material, the New Revised Standard Version is quoted.

With regard to the Psalms, these are numbered according to English translations of the Bible, following the Hebrew Bible. This means that the numbering of Psalms 9–147 will be one ahead of the numbering found in the Greek and Latin versions of the Bible, which combined Psalms 9 and 10 and also 114 and 115, but divided Psalms 116 and 147 into two.

Citations are occasionally made from books of the Bible regarded as apocryphal in the Hebrew and English versions, e.g. Ecclesiasticus, the Wisdom of Solomon and parts of the Book of Daniel.

Although I have tried to identify all obvious biblical quotations in the Notes, it has been impossible to annotate all Jerome's references to places referred to in the Bible (especially plentiful in his letter to Paula the elder).

Lives of Roman
Christian Women

THE MARTYRDOM OF
PERPETUA AND FELICITAS

Perpetua and Felicitas

The little we know about Vibia Perpetua and Felicitas is derived from this account – anonymous, but containing some autobiographical material from two of the protagonists – of the days leading up to their martyrdom, along with a small group of other Christians, probably on 7 March 203, in the arena at Carthage. Perpetua came from a well-to-do family and converted to Christianity. Her father was probably a pagan for he tried to dissuade her from refusing to make the sacrifice required by the Roman emperor. She was the mother of a baby whom she kept with her in prison until he was weaned. Felicitas was Perpetua's slave who gave birth to a daughter while in prison. Theirs is a world depicted in the writings of the first major Christian writer in Latin, Tertullian, who was not only their contemporary but who also lived in Roman North Africa: indeed, it has been suggested that he is the author of the introductory and concluding framework of this account which includes the prison diary of Perpetua (sections 3–10) and of Saturus (11–13), one of the four men martyred alongside the two women. Tertullian mentions Perpetua as 'the most heroic martyr' in chapter 55 of *On the Soul*, and Augustine preached four sermons on the feast day of these two martyrs, some two hundred years after their deaths (Augustine, *Sermons* 280–83). There exists also a Greek text of the account which is probably a translation from the Latin. Although other martyrdom narratives, usually known as 'Passions', exist, this is probably the most famous, largely because of the vividness of Perpetua's own account of her time in prison and the visions experienced by her and by Saturus, and of the courage and solidarity displayed by all these martyrs.

1 In the past people used to record examples of behaviour that had been inspired by faith for these were considered a sign of God's grace. Such examples were thought to provide others with spiritual strength because by reading such accounts people would remember those deeds, and as a result they would honour God and derive encouragement for themselves. So why should one not record recent examples, too, seeing that they are just as likely to have the same effect?

At some stage these recent examples will also become things of the past and be important to people of later generations, even if those who are contemporary with these events do not esteem them as highly because there is a tendency to value more highly things from the past. But those who gauge the power of the one Holy Spirit according to the period when it manifested itself should consider this: more recent events should be regarded as more impressive for the very reason that they are recent, because it was for the final period of time that most grace was promised.

For 'in the last days, says the Lord, I will pour out my spirit on all flesh and their sons and daughters will prophesy, and I will pour out my spirit on my servants, both men and women, and the young men will see visions and the old will dream dreams'.[1] We, too, recognize and value not only prophecies but also new visions which have been promised to us. We consider all the other powers of the Holy Spirit to be for the good of the church, for the Holy Spirit was also sent to the church to distribute all gifts to everyone, as the Lord hands them out to each person. We therefore consider it necessary to write down these things and to make them known to prevent people of weak or despairing faith from believing that God's grace was only active in the past, whether in martyrdom or visions. God always carries out his promises, as proof for non-believers and as a benefit for believers.

And so, my brothers and little children, we will tell you what we have heard and touched, so that those of you who were present may recall the glory of the Lord, while those of you who hear about it now may have fellowship with the holy martyrs and through them with our Lord Jesus Christ, to whom belong splendour and honour for ever and ever. Amen.

2 It happened that a number of young candidates for baptism were arrested – Revocatus and his fellow-slave Felicitas, together with Saturninus and Secundulus; they were accompanied also by Vibia Perpetua, a married woman of good family who was well educated. Perpetua, who was about twenty-two years old, had a father, a mother and two brothers – one of them a candidate for baptism like her – and a baby son at her breast. From this point on the account of the events leading up to her martyrdom is hers, as she wrote it down in her own words.

3 While we were still up before the prosecutors, my father, out of love for me, came to try to shake my resolve and persuade me to change my mind. 'Father,' I said, 'You see this jar lying here, a water pot or whatever it is?' 'Yes, I do,' he replied. 'Surely it cannot be called anything other than what it is?' And he replied, 'No.' 'Well, in the same way I cannot call myself anything other than what I am, namely a Christian.' My father got so angry when he heard the word Christian that he came at me as if he were going to tear my eyes out, but he just shouted at me and then left, defeated, as were his diabolical arguments. For the next few days I gave thanks to God because my father had left me alone: I was relieved that he was not there. During those few days we were baptized and I was inspired by the Holy Spirit not to pray for anything afterwards other than the ability to endure physically. A few days later we were taken to prison. I was terrified as I had never experienced such a dark place.

What a difficult time that was! Stiflingly hot because of the huge crowds; soldiers extorting money; and during the whole time I was there I was tormented by worries about my baby. Then Tertius and Pomponius, those kind deacons who were looking after us, bribed someone to allow us to be moved to a better part of the prison for a few hours so that we could recover a bit. Everyone then left the prison cell and we had a rest. I fed my baby who was weak from hunger. In my anxiety about him I spoke to my mother, tried to comfort my brother and entrusted my son to them, but I suffered because I saw them suffering on my account.

Such were the worries that tormented me for many days. Then I managed to get permission for my baby to stay with me in prison and as a result I immediately felt better, relieved as I was of my discomfort and of worry for the child. Suddenly the prison had become a palace, and I preferred to be there rather than anywhere else.

4 Then my brother said to me, 'My dear sister, you are already greatly privileged – so much so that you can surely ask for a vision to find out whether you will be condemned or set free?' I faithfully promised that I would, for I knew I could talk with the Lord, whose great blessings I had experienced. I told my brother I would give him an answer the following day. I then asked for a vision and this is what I saw. I saw an amazingly tall ladder, made of bronze, reaching right up to heaven. It was so narrow that only one person could climb it at a time. All kinds of metal objects had been fixed into the sides of the ladder: there were swords, spears, hooks, daggers and spikes, so that if the person climbing up were not careful or if he failed to look where he was going, he would be gashed and his flesh would stick to the metal spikes. Under the ladder lay an enormous dragon, waiting to attack those who climbed it and to frighten them off any attempt to climb. Saturus was the first to climb up – he who later surrendered voluntarily out of consideration for us (for it was he who had been our spiritual teacher), and so he had not been with us when we were arrested. When he got to the top of the ladder, he turned round and said to me, 'Perpetua, I will help you up. But be careful that the dragon does not bite you.' I replied, 'He will not hurt me, in the name of Jesus Christ.' Then hesitantly, as if it were afraid of me, the

dragon stuck its head out from under the ladder and I trod on its head as if it were the first rung, and began to climb up.

Then I saw a very large garden and a tall man with grey hair sitting in the middle of it dressed as a shepherd, milking his sheep. Standing around him were thousands of people dressed in white. He raised his head, looked at me and said, 'Welcome, my child.' He called me over to him and gave me a mouthful of fresh milk; I took it in my cupped hands and drank it and all those who were standing around said, 'Amen.' At the sound of this word I woke up, with the taste of something sweet still in my mouth. I immediately told my brother and we realized that I would be condemned. From that time on we began to relinquish all hope in this life.

5 A few days later a rumour circulated that we were going to be given a hearing. My father also arrived from the city, worn out with anxiety. He came up to me to try to shake my resolve and said, 'Dear daughter, have pity on me in my old age. Have pity on your father – if I deserve to be called your father, if I have raised you to reach the prime of your life, if I have favoured you more than your brothers. Do not cause me disgrace. Think of your brothers, think of your mother and your aunt, think of your son who cannot live without you. Stop being so proud and stubborn! Do not destroy us all! For none of us will be able to speak freely again if anything happens to you.' This was the way my father spoke out of love for me, kissing my hands and throwing himself down in front of me; in tears, he talked to me no longer as a daughter but as a woman. I was sorry for my father because he was the only one of all my relatives who would not be happy for me in my suffering. I tried to comfort him, saying, 'Let God's will be done in the prisoner's dock. For you must remember that things are not in our power but in God's.' And he went away, deeply upset.

6 One day, while we were eating breakfast, we were suddenly rushed off to a hearing. When we arrived at the forum the news immediately circulated around that area and a large crowd turned up. We went up into the prisoner's dock and when interrogated, all the others admitted their guilt. Then it was my turn. Suddenly my father appeared with my son and pulled me off

the platform, saying, 'Perform the sacrifice! Have pity on your baby!' The governor Hilarianus, who had received his judicial powers as successor to the late proconsul Minucius Timinianus, said to me, 'Have pity on your father's grey hairs, have pity on your baby son. Make a sacrifice for the emperors' welfare.'[2] I answered, 'No, I will not.' Hilarianus asked me, 'Are you a Christian?' and I answered, 'Yes, I am.' When my father persisted in trying to shake my resolve, Hilarianus gave orders that he be thrown to the ground and beaten with a rod. I was upset by what was happening to my father, for it was as if I myself was being beaten; I felt really sorry for him, so pathetic was he in his old age. Then Hilarianus passed sentence on us all, condemning us to the wild beasts. We went back down to the prison cell in good spirits. Then, because my baby was used to being breastfed and to being with me in prison, I at once sent the deacon Pomponius to ask my father for the baby but he refused to hand him over. However, it was God's will that the baby should no longer want the breast. Fortunately my breasts did not become inflamed so I was not tormented by worry for the baby nor by discomfort in my breasts.

7 A few days later, while we were all praying, I suddenly shouted out the name Dinocrates. I was shocked, for this name had never entered my mind until that moment, and I was upset when I recalled what had happened to him. I realized at once that I was privileged and ought to pray for him. I began to pray at length and to sigh for him before the Lord.

That night I had the following vision. I saw Dinocrates coming out of a dark hole where there were also many others with him. He was very hot and thirsty, pale and dirty. On his face he had a sore, the one he had when he died. This Dinocrates was my brother according to the flesh. He had died of skin cancer when he was seven years old, a death that everyone found horrifying. It was for him that I prayed but we were separated by a great gulf which prevented us from reaching each other. There was a pool full of water where Dinocrates was standing. Its rim was higher than the child's height and Dinocrates was reaching out to try and drink from it. It upset me that the pool was full of water and yet he could not drink it because he was not tall enough.

Then I woke up and realized that my brother was suffering. But I was confident that I could help him in his trouble. I prayed for him every day until we were transferred to the military prison (for we were going to engage with the wild beasts at the military games held on the Emperor Geta's birthday).[3] Sighing and weeping I prayed night and day that my brother should be given to me.

8 On one of the days when we were still in custody, I had the following vision: I saw the same place I had seen before and Dinocrates was there, clean, well dressed and refreshed; where the wound had been, I now saw a scar. The rim of the pool I had seen earlier reached only to the boy's waist and he could now draw water from the pool. On the rim stood a golden bowl full of water. Dinocrates went up to it and began to drink from it but the bowl never became empty. When he had had enough he left the water and happily went off to play as children do. Then I woke up and I realized that he had been delivered from his suffering.

9 A few days later the junior officer Pudens, who was in charge of the prison, began to treat us really well for he could see that some great power was at work in us. He allowed us to have many visitors so that we could comfort each other. When the day of the games was close at hand, my father came to see me, worn out with anxiety. He began to tear the hairs from his beard and fling them to the ground; then he threw himself down, cursing his old age and saying things that would move any living being, causing me to grieve that he should be so unhappy in his old age.

10 On the day before we were due to face the wild beasts, I saw the following vision: Pomponius the deacon had come to the door of the prison and was knocking on it furiously. I went out and opened the door for him. He was wearing a loose white tunic and elaborate sandals. He said to me, 'Perpetua, we have been waiting for you. Come on.' He took me by the hand and we began to walk along uneven and winding paths. Finally, out of breath, we managed to reach the amphitheatre. He led me to the centre of the arena and said to me, 'Do not be afraid. I am here with you and I will share your suffering.' Then he went

away and I saw a huge crowd of people looking on in amazement. And because I knew that I had been condemned to the beasts, I was surprised that they were not brought in to attack me.

Then an Egyptian, of terrifying appearance, came out with his assistants to fight me. Some good-looking young men also came out to join me, to give help and support. I was then stripped and I found I was a man. My supporters began to rub me down with oil, as is the practice before a contest. Then I saw the Egyptian on the other side rolling in the dust. Next a man came out who was so extraordinarily tall that he stood higher than the roof of the amphitheatre. He wore a loose robe of purple with two stripes across the chest, and sandals made of gold and silver. He carried a rod, like a gladiatorial trainer, and a green branch on which hung golden apples. He called for silence and said, 'If the Egyptian beats this woman he will kill her with this sword, but if she beats him, she will receive this branch.' Then he withdrew and we approached each other to begin the fight. The Egyptian tried to catch hold of my feet but I kept kicking him in the face. Then I was lifted up in the air and began to punch him without as it were touching the ground. When I saw him pause, I joined my hands together by intertwining my fingers and grabbed his head. He fell on his face and I trod on his head. The crowds began to shout and my supporters began to sing psalms. I went up to the gladiatorial trainer and he presented me with the branch. He kissed me and said, 'My daughter, peace be with you.' I began to walk triumphantly towards the Gate of Life. Then I woke up and realized that it was not beasts that I was going to fight against but the devil, though I also knew that I would win.

This was what I did until the day before the gladiatorial games. If anyone wants to write about what happened at the games, let him do so.

11 The blessed Saturus also told of his own vision and wrote it down himself, as follows. We had died and been stripped of our bodies and we began to be carried towards the east by four angels whose hands did not touch us. We were not being carried on our backs facing upwards but leaning forwards as if we

were climbing a gentle hill. When we had got free from the world, we saw an immeasurably bright light, and I said to Perpetua (for she was at my side), 'This is what the Lord promised us. We have received what he promised.' And while we were being carried by those four angels, a huge space appeared before us, like a garden with rose trees and all kinds of flowers. The trees were as tall as cypresses and their leaves were falling without cease. There in the garden were four more angels, brighter than the others. When they saw us, they bowed down before us and said to the other angels in admiration, 'Look, here they are!' The four angels who were carrying us became frightened and put us down. Then we walked to the arena along a broad path and there we found Jocundus and Saturninus and Artaxius (who were burnt alive in the same persecution) and Quintus who had died as a martyr in prison. We asked them where they were. The other angels said to us, 'Come here first; go in and greet the Lord.'

12 We came to a place with walls that looked as if they were built of light. In front of the door stood four angels who went in and put on white robes. Then we went in and heard a chorus of voices continuously chanting, 'Holy, Holy, Holy.' There we saw an old man seated, with snow-white hair. His face was youthful but we could not see his feet. On his left and on his right were four elderly men and behind them were several others. We went in, full of wonder, and stood in front of the throne. Then the angels lifted us up and we kissed the old man and he touched our faces with his hand. The other elderly men told us to go and play. I said to Perpetua, 'You have got what you want.' And she replied, 'Thanks be to God! Although I was happy while alive, now I am even happier.'

13 We went out and in front of the doors we saw Bishop Optatus on the right and Aspasius the priest and teacher on the left. They were standing apart, looking miserable. They threw themselves at our feet and said, 'Make peace between us for you are going away and leaving us.' We said to them, 'Are you not our bishop and you our priest? Why do you throw yourselves at our feet?' And we moved forward to embrace them. Perpetua began to speak to them in Greek while we took them aside into

the garden under a rose tree. While we were talking with them the angels said to us, 'Let them rest. If you have any disagreement, sort it out among yourselves.' They were upset and said to Optatus, 'Tell these people off for coming to you as if they were on their way back from the races and were just having an argument about the different teams.' It seemed to us that they wanted to shut the gates. We began to recognize many brothers there, including some martyrs. We all felt nourished by a wonderful fragrance that seemed to satisfy us. Then I woke up, feeling really happy.

14 These were the remarkable visions of those most blessed martyrs Saturus and Perpetua, which they themselves wrote down. As for Secundulus, by a special grace God called him out of this world earlier than the others while he was still in prison so that he would not have to face the beasts. Although his soul did not experience the sword, his body certainly did.

15 As for Felicitas, the Lord's grace touched her too in the following way. When she was eight months pregnant (for she had been pregnant when she was arrested) and the day of the games was approaching, she became very upset at the thought that her martyrdom would be postponed because of her pregnancy (for it was against the law for pregnant women to be executed) and that she would have to shed her holy and innocent blood afterwards in the company of people who were common criminals. Her fellow martyrs were also very upset at the thought that they would have to leave such a good friend alone on the road to the same hope. And so a couple of days before the games they shared in her sorrow by saying a prayer to the Lord together. As soon as they had finished the prayer she went into labour. Since she was in great pain because of the natural difficulty of giving birth in the eighth month, one of the assistants of the prison guards said to her, 'You are in great pain now but what will you do when you are up against the beasts? Did you not think of them when you refused to sacrifice?' She replied, 'Now it is I who suffer this, but there it will be someone else in me who will suffer for me, just as I will suffer for him.' Then she gave birth to a girl whom one of her sisters brought up as her own daughter.

16 Since the Holy Spirit has allowed the events of the games to be recorded, and by allowing it has willed it, even if I am unworthy of adding anything to this glorious story, I shall still carry out the order, so to speak, or rather the commission of the most holy Perpetua, and I will add one more example of her perseverance and nobility of soul. At the time the tribune was treating them very harshly because, as the result of some information given by certain misguided people, he was afraid that they would be spirited away from prison by means of magic spells. So Perpetua said to his face, 'Why do you not allow us to have a proper rest, seeing that we are the most valuable of the criminals, namely those belonging to the emperor, and we are to engage with the beasts at the games in celebration of his birthday? Or does it not redound to your credit if we are brought out on the day in a healthier condition?' The tribune was disturbed and embarrassed by this. So he gave orders for them to be treated more humanely and gave permission for her brothers and other people to visit and eat with them. By now the junior officer in the prison was also a believer.

17 On the day before the games when they ate their last meal, usually known as the meal of freedom, they held instead a love feast.[4] They called to the crowd with the same steadfastness, warning them of God's judgement, firmly maintaining that they were happy to die, and were amused by the curiosity of those who had gathered to look at them. Saturus said, 'Is tomorrow not soon enough for you? Why are you keen to look at something you hate? Our friends today will be our enemies tomorrow. But make a careful note of what we look like so you can recognize us on the day.' Then the crowd dispersed in amazement and many of them began to believe.

18 The day of their victory dawned and they were led out of the prison into the amphitheatre, as cheerful as if they were on their way to heaven. Their looks were composed and if they trembled they did so out of excitement rather than fear. Perpetua proceeded calmly, her countenance radiant, like a wife of Christ, like the beloved of God. The intensity of her gaze forced everyone who looked at her to avert their eyes. Then came Felicitas who was relieved that she had safely given birth so

that she could fight the beasts, going as it were from one bloody event to another, from the midwife to the gladiator, preparing to wash after childbirth in a second baptism. When they had been led in through the gates they were forced to put on robes – the men putting on those of the priests of Saturn and the women those of the virgins dedicated to Ceres. But Perpetua, that noble woman, continued to refuse to do so right to the end. For she said, 'We came to this of our own free will, to prevent our freedom being violated. We agreed to hand over our lives to you, on condition that we would not have to do this: you agreed to this.' Injustice recognized justice and the tribune gave in. They were led in just as they were. Perpetua was singing a psalm, already crushing the Egyptian's head underfoot. Revocatus and Saturninus and Saturus began to threaten the crowd of onlookers. Then when they came within sight of Hilarianus, they began to communicate with him by gestures and nods: 'You have condemned us, but God will condemn you.' At this the people became enraged and demanded that they be whipped by a line of gladiators; but this just made them happy because they had managed to share something of the Lord's sufferings.

19 But he who said, 'Ask and you will receive',[5] granted them what they asked for by giving each what he wanted. For every time they had discussed their desire for martyrdom, Saturninus had claimed that he wanted to be thrown to all the wild beasts, so that he would win a prize of greater glory. And so when they were brought to the games, he and Revocatus were matched with a leopard, and then when they were on the platform they were attacked by a bear.

Saturus on the other hand hated the thought of a bear and claimed that his life would be ended by the single bite of a leopard. Then he was matched with a boar but the gladiator who had tied him to the boar was himself gored by the beast and died a few days after that contest, while Saturus was only dragged along. Then when he was bound on the platform for the bear to attack him, the bear refused to come out of its cage. As a result Saturus, unharmed, was called back a second time.

20 For the girls, however, the devil had prepared a very fierce

heifer. This was an unusual animal but one that had been chosen as appropriate for their sex. So they were stripped and covered with nets and brought out. The crowd was shocked to see a pretty young girl and another young woman with breasts swollen with milk after recently giving birth. So they were called back and dressed in loose tunics. First, Perpetua was tossed by the heifer and fell on her back. Her tunic had been ripped along the side and when she sat up she pulled it down to cover her thigh, more concerned with her modesty than the pain. Then she asked for a pin to clip back her hair which had become dishevelled; for it was not right for a martyr to die with her hair in a mess, lest she should seem to be mourning in her hour of glory. She got up and when she saw that Felicitas had been dashed to the ground, she went up to her and held out her hand to help her up, and the two of them stood side by side. The crowd was now no longer keen to see them suffer and the two women were called back to the Gate of Life. There Perpetua was held up by a man called Rusticus, a candidate for baptism at the time, who was devoted to her. It was as if she had woken from sleep (in such ecstasy of spirit had she been) and she began to look round. Then to everyone's amazement she said, 'When are we going to be taken out to that heifer or whatever it is?' When she heard what had happened, she did not believe it until she noticed some marks on her body and clothes, which proved that she had been roughly treated. Then she summoned her brother and that candidate for baptism and said to them, 'Keep firm in the faith[6] and love each other, all of you. Do not let the sufferings we have been through cause you to stumble.'

21 At another gate Saturus was speaking to the soldier called Pudens, saying, 'It is exactly as I thought would happen and as I foretold: so far not a single wild beast has touched me. Now you must believe with all your heart: look, I am going in and one bite from the leopard will finish me off.' As the contest was coming to a close, Saturus was thrown to a leopard, and after one bite he was so covered in blood that as he turned round, the crowd claimed this as evidence that he was being baptized for a second time. 'A good way to wash! A good way to wash!'

they cried, and it certainly was. He said to the soldier Pudens, 'Farewell. Do not forget your faith or me. Do not let these events upset you but rather inspire you.' He asked Pudens for the ring off his finger, dipped it in the blood from his wound and gave it back to him, leaving it to him as a pledge and reminder of his bloodshed. Then he was thrown to the ground unconscious along with the others for his throat to be cut. But the crowd demanded that they be brought into the middle so that the people could feast their eyes, as guilty partners in murder, on the sight of the sword piercing their bodies. So the prisoners got to their feet of their own accord and moved to where the crowd wanted them to go, kissing each other first, for they wanted to complete their martyrdom with the ritual kiss of peace. The others stood motionless and accepted the sword wound in silence, especially Saturus who had been the first to climb the stairs and was the first to die for he was also supporting Perpetua. But Perpetua shouted out with joy as the sword pierced her, for she wanted to taste some of the pain and she even guided the hesitant hand of the trainee gladiator towards her own throat. It was as if such an extraordinary woman, feared as she was by the unclean spirit, could not have died in any other way except as she wished. You brave and blessed martyrs! Truly called and chosen to share in the glory of our Lord Jesus Christ! Anyone who glorifies and reveres and worships Christ's glory should also read these examples for the edification of the church, for they are no less marvellous than those from the past. In this way recent examples of goodness can also serve to prove that the one Holy Spirit is always at work even now, together with God the omnipotent father and his son Jesus Christ our Lord, to whom is splendour and limitless power for ever and ever. Amen.

THE LIFE OF MACRINA

by Gregory of Nyssa

Macrina

Macrina was born in about 325 and died in 380, living her whole life in what is now central Turkey. She was the eldest child of Christian parents from families that had suffered much for their faith. Gregory wrote an account of his sister's life shortly after her death and also mentions her in his *Letter* 19 and in *On the Soul and the Resurrection*, but strangely, her brother Basil never refers to her in his writings.

Macrina was given a Christian education at home by her mother. Her parents intended her to marry, but her fiancé died and Macrina refused to be married to anyone else. Instead, she chose at the age of twelve to live a sheltered life with her mother, helping to administer her mother's property and bring up her own younger brothers whom she inspired in their spiritual lives. Her holiness, generosity and learning drew many women who came to live with her and adopt the same life of austerity, humility and Christian devotion. A large part of Gregory's account is taken up by a description of his visit to his sister after their mother's death, when Macrina herself is ill. Gregory tells of her calm courage in facing death, of his own emotions and of the events surrounding her death. Included are Macrina's healing of herself from a breast abscess, and of a little girl from a chronic eye complaint.

Gregory of Nyssa

Gregory was born in 331, the younger brother of Macrina. His brother Basil (see also note 3) made him bishop of Nyssa in 372. Together with Basil and Basil's friend Gregory of Nazianzus, Gregory is regarded as one of the leading churchmen and theological writers in Greek of the fourth century: collectively these three are often referred to as the Cappadocian Fathers. His greatest contributions to Christian theology lie in his work on the Trinity and on the spiritual life. He engaged with Platonic philosophy and was influenced by Philo and Origen. He died after 385.

According to some manuscripts his biography of Macrina is addressed to the monk Olympios.

1 You might think from the title that this is a letter, but since it is as long as a prose monograph it is too long to be a letter. My excuse is that the subject you have asked me to write about is too big to fit into a letter. At any rate you will not have forgotten our meeting when I was about to set out for Jerusalem in fulfilment of a vow, for I wanted to see for myself the evidence for our Lord's life on earth in the actual places where he stayed. I came across you near the city of Antioch, and all kinds of topics for conversation bubbled up in us (for it was hardly likely that our meeting would take place in silence when your lively mind triggered numerous starting points for discussion) as often happens on such occasions. In the course of our conversation we recalled the life of a person who was highly thought of. This person was a woman – if indeed she was a woman, for I am not sure it is right to refer to someone by their sex when she had transcended her sex. Our account was not based on hearsay but was an accurate description of things we had learned from personal experience. We did not need to rely on what other people can tell us for the young woman who was the subject of our reminiscences was not a stranger to our family. If she had been it would have been necessary to learn from others about the wonders associated with her, but in fact she was from the same family, being as it were the first product of our mother's womb. You decided that it would be worth telling the story of her achievements so that a life of this kind would not remain unknown in times to come. You considered it wrong that a woman who by means of the Christian faith raised herself to the highest peak of human virtue should be consigned to oblivion

and neglected without benefiting anyone. So I thought I ought to do as you asked and tell her story, as briefly as I can, in a straightforward and unpretentious style.

2 This young girl's name was Macrina. There had been another Macrina in the past who was much admired in our family – she was our father's mother and had bravely endured the persecutions, standing firm in her faith in Christ – and it was after her that this little girl had been given the name Macrina. This was her official name, the one used by those who knew her, but she had another name given to her in secret as the result of a vision before she was born. For her mother was so virtuous that she was guided in all matters by the will of God. In particular she adopted a pure and spotless way of life to the point that she had chosen of her own accord not to get married. But as she lost both her parents at a stage when she was blossoming into such a lovely young girl that her beauty inspired many men to want to marry her, she ran the risk, if she did not agree to marry someone, of being forced to do something against her will; for some of those who were attracted by her beauty were planning to abduct her. So she chose a man who was clearly serious-minded – in fact he was well known for it – so that she would have someone to protect her in her private life. Soon afterwards, as the result of her first pregnancy, she became the mother of this girl Macrina. When the time came for the birth to put an end to her labour pains, Macrina's mother fell asleep and dreamed that she was carrying in her arms the child she was still carrying in her womb. Then there appeared to her a person looking much more majestic and taller than any human being, who addressed the unborn child by the name of Thecla, alluding to that famous virgin also called Thecla.[1] The person did this three times and then vanished, granting the pregnant woman a pain-free birth. She woke up and realized that she had had a vision while she was asleep. This is how Thecla came to be Macrina's secret name. It seems to me that the person in the vision made this announcement not to help the mother choose a name for her baby but to indicate the kind of life the child would lead, for having the same name as Thecla signified that she would choose the same way of life.

3 And so the little girl grew. Although she had her own nurse it
was in her mother's arms that she was usually nursed. When
she had passed the stage of infancy the little girl was ready to
learn those things that small children are taught, and she proved
to be exceptionally clever at whatever subject her parents
decided she should study. Her mother was committed to educating her daughter, though not by means of the general education system taught by the non-Christians in which poetry is
used to instruct children from their earliest years. For Macrina's
mother considered it degrading and altogether unsuitable for a
delicate and impressionable nature to learn from the passions
of tragedy or from obscene comedies or from the causes of
Troy's suffering: such stories of women, which provided the
poets with their subjects and inspiration, would be likely to
corrupt her in some way. Instead, everything in the divinely
inspired Scriptures that seemed comprehensible to a child
became the subject of the girl's studies, in particular those passages of the Wisdom of Solomon that were conducive to a
moral life. The little girl also studied the Psalms, and she would
chant every part of them at the appropriate times: when she got
out of bed, when she applied herself to her studies or when she
had a break, when she went to eat and when she left the table,
when she went to bed and when she got up to pray, at all times
she had the Psalms with her like a good companion who was
always there to support her.

4 Growing up amid these pursuits as well as becoming skilled
at processing wool, she reached her twelfth year, an age at
which the flower of youth begins to blossom. At this point one
may marvel at how her youthful beauty, even when kept out of
the public eye, did not remain unnoticed. It seemed that nowhere
in that country was there anything as marvellous as her loveliness: even skilful painters could not do justice to her grace.
Although the art of the painter is able to produce anything,
venturing to deal with the most challenging subjects and by
means of imitation representing the images of the heavenly
bodies themselves, it was unable to provide an accurate depic-
tion of her beauty. It attracted a great swarm of suitors and in
their eagerness to marry her, they besieged her parents. Her

father (who was wise and skilled at discerning what was good) had picked out from the rest a man from a reputable family, well known for his good sense, who had recently left school. This was the man whom he decided should marry his daughter when she came of age. Meanwhile the man showed promise for the future and brought to the girl's father his fame in public speaking as if it were one of the wedding gifts, demonstrating his eloquence in lawsuits on behalf of those who had been unjustly treated. But Envy destroyed these promising hopes, snatching him from life while he was still tragically young.

5 The girl knew of her father's plans but when they were cut short, she spoke of the young man's death as if it were marriage and as if her father's plans had already been fulfilled. In future, she announced, she would live on her own. In taking this decision she showed a determination stronger than one would expect from someone of her age. Her parents often tried to bring up the subject with her because of the many men who, after hearing of her beauty, sought to marry her, but Macrina answered that it was unnatural and unlawful not to be content with the marriage her father had arranged for her; she should not be forced to set her sights on another, since marriage is by nature unique, as are birth and death. She asserted confidently that the man to whom her parents had decided to marry her had not died. She believed he was living for God through his hope of the resurrection: he was not a corpse, he was just absent. She claimed it was right to remain faithful to a husband while he was away. Using these arguments to repel those who tried to persuade her, she decided that there was one way of safeguarding her noble resolve, namely never to be separated from her mother, not even for a moment. Her mother would often say to her that she had carried her other children for the normal length of time in pregnancy, but that when it came to Macrina she carried her always because she had her with her all the time. But her daughter's company was not a burden to her – in fact it was very useful, for her daughter helped her, replacing the work of several maids. Indeed both mother and daughter derived mutual benefit: the mother took care of her daughter's spiritual needs, while Macrina took care of her mother's physical

needs, and in all other matters she carried out the required tasks, in particular often making bread for her mother with her own hands. This was not her main activity for it was only after she had performed the liturgical tasks that she used her spare time to cook for her mother, believing this was appropriate to her way of life. Not only this, but she would also share her mother's responsibilities, which were quite a burden for her mother had four sons and five daughters and had to pay tax to three governors because her estates were in three different regions. As a result her mother was plagued by many worries (Macrina's father having already passed away), and so Macrina became her companion in all these tasks, sharing her mother's anxieties and easing the burden of her sufferings. At the same time she managed to retain her pure way of life under her mother's guidance and watchful eye. In return, Macrina gradually led her mother towards the same ideal, I mean the philosophical ideal,[2] by means of her own way of life, inspiring her mother to adopt a simple existence detached from material things.

6 But after her mother had made suitable arrangements for Macrina's sisters in accordance with the expectations of each, her brother Basil,[3] a most impressive man, returned after having spent a long time studying rhetoric at university. Macrina found him excessively proud because he was very aware of his own rhetorical talent. He despised those in high office and arrogantly considered himself superior to the leading men of the province. But his sister soon persuaded him to focus on philosophy with the result that he rejected his celebrity status and came to despise the admiration accorded his rhetorical skills. Instead he adopted a way of life that involved hard manual work, preparing for himself a clear path towards a life of virtue by means of total poverty. It would, however, take too long to give an account of his life and the subsequent activities that made him famous everywhere under the sun with the result that his reputation eclipsed that of everyone else who was renowned for virtue, but I hope to return to this subject later.

7 As they no longer had any excuse for leading a materialistic life, Macrina persuaded her mother to renounce the life she was used to and give up her extravagant style of living and the

services of her servants to which she had grown accustomed. Instead she came to regard herself as being on a level with the mass of ordinary people, sharing a life in common with the young girls who worked in her house, making them her sisters and equals. Here I would like to make a brief digression because I do not want to leave unrecorded the following episode which provides proof of Macrina's high ideals.

8 The second of her four brothers after Basil was called Naucratios: he surpassed the others in being lucky enough to have a cheerful personality, good looks, strength, agility and all-round ability. At the age of twenty-two he gave a demonstration of his own work at a public gathering and the whole audience was hugely impressed by him. But divine providence seems to have led him to despise everything he had, and he was suddenly inspired to go off to live a life of solitude and poverty, taking nothing with him – just himself. One of his servants, called Chrysaphios, followed him both because of his affection for Naucratios and because he had decided to lead the same kind of life. And so Naucratios adopted a life of solitude in a remote area beside the Iris, a river that rises in Armenia and then flows through the Pontus (the region where we live), and then pours into the Black Sea. Near the river the young man found a place surrounded by dense woodland and hidden in a hollow beneath an overhanging rock: he decided to live here, far from the noise of the city and the distractions of life as a soldier or as an advocate in the law courts. After he had detached himself from all the noise and cares of human existence, he took to caring for some old men who lived together in poverty and sickness, for he thought that this was a suitable way to spend his time. Being skilled at every kind of hunting, he was able in this way to acquire food for the old men, while at the same time working off his youthful energies. He was also very happy to obey his mother's wishes whenever she asked him to do something. In this way he lived a double life for the hard physical work allowed him to control his youthful impulses, while his devotion to his mother meant that he was obedient to the divine commandments, thereby travelling on a straight path towards God.

9 Naucratios spent five years in this way, leading the life of a philosopher – a way of life that made his mother very happy, because he was managing both to live in a self-disciplined way and also to put all his energy into doing what his mother asked. But then a terrible tragedy befell his mother – no doubt the result of the adversary's[4] scheming – something that was enough to plunge the whole family into disaster and sorrow. Naucratios was suddenly snatched from this life, without having had any illness that might have provided a warning of what was going to happen; nor was it as if he had fallen victim to any of the usual things that cause a young man to die. He had gone off hunting to get the food necessary for the old men in his care, but then his dead body was carried home, together with that of his companion Chrysaphios. His mother was totally unaware of these events, for she was at a distance of three days' journey from the accident, and so someone had to go to tell her what had happened. Despite the fact that she was so perfect when it came to virtue, she was as susceptible to emotion as other people. She immediately fainted, unable to breathe or speak, and sorrow took the place of reason. Struck down by this terrible news she lay there like a champion boxer floored by an unexpected blow.

10 In this situation the great Macrina showed what a strong person she was: using her reason to withstand her strong emotions, she prevented herself collapsing and instead she became a support to her mother, raising her up again from the depths of sorrow. By means of her firm and unyielding attitude she trained her mother to be brave. Not that her mother was swept away by her feelings nor did she behave in a womanish or vulgar way: she did not shout abuse at misfortune or tear her clothes or lament over what had happened or encourage the singing of mournful dirges. She patiently endured the assaults of nature, pushing them away by means of her own reasoning and that of her daughter, which helped to heal her suffering. For it was at this time in particular that the young woman's sublime and noble soul was revealed, for she was naturally suffering in the same way – after all, it was her brother, her dearest brother, whom death had snatched away like this. But she

overcame her human nature and by means of her own reflections she raised up her mother, too. She helped her to overcome her sorrow, leading her by her own example to be patient and brave. In addition Macrina's life was becoming increasingly virtuous, and this allowed her mother not to grieve so much for the son she had lost but rather to be happy for the goodness she could see in her daughter.

11 When Macrina's mother no longer needed to worry about her children's upbringing or be concerned about educating or setting them up in life and when she had divided most of her material wealth between her children, then (as has already been mentioned) the young woman became her mother's guide to this kind of philosophical and spiritual way of life. Macrina, who had already given up all the norms of society, inspired her mother to strive for the same humility: she persuaded her to live as an equal with the female domestic servants, sharing the same table, the same kind of bed, and all the same necessities of life on an equal footing. All differences of rank were removed from their way of life. Indeed it would be impossible to describe their noble way of life, its order and the loftiness of their philosophy, both by day and by night. Just as the soul released from the body by death is also released from worries about this life, so their life was lived apart, far removed from all trivialities, and organized in imitation of the angelic life. You could find no evidence of anger, envy, hatred, contempt, or anything similar among them; they had rejected all desire for trivial things, for fame or reputation, or anything that led to pride or arrogance. Their self-indulgence was to be self-disciplined; their fame was to remain unknown; their wealth was to be poor and to shake off from their bodies all material abundance as if it were dust. They occupied themselves with none of those tasks that people busy themselves with in this life, except incidentally; instead they focused completely on God, on unceasing prayer and the continual singing of hymns, extended equally throughout the day and night in such a way that it was for them both work and a break from work. What human words could adequately describe such a way of life, lived by people existing on the borders between human and incorporeal nature?

The fact that they had freed their nature from human feelings made them superhuman, but on the other hand the fact that they appeared in bodies and were encased in human form, equipped with sense organs, meant that they had a nature lower than the incorporeal nature of the angels. One might dare to say that the difference was minimal because living in the flesh in the likeness of incorporeal powers they were not weighed down by the burden of the body; instead their life was sublime and uplifted, walking on high with the heavenly powers. They led this kind of life for a long time and their good qualities increased with time as their philosophy advanced towards a greater purity with the help of other blessings they discovered on their way.

12 Macrina had another brother who particularly helped her to achieve her great purpose in life: his name was Peter[5] and he was the last child for whom our mother endured labour pains. He was my parents' youngest child and he became an orphan and a son at the same time for his father died when he was born. But his eldest sister, the subject of this account, took him from the nurse when he was weaned soon after his birth and looked after him herself, even though she herself was still very young. Macrina educated him in all the higher forms of learning, training him from childhood in the Scriptures so as not to allow his soul any leisure to spend on trivial things. She became everything to the young boy – father, teacher, mentor, mother, giver of all good advice – and managed to bring him to such perfection that before he left childhood behind, while he was still a delicate youth, he was already blossoming and making excellent progress in the spiritual life. He was lucky enough to have a natural aptitude for all forms of manual work, and without having anyone to teach him he achieved a perfect understanding of things that most people spend a lot of time and effort in learning. Peter despised the study of secular subjects, believing that nature was a good enough teacher of everything one needed to know. He always looked to his sister as the ideal at which he should aim. In this way he made such progress in virtue that he was respected for his goodness as much as his brother Basil. These things belong to a later time but at this

period he was everything to his sister and mother, helping them in their progress towards the angelic life. Once when there was a severe famine and many people came from all over to the region where they lived, having heard of their generosity, Peter was able, due to his imaginative thinking, to provide so much food that the large numbers of visitors made that remote area look like a city.

13 At about this time their mother, who had reached a comfortable old age, departed for God, dying in the arms of two of her children. It is worthwhile recording the words of blessing she pronounced over her children. As was proper, she mentioned each one who was not there so that no one was deprived of her blessing, but it was those who were with her whom she specially commended to God in prayer. Her two children sat on either side of her bed, and she took the hand of each in her own and spoke her last words to God, saying: 'To you, O Lord, I offer the first fruits and pay a tithe on the fruit of my labour pains. My first fruits are my eldest daughter and my tithe is my last-born son. Both these offerings are dedicated to you according to your law. May your blessing come upon both the first fruits and the tithe.' By these words she meant her daughter Macrina and her son Peter. Her life came to an end as she finished her blessing, after getting her children to promise to bury her body in their father's tomb. When they had done as she asked they were even more resolved to live an ascetic life, and struggling against their personal inclinations, they eclipsed their earlier achievements by means of subsequent success.

14 At about this time Basil, one of the most saintly men, was elected bishop of the great church at Caesarea. He himself ordained his brother Peter a priest, consecrating him with the sacred rites. As a result their lives became yet more solemn and holy, for the priesthood caused them to lead an even more ascetic life. Eight years later, Basil, by now world-famous, departed this life and went to be with God. His death was lamented equally in his own country and the world at large. When news of his death reached Macrina in her distant home, her heart was broken by this loss (for how could she not be affected by this misfortune when even the enemies of truth were

affected?). It is said that gold is purified in different furnaces so that if any impurity is left after the first melting process it will be separated in the second, and once more in the final smelting when the metal is purged of all the impurities mixed in with it: the most accurate proof that the gold has been properly tested is if it no longer produces any impurity after it has passed through every furnace. Something similar happened to Macrina for her lofty ideas were put to the test by the repeated onslaughts of grief: her soul was thereby proved to be genuine and firm, first by the death of her brother Naucratios, then by the separation from her mother and finally when Basil, of whom our whole family was proud, departed this life. But Macrina remained unbeaten like a boxer, never cowering or brought to her knees by the blows of misfortune.

15 Nine months or slightly more after Basil's death a council of bishops was held at Antioch,[6] which we attended, and before a year had passed, when we were free once again to return home, I, Gregory, conceived a longing to go and visit my sister. For a long time had elapsed during which I had been prevented from going to her by the difficulties caused by the persecutions. I had endured these difficulties everywhere, exiled as I was from my country by the heretics. When I reckoned the intervening time during which the persecutions had prevented me from meeting her in person, it seemed like a long interval – a little less than eight years. After travelling most of the way I found myself only a day's journey away. Then a vision came to me in a dream and made my hopes for the future full of apprehension: I seemed to be carrying the relics of a martyr and from them there shone a bright light like that which is reflected off a clean mirror when it is held up to the sun – indeed it was so bright that it dazzled my eyes. That night the same vision appeared to me three times: I could not understand clearly the dream's hidden meaning, but I foresaw that my soul would encounter some sorrow. I waited to see what would happen next so that I could judge its significance. When I came close to the remote area where Macrina lived her angelic and heavenly life, I asked one of the servants whether my brother Peter was there. He told me that he had set off to meet us three days ago, from which I surmised that he

had taken a different route from mine. Then I asked about Macrina. When the servant told me she was ill, I hurried to reach my destination for some premonition of the future crept over me and filled me with fear.

16 When I got there and news of my arrival reached the brothers, the whole community came out of the monastery [on their estate] to greet me (for it is usual for them to honour their friends by coming to meet them). From the women, a group of young girls, carefully arranged in order, were waiting by the church for my arrival. When the prayers and blessing were finished the girls, after respectfully bowing their heads to receive a blessing, withdrew to their quarters, leaving not a single one with us, from which I inferred that their leader was not among them. Someone led me to the house where Macrina was. The door was opened and I entered that holy place. She was already seriously ill but was resting not on a bed or a cover but on the ground itself, on a board covered with sacking, with her head on another board, which was used as a pillow for her head, for it had been set at an angle to support her neck.

17 When she saw me near the door, she raised herself up on one elbow: there was no way she could run towards me, for the fever had already sapped her strength. Instead she carried out her duty to come and meet me by putting her hands firmly on the ground and leaning out of bed as far as she could. I ran up to her and took her face, which was turned towards the ground, in my hands. I raised her up and helped her to lie back again as she had been. She stretched out her hand to God and said: 'God, you have filled me with this grace and have not failed to grant my desire, for you inspired your servant, my brother, to visit me, your servant girl.' She did not want to upset me further so she tried to control her groans and conceal how much her breathlessness distressed her, and attempted to put on a brave face, making cheerful remarks and giving us the opportunity to do the same by asking us questions. When Basil was mentioned in the course of the conversation, I lost heart, my face fell in dejection and tears streamed from my eyes. But Macrina was so far from sharing my sorrow that she made the mention of our saintly brother an opportunity for making greater progress in

the philosophical life. She talked to us at length, seeking to explain the nature of man and revealing the workings of the divine plan, hidden though it was during these sorrowful times. She told us about things to do with the future life as if she were inspired by the Holy Spirit. As a result of her talk my soul seemed almost to be freed from my human nature, elevated by her words, and to take its place within the heavenly sanctuary.

18 We hear in the story of Job that although this man's whole body was consumed by infected and suppurating sores, he did not allow himself to indulge in self-pity, but while suffering physically he remained as active as ever and did not cut short his discussions which were concerned with lofty matters. I noticed something similar happening in the case of Macrina when the fever was consuming all her energy and dragging her towards death, and yet she managed to refresh her body with a kind of dew and in this way she kept her mind clear for the contemplation of higher things, unaffected by the terrible illness. If I did not have to keep my account within limits, I would set down in order everything that she said and describe how she was so exalted by her own words as to enter upon a philosophical discussion regarding the soul and an explanation of the cause of life in the body: she told us why man exists and how it is that he is mortal and where death comes from and how we are released from this life into a new one.[7] In all of this she was inspired by the Holy Spirit, explaining everything clearly and logically, as fluently as water flowing downhill from a spring without any hindrance.

19 When she had finished, she said, 'Now, my brother, it is time for you to rest a while for you are very tired after your journey.' In fact I felt genuine relief at seeing her and hearing her uplifting words, but because I knew it would please her if I complied with her wishes, I went into a nearby garden and found a beautiful place prepared for me. There I rested beneath the shade of the climbing vines. But it was impossible for me to enjoy the pleasant surroundings when my soul was troubled within by the thought of the sad events that were soon to occur. What I saw seemed to explain the mystery of my dream. For the vision before me really seemed to be the remains of a saint who had

died to sin, and was radiant with the grace of the Holy Spirit
dwelling in him. I told this to one of the people who had heard
me describing my dream. We were feeling depressed, as was
natural seeing that we were worried about what would happen,
but somehow Macrina guessed our state of mind and gave us a
more cheerful message. She told us to take heart and to have a
more positive attitude for she claimed that she actually felt she
was getting stronger. She was not saying this to deceive us –
what she said was based on the truth, even if we did not know
it at the time. Macrina's attitude was like that of an athlete
overtaking his rival in the stadium: he is already on the home
straight and is close to getting the prize; he can see the victor's
wreath and is terribly excited as if the prize were already his; he
even shouts out in triumph to his watching supporters. In a
similar way Macrina gave us reasons to be excited over her success now that she was close to winning the prize of the heavenly
calling and could almost apply the Apostle's words to herself:
'There awaits for me a crown of righteousness which the righteous judge will offer me', since 'I have fought the good fight
and I have finished the race and kept the faith.'[8] Her positive
attitude cheered us up and as a result we were able to take
pleasure in the food set before us: Macrina had up till now put
a lot of effort into the careful preparation of a variety of dishes
to offer us.

20 When we were in her company again (for she would not
allow us to spend our spare time by ourselves), she resumed her
account of her life starting from her childhood and describing
everything in order as if it were a historical narrative. She told
us what she remembered of our parents' lives, both before my
birth and in the years following. Her aim was to express thanks
to God. She showed that our parents' contemporaries did not
admire them because of their wealth but for their divinely
inspired philanthropy. Our father's parents had their property
confiscated because they were Christians, while our mother's
father was put to death because he provoked the emperor's
anger and all his property was transferred to other owners.
Nevertheless, their wealth had increased so much through their
faith that no one could name anyone wealthier than they. Later

on, when our parents' property had been divided up among
their nine children, each child's share was increased by God's
blessing in such a way that they each had a greater share than
their parents had had. Macrina kept nothing of the share allotted to her when the estate had been divided up between her and
her siblings – instead she arranged for it all to be put in the
hands of a priest, in accordance with the divine command.
Thanks to God's guidance her life was such that she never ceased
to work to carry out his commandments, nor did she ever rely
on any human being, nor did her ability to lead a virtuous life
depend on other people's resources. On the other hand she never
turned away beggars nor she did go in search of benefactors, for
God, by his blessings, secretly increased the meagre resources
produced by her efforts, turning them to abundant fruits.

21 Then I told her of the troubles I was experiencing – first,
being sent into exile by the Emperor Valens[9] because of my
faith and then finding myself being drawn into distressing controversies because the churches had been thrown into confusion. She reacted by saying: 'Will you not stop being so stubborn
and ignoring God's blessings? Will you not heal your ungrateful soul? Why do you not compare your situation with that of
your parents? From a worldly point of view at any rate we can
be proud of the fact that we are nobly born and come from a
good family. Our father was highly regarded in his day for his
learning but his reputation only extended as far as the local law
courts; despite his outstanding skill at rhetoric, his fame did not
go beyond the Pontus, but he was content to be admired in his
own region. But you are famous throughout many cities, provinces and countries, and it is you whom the churches call on
and send out as their negotiator and troubleshooter – do you
not realize how much you are appreciated? Can you not see
where all these blessings come from? It is your parents' prayers
that have raised you to these heights for you yourself have little
or no natural predisposition for such things.'

22 While she was saying this I felt that I would very much have
liked to extend the day so that she could continue to charm our
ears with her delightful words. But the sound of the chanting
of psalms was summoning us to the evening service, and so

Macrina sent me to the church while she herself withdrew to be with God in her prayers. Then night fell. When the next day dawned it was clear to me from what I saw that this would be her last day on earth, for the fever had consumed all her natural strength. When she saw how depressed we were, she made an effort to distract us from our gloomy thoughts, dispelling the grief from our hearts by means of her sweet words, even though her breathing was now weak and distressed. My soul was weighed down by sadness, as was natural, because I could no longer hope to hear such a voice again, and I was expecting this woman, our family's pride and joy, to pass from human life. On the other hand I was inspired by what was happening, sensing that she had transcended our common human nature. It seemed to me that she was no longer part of human reality in that she experienced nothing strange in waiting for death, even though she had almost breathed her last, and did not fear separation from this life. Instead she was meditating on the most important things right to the very end. It was as if some angel had providentially taken on human shape, an angel who had no connection or familiarity with life in the flesh and for whom a state of incapability of feeling pain was perfectly natural for the flesh did not drag her towards physical passions. For this reason it seemed to me that she revealed to those who were with her at the time that divine and pure love for the unseen Bridegroom which she kept hidden in the secret recesses of her soul. It seemed that she made public her heart's desire to rush forward to join her beloved as quickly as possible, as soon as she was released from the ties of the body. For it was really her lover towards whom she was running, not allowing any of the pleasures of life to distract her.

23 Most of the day had already passed and the sun was setting, but her eagerness showed no signs of flagging. Indeed, as the time of her departure approached it was as if she could see more clearly the beauty of her Bridegroom and was hastening all the more towards her beloved. She no longer spoke to us who were present but to him on whom her gaze was fixed. Her bed had been turned towards the east, and she had withdrawn from conversation with us and was now addressing

God in prayer, with her hands stretched out in supplication. She was whispering so faintly that we could hardly hear what she was saying. I will record the words of her prayer so that there can be no doubt that she was with God and that he was listening to her.

24 'You, O Lord, have freed us from the fear of death.[10]

You have made the end of this life to be the beginning of our true life.

You allow our bodies to rest for a time in sleep and wake us up again at the last trumpet.[11]

You have given in trust to the earth our earthly bodies which you have shaped with your own hands.

You have restored what you have given, transforming what is mortal and shapeless in us by means of immortality and beauty.

You have redeemed us from the curse of the law and from sin, becoming both for us.[12]

You have crushed the heads of the dragon[13] which seized us in its jaws, dragging us through the yawning gulf of disobedience.

You have prepared the way for the resurrection, smashing down the gates of hell, and have destroyed the one who had power over death.[14]

You have given as a token to those who fear you the sign of the holy cross so that we can destroy the enemy and bring stability to our lives.

God eternal, at whom I threw myself from the moment I left my mother's womb,[15]

You whom my soul has loved with all its strength, you to whom I dedicated my flesh and my soul from my youth until this moment, give me as companion a bright angel who will take me by the hand and lead me to the place of refreshment where flows the water of repose[16] in the bosom of the holy fathers.

You have cut through the flame of the fiery sword[17] and have allowed the man who was crucified with you and who threw himself on your mercy to enter paradise.[18]

Remember me, too, in your kingdom when I am crucified with

you, I who out of fear of you have nailed down my flesh and
have feared your judgements.[19]

Do not let the terrifying chasm separate me from your chosen
    ones.

Do not let the jealous one block my way.

Do not let my sin be revealed before your eyes, if I have sinned
    in word or deed or thought, led astray by the weakness of my
    nature.

You who have power on earth to forgive sins,[20] forgive me so
    that I may draw breath.

Grant that I may come into your presence when I shed my body
    and that my soul, holy and without blemish, will be received
    into your hands like incense before your face.'[21]

25 As she finished her prayer she traced the sign of the cross
over her eyes, her mouth and her heart. Little by little her
tongue, parched by the fever, lost the ability to form the words
clearly. Her voice failed and it was only from the parting of her
lips and the gestures of her hands that we realized she was praying. Then, as evening drew on and a lamp was brought in,
Macrina suddenly opened her eyes wide and looked towards
the light, indicating that she wanted to sing the hymn set for the
lighting of the lamps. But her voice failed her and so she
achieved her purpose in her heart and by the gestures of her
hands: her lips moved in harmony with her inner activity. When
she had finished the hymn of thanksgiving and she moved her
hand to her face to make the sign of the cross to indicate the
end of the prayer, she gave a deep sigh: she had reached the end
of her life at the same time as her prayer. When she stopped
breathing and moved no more, I recalled the request she had
made when we first met again. She had said she would like me
to close her eyes with my hands and carry out the customary
treatment of her body. So I put my hand, numb with grief, to
her saintly face, because I did not want to appear to be disregarding her request. Her eyes did not need any adjustment for
they were as they would be if she had been sleeping naturally,
decently covered by her eyelids; her lips were firmly closed and
her hands rested on her breast in the proper way. Indeed her

whole body had of its own accord adopted a graceful posture and did not need my hands to make any improvements.

26 My soul was paralysed both by what I saw before me and by the distressing sound of lamentation I could hear from the women. Until then they had restrained themselves calmly, keeping their pain deep inside their hearts and stifling their impulse to weep for fear of encountering Macrina's reproachful look, even if she did not say anything, if one of them failed to stifle a cry, and thereby disobeyed her. They had not wanted to upset her. But when they could no longer calmly control their feelings, like a fire smouldering in their hearts a bitter and irrepressible cry burst forth which knocked me completely off balance. I felt as if I were being dragged under water by a fast-flowing stream as I was swept away by my grief. Forgetting what I had been doing, I joined in their lament. The women's grief did in fact somehow seem right and reasonable to me. They were not crying because they had lost a close friend or someone with whom they had had a physical relationship or anything of that sort which makes it intolerable when tragedy strikes. No, it was rather as if they had lost their hope in God and in the salvation of their souls – this was what they were crying for and loudly bewailing in their lamentations. 'The light of our eyes has been put out,' they said, 'and the lamp that guided us has been taken away. The stability of our life has been destroyed and the seal of our immortality has been snatched away. That which bound us together in harmony has been torn apart, that which supported us in our exhaustion has been shattered, and we have lost the one who cared for the weak. When we were with you night seemed to us as bright as day because of your pure life; but now daylight itself has turned to darkness.' Those women who called her mother and nurse expressed their grief even more passionately. They were the ones whom she had found wandering along the roads during the famine: she had taken them home and fed and cared for them and led them towards a pure and uncorrupted life.

27 When I had somehow managed to lift my soul out of the abyss, I looked closely at this saintly woman, and I felt I was being rebuked for the lack of discipline of those who were

making such a noise with their wailing. 'Look at her,' I called to the women in a loud voice, 'and remember what she taught you about what was proper and correct in each situation. Her holy soul prescribed a specific time for tears; you were told to limit your crying to the time set aside for prayer. You can obey her now, by turning the wailing of your laments into the harmonious singing of hymns.' I said this in an even louder voice, so that I could be heard over the sound of their grief. Then I asked them to move to the building next door for a few moments, while some of the women whose care she had been happy to accept during her lifetime stayed behind.

28 Among these women there was one who was wealthy and nobly born and whose physical grace and general distinction had made her a celebrity in her youth. She had married a man of high rank and had lived with him for a short time but their union had been torn apart while she was still young. After that she had made Macrina the guardian and teacher of her widowhood. She lived most of the time with the women who had adopted a life of chastity, learning from them how to live a life of virtue. Vetiana was the name of this woman and her father, Araxios, had been a member of the senate. I told her that now, at any rate, we could not reproach ourselves for dressing Macrina's body in bright clothes and adorning her pure and spotless body with colourful garments. Vetiana replied that we must find out what the saintly woman had thought right in these circumstances for it would not be a good idea to go against her wishes; but certainly she would be happy to do whatever was pleasing to God.

29 There was one woman who had been put in charge of the women dedicated to chastity – a deaconess called Lampadion who claimed to know precisely what Macrina's wishes had been with regard to her own burial. When I asked her about it (for she happened to be present at our discussion), she replied in tears, 'The only adornment that this saintly woman longed for was a pure life. This was to be what adorned her in life and her shroud in death. As regards the adornment of her body she was not concerned with such things during her lifetime nor did she make arrangements for the present situation: even if we

wanted it we would find nothing more than what we have here.'
'But has nothing been put away,' I asked, 'which we could use
to decorate the coffin?' 'How do you mean, "put away"? What
you are holding is everything that she put away. Look at the
cloak, look at the veil for her head, the worn-out shoes on her
feet. These are her riches, this is her fortune. There is nothing
other than what you can see, nothing put away and locked in
secret chests or rooms. She knew only one place to store her
personal wealth and that was the heavenly treasure-chest. It
was there that she stored everything, leaving nothing on earth.'
'Well then,' I said to her, 'what if I were to offer her one of the
things I had put away for my own burial – would that be contrary to her wishes?' Lampadion replied that she did not think
this would be against Macrina's wishes. 'While she was still
alive she would allow you to pay her such honour for two reasons, because of your priesthood which she always respected
and because of your close family tie. In her opinion what
belonged to her brother also belonged to her. That is why she
asked that her corpse be dressed for burial by your hands.'

30 When this had been decided it was time to dress her saintly
body in linen for burial. We divided the tasks between us, each
person taking on a different one. For my part I gave instruc-
tions to a servant to bring the garment, and Vetiana, whom I
mentioned, prepared the saintly woman for burial. As she put
her hand to Macrina's neck she turned to me and said, 'Look at
the necklace she's wearing!' She unfastened the chain at the
back and stretched out her hand to show me a cross and a ring
both made of iron. Macrina had clearly worn them both all the
time, hanging by a thin thread over her heart. I said to Vetiana,
'Let us share these. You take the cross to protect you; I will be
happy to take the ring as my share.' Vetiana looked carefully at
the ring's signet which had a cross engraved on it and then she
said to me, 'This was a good choice of yours. Look, the hoop of
the ring is hollow and there is a sliver of the Tree of Life[22] inside
it. So the cross engraved on the outside is an indication of what
the ring contains inside.'

31 When the time came to dress that pure body in the linen
clothes, Macrina's request to me meant that I had to do it

myself, though I was assisted by the woman who had shared with me Macrina's legacy. 'You should be aware of the greatest miracle this holy woman performed.' 'What was that?' I asked. Vetiana bared part of Macrina's breast. 'Can you see this slight mark under the skin? It is hardly noticeable – it just looks like a hole made by a fine needle.' She brought the lamp up close to the spot she was indicating. 'What is so miraculous about her body having this mark here which you can hardly see?' I asked. 'This was left on her body as a reminder of the great help given to her by God. For at one time a painful abscess appeared here: it was equally risky to cut out the tumour or to leave it to develop until it spread to the area around her heart, for then it would be completely incurable. Her mother often begged her to allow a doctor to examine her, arguing that God had given the doctor his skill to help people. But Macrina thought that laying bare that part of her body to another person's eyes would be worse than the pain of the abscess. One evening when she had finished helping her mother with the housework as usual, she went into the sanctuary and spent the whole night prostrate before the God of healing. As the water that flowed from her eyes dripped on to the ground, she used the mud created by her tears as an ointment on her abscess. When her desperate mother begged her again to go to the doctor, she replied that it would be sufficient to heal her of her pain if her mother were to make the sign of the holy cross on the spot with her own hand. And when her mother put her hand on Macrina's breast, the sign of the cross had an immediate effect and the abscess vanished. But this little mark,' Vetiana told me, 'appeared just where the terrible abscess had been and remained there till the end, as a reminder, I believe, of the divine visitation, and as a reason for everlasting thankfulness to God.'

32 When we had finished adorning the body as best we could, the deaconess again said that it was not appropriate for the women to see Macrina dressed as a bride. 'I have a dark cloak of your mother's which I have kept,' she said. 'I think it would be a good idea to put this over Macrina so that the attractiveness of the clothes she is wearing does not unnaturally enhance her saintly beauty.' I was persuaded by what she said and so we

spread the cloak over Macrina. But even when wearing the dark cloak she was still radiantly lovely. I am convinced that the divine power added this grace to her body, so that her beauty seemed to shine with a bright light just as in the vision I had had in my dream.

33 While we were busy with these things and the women's psalm singing, mingled with lamentations, echoed round the place, the news of her death had quickly spread – I am not sure how – all over the surrounding area. All the people living nearby were hurrying here in response to this tragic news; in fact the hall was not large enough to contain all those who came running. We spent the whole night singing hymns around her, just like those hymns sung in praise of the martyrs, and when dawn broke, the crowd of both men and women who had gathered from the surrounding areas disturbed the psalm singing with its wailing. For my part, although my heart was suffering as a result of this sad event, I nevertheless decided that as far as our resources permitted we should do all the things appropriate for such a funeral. So I divided the crowd according to sex, putting the many women with the virgins and the men with the monks, thereby creating a rhythmic and harmonious choir to sing the psalms. A little later in the day, when the whole area around this remote spot became too small for the large number of people gathered there, the bishop of that area, a man by the name of Araxios who was there with all his clergy, suggested that the funeral procession should set off slowly because the distance we had to go was considerable and the crowds of people would prevent it moving any faster. At the same time he gave orders that all his priests should help to carry the bier.

34 When these decisions had been made, we began to carry them out. I went to stand in front of the bier and invited Araxios to stand beside me, while two other members of the higher clergy took up position at the back. The slow procession then set off, as is the custom, and we moved forward step by step. The people crowded round the bier, each person finding it hard to tear their eyes from that holy woman, and this meant that it was not easy for us to proceed. On each side long lines of

deacons and clergy of the lower orders led the procession, each carrying a candle. It was like a liturgical procession for the sound of the psalms being sung in harmony could be heard the whole length of it, as in the Song of the Three Children.[23] It was about a mile from our remote home to the chapel of the holy martyrs where our parents were buried, and the journey took us nearly the whole day. For the ever-increasing number of people accompanying us hindered our progress and we could not go as fast as planned. Once inside the building we stopped, put down the bier and immediately began to pray. But our prayer caused people to start crying. When there was a pause in the singing of the psalms, the women turned to look at that saintly face. At that moment our parents' tomb (in which Macrina was to be buried) was being opened and some woman cried out desperately that we would never see that divine face again. Then the rest of the women joined her in crying out in the same way, and a wild confusion broke out, disrupting the ordered and sacred character of the psalm singing, as everyone echoed the women's laments. We signalled to them to be quiet but it was hard to get them to do so. Then the cantor led them in prayer, starting with the proper liturgical chants while the people composed themselves to pray.

35 When the prayer had reached its proper conclusion, I was seized by a fear that I would break the divine command against uncovering one's father's or mother's nakedness.[24] 'How will I avoid this kind of condemnation if I see in my parent's bodies that nakedness which all humans share? No doubt their bodies will have decayed and become disgusting and foul.' As I thought about this, I became even more worried when I remembered Noah's anger at his son, but it was actually the story of Noah that advised me what to do.[25] Before the bodies were exposed they were covered with a clean shroud, which was pulled right down to each corner before the lid of the tomb was lifted off. When the shroud covered the bodies, the local bishop and I lifted Macrina's saintly body from the bier and laid her beside her mother, thereby carrying out the wishes of both women. For together they had prayed to God their whole lives long, asking that their bodies should be joined

after death and that the intimacy they had shared during their
lives should not be disrupted in death.

36 When we had performed all the funeral rites and it was time
to go home, I lay down on the tomb and kissed the dust before
starting the return journey. I felt dejected and tearful when I
thought of all that my life had now lost. On the way I came to
Sebastopolis, a small town in the Pontus, where I was courte-
ously met by a man who was a high-ranking army officer in
charge of a garrison there, where he lived with his subordi-
nates. He had heard of my misfortune and was very upset (for
he was connected to our family as a relative and a friend), and
he described to me a miracle that Macrina had performed. I
will just add this one miracle to my account and then I will
bring my story to an end. When we had stopped crying and
started to talk, he said to me, 'Let me tell you how good Macrina was, she who has been set free from human existence', and
with these words he began his story.

37 My wife and I once conceived a desire to visit the 'school of
virtue' – that is, I believe, the name one should give the place
where that blessed soul lived. We had our daughter with us
who was suffering from an eye infection. She looked really ugly
and pitiable for the cornea around her pupil had swollen and
turned milky. On entering the holy house, my wife and I went
off separately to visit the men and women who were living an
ascetic life there: I went to the men's monastery which was
headed by your brother Peter, while my wife went to the wom-
en's monastery to meet the saintly Macrina. After some time,
we judged it was time to leave that remote place and we were
just about to depart when we both experienced an act of friendship, each in our separate place. For your brother invited me to
stay and share their austere meal, while the blessed Macrina
refused to let my wife go. Holding my daughter on her lap, she
said she would not let them leave until they had been offered a
meal and the riches of the ascetic life. Macrina caressed the
child as was natural and as she put her lips to the girl's eyes, she
noticed the medical condition around the pupil. 'If you do me
the favour of joining me for the meal, I will give you in return
a suitable reward for the respect you have shown me.' 'What

kind of reward?' asked the child's mother. 'I have an ointment,' said the great one, 'which has the power to heal this eye condition.' When a message from the women's monastery informed me of Macrina's promise, my wife and I were happy to stay without worrying too much about the need to return home.

38 When we had finished the meal and our hearts were full – for the great Peter had produced the food for us with his own hands and had cheered us up, while the saintly Macrina had said goodbye to my wife with real friendliness – we resumed our journey, eager and cheerful. As we travelled along we told each other of what we had experienced. For my part I told her what I had seen and heard in the men's quarters, while my wife described everything to me in great detail, convinced that she should not leave out even the smallest detail, as if she were giving a blow-by-blow account. She gave me an account of events as in an historical monograph, and when she got to the promise of a cure for our daughter's eyes, she suddenly stopped and said, 'What's the matter with us? How could we forget her promise and the eye ointment she told us about?' I was upset by our carelessness and I asked someone to run back quickly and fetch the medicine. Then the child who was being carried by her nurse happened to look at her mother, and her mother, staring at her daughter's eyes, said, 'Do not be upset any longer at our carelessness.' (Her excitement and surprise caused her to shout out these words.) 'Look! We have got everything she promised us! She has already given us the true medicine which can heal the medical condition! It is the medicine of prayer and it has already had an effect: there is not the slightest trace of the problem affecting her eyes! That saintly woman's remedy has cleared her eyes completely!' As she said this, she took the child and put her in my arms. Remembering the incredible miracles in the Gospels I said, 'Is it surprising that God's hand causes the blind to recover their sight, when today his servant Macrina, in curing this disease by means of her faith in God, has performed a miracle almost as wonderful as the ones in the Gospel?'

As he said this his words were choked by sobs: what he had told me made him burst into tears. This was the story I heard from the army officer.

39 We heard many similar stories from those who lived with Macrina and who knew her very well, but I do not think it is a good idea to add them to this account. Most people judge the credibility of what they are told from their own experiences, and anything that goes beyond what they can grasp they disparage as unbelievable, suspecting it of being a lie. For this reason I will not say anything about that incredible harvest during the famine, when the amount of grain available seemed to remain the same even after everybody had got as much as they needed. Nor will I mention other things even stranger than this – the healing of illnesses, the expulsion of demons and the prophecies that proved to be true. All these things, incredible though they may seem, are believed to be true by those who know all the details. But such stories are regarded as unacceptable by people who have a less spiritual view, those who do not know that grace is distributed according to the measure of faith, and is granted in small amounts to those who have little faith, but in abundance to those who have a lot of room for faith in them. So that those who have less faith will not be harmed by being given the opportunity to deny faith in God's gifts, I have decided to leave out Macrina's more remarkable miracles, thinking it sufficient to outline her story in the way I have done here.

THE LIFE OF MELANIA THE ELDER

by Palladius

Melania the elder

Melania was born in Spain in about 340, into a wealthy Roman family. Some time after she was widowed, she decided to abandon her luxurious life in Rome, leaving her young son Publicola behind and travelling to Egypt in 374, where she spent some months living with the desert monks. She then moved to Palestine, where she stayed for more than twenty-five years, establishing monasteries for men and women on the Mount of Olives in Jerusalem with her friend Rufinus of Aquileia. Melania returned to Rome in 400 but a few years later she went back to Palestine where she died in 410. There is no full-scale biography of her; in addition to the chapters in Palladius' *Lausiac History*, she is mentioned in Paulinus' *Letter* 29 and *Poem* 21; Jerome's *Letters* 3, 4 (in which he says that she has reached Jerusalem with Rufinus, who had once been his best friend), 45, 133; and Augustine's *Letter* 94. Jerome had called her 'a second Thecla' in his *Chronicle* but deleted this when he fell out with her companion Rufinus, and later, in his *Letter* 133, he alludes to her by saying that her name, which means 'black' in Greek, accurately reflects the dark treachery of her character.

Palladius

Palladius was born in about 363 in what is now Turkey. Interested in the growing monastic movement, he lived for a time in a monastery on the Mount of Olives and came into contact with Melania the elder. He then spent nine years in monastic communities in Egypt, and witnessed the outbreak of the bitter dispute between those who were enthusiastic about the writings of the third-century theologian Origen and those who considered some of his doctrines suspect. Palladius seems to have been made bishop of Helenopolis in Turkey but he still became embroiled in the spreading Origenist controversy. As a supporter of John Chrysostom who was deposed from his post as bishop of Constantinople in 404 for alleged Origenism, Palladius was sent into exile in Egypt for a time. In 419–20 he wrote the *Lausiac History*, dedicated to an official at the emperor's court: this takes the form of a series of thumbnail sketches of ascetics, both men and women, many of whom Palladius had met. He died before 431.

Melania, that most fortunate woman, was a Spaniard by birth and as such she qualified for Roman citizenship. She was the daughter of Marcellinus, a man of consular rank, and the wife of a man of high status, whose name I do not remember. Melania was widowed at the age of twenty-two, at which time God considered her worthy of divine love. She said nothing to anyone – for she would have been prevented from doing so at that time when Valens was the emperor – but arranged for a guardian for her son[1] and, taking all her movable belongings and loading them on board ship, she sailed directly to Alexandria with a group of remarkable young men and women. There she sold her material possessions, exchanging them for gold, and then went to Mount Nitria to meet the fathers who lived with Pambo, Arsisius, Sarapion the Great and Paphnutios of Scete, Isidore the Confessor, who was bishop of Hermopolis, and Dioscurus. She spent six months with them, travelling around the desert and questioning all the holy men. After this, when the prefect of Egypt sent Isidore, Pisimios, Adelphios, Paphnutios and Pambo, together with Ammonius the one-eared, and twelve bishops and priests, into exile near Diocaesarea in Palestine, she followed them and acted as their servant, using her own money. When servants were forbidden, so the story goes (for I happened to meet the holy Pisimios, Isidore, Paphnutios and Ammonius), she would put on the hooded cape worn by servant boys and in the evenings would bring them what they needed. The consular governor of Palestine heard about her and wishing to fill his pockets, he decided to blackmail her. Not realizing that she was a freewoman, he seized her and threw her into prison, but she made it clear to him who her father was and whose wife she had been. She said to him, 'I am Christ's servant. Do not look down on my shabby appearance; I can make myself look impressive if I want. You cannot terrify me or take anything away from me. I have made this clear to you so that you do not commit a crime as the result of ignorance. For in dealing with idiots you need to be as sharp as a hawk.' Then, when the judge understood the situation, he apologized and treated her with respect, telling her she could associate with the holy men without restriction.

After these men had been recalled from exile, Melania founded a monastery in Jerusalem where she lived for twenty-seven years in the company of fifty virgins. A man called Rufinus[2] who came from Aquileia in Italy lived there too. He came from a very good family, held similar views to Melania's and was most energetic. Later he was considered worthy to become a priest. There was no more knowledgeable and capable person to be found. During these twenty-seven years they welcomed people who visited Jerusalem for the sake of their vows – bishops, monks and deacons – providing all their guests with hospitality at their own expense. They healed the schism of Paulinus[3] which involved about four hundred monks, and together they won over all the heretics who denied the divinity of the Holy Spirit and brought them into the church. They showed respect to the local clergy and lived out their lives without offending anyone.

*

I have already given a superficial description of that wonderful, saintly woman, Melania in this book; nevertheless I wish to weave into this account the remaining elements of her story. It is not for me, but for the inhabitants of Persia, to describe how much of her wealth she spent with God-given generosity, as though she were throwing it on a fire, so to speak. No one failed to benefit by her good works, whether in the east or west, north or south. For thirty-seven years she lived in exile, supporting churches, monasteries, refugees and prisoners with her private fortune; she was also provided with funds by her own financial administrators and those of her family and son.

Because she persisted so long in her life of isolation from the
world, she did not possess so much as a square metre of land.
Nor was she distracted by longing for her son: indeed, her love
for her only son did not separate her from her love for Christ.
By means of her prayers the young man attained a high standard of education, developed an excellent character and made a
distinguished marriage. He achieved a high-ranking position
in a secular career and had two children. Much later, Melania
heard about the situation of her granddaughter Melania the
younger, how she was married and had decided to withdraw
from the world. As she was afraid that the couple might fall
victim to incorrect teachings or heresy or bad ways, she set sail
from Caesarea, although she was already an old woman of
sixty, and reached Rome twenty days later. There she met
Apronianus, a Greek and a most blessed and distinguished
man. She gave him religious instruction and made him a Christian, having persuaded him to live in chastity with his wife
Avita, who was Melania's cousin. Then having strengthened
her granddaughter Melania and her husband Pinianus in their
resolve, and having given instruction to her daughter-in-law
Albina (her son's wife), she persuaded them all to sell their
possessions. She took them away from Rome and brought
them to the haven of a consecrated and peaceful life. In doing
this she so to speak fought with the wild beasts, in other words
with the senators and their wives, who tried to prevent her
from persuading the rest of her family to withdraw from the
world. This is how she responded to their attempts. She said,
'My children, it was written four hundred years ago that "the
last hour has come". Why do you cling to your empty lives?
Are you not afraid that the days of the Antichrist[4] will catch up
with you and prevent you from enjoying your own wealth or
what you have inherited?'

She set all these people free and brought them to the monastic life. She gave religious instruction to the younger Publicola
and took him to Sicily. When she had sold all her remaining
property and received the money for it, she went on to Jerusalem. Forty days after distributing all her worldly goods, she
passed away at a fine old age and in the deepest peace. She left

behind a monastery in Jerusalem together with the money for
its endowment.

After all these people had left Rome, the barbarian deluge
fell upon that city [in 410], as mentioned long before in prophecy, and did not spare even the bronze statues standing in the
forum, but ravaged everything in their barbaric fury, consign-
ing it to destruction. The result was that Rome, which had been
adorned with beauty for twelve hundred years, collapsed in
ruins. Then both those who had received religious instruction
from Melania and those who had been opposed to this instruction glorified God, who won over the unbelievers by overturn-
ing the accepted order of things, for of all the other people who
had been taken prisoner, only those households were saved that
had offered themselves as sacrifices to the Lord as the result of
Melania's efforts.

*

It happened that we made a journey from Jerusalem to Egypt,
accompanying Silvania, the sister-in-law of Rufinus, the ex-
prefect. Jovinus also went with us: he was a deacon at the time
but is now bishop of the church at Ascalon, a pious and learned
man. We found the heat really oppressive and when we arrived
at Pelusium, Jovinus took a basin and gave his hands and feet a
thorough wash in very cold water. Then he lay down to rest on
a leather cushion thrown on the ground. Melania went up to
him like a sensible mother approaching her own son and scoffed
at his weakness, saying, 'How can a warm-blooded young man
like you dare to pamper your body in that way? Do you not
realize that this is a potential source of great harm? Look, I am
sixty years old and neither my feet nor my face nor any of my
limbs except for the tips of my fingers have touched water,
although I suffer from many ailments and my doctors urge me
to wash properly. I have not yet made concessions to my body
nor have I slept on a bed or ever travelled in a litter.'

Melania was very learned and loved literature. She would
turn night into day by going through all the writings of the
ancient commentators – three million lines of Origen and a
quarter of a million of Gregory, Stephen, Pierius and Basil as
well as other admirable writers. She did not read them only

once or in a casual way but worked hard on them, ploughing her way through each seven or eight times. So she was able to be liberated from what is falsely called knowledge[5] and to mount on wings, thanks to those books: elevated by good hopes she transformed herself into a spiritual bird and so made the journey to Christ.

THE LIFE OF MARCELLA

by Jerome

(Letter *127 to Principia*)

Marcella

Marcella was born in Rome in 325 and lived there until her death some months after Alaric's invasion in 410. Jerome's *Letter* 127 is the primary source of information about her life, but during her lifetime she received his *Letters* 23–9, 32, 34, 37–8, 40–44, 59 and 97; is mentioned in 22, 30, 45, 47, 48, 54, 65 and 107; and is the recipient of Paula and Eustochium's letter (*Letter* 46 in Jerome's collection), included in this volume (*On Visiting Jerusalem*). She was one of the first wealthy aristocratic women to decide to adopt a life of austerity in Rome itself, inspired by the desert fathers and doing for Rome what Antony had done for the desert of Egypt. Widowed after only seven months she chose to live a life of poverty, chastity and biblical study, first in the company of her mother Albina and then of her companion Principia, inspiring other women to adopt a similar life, among them Paula and Eustochium.

The letter is addressed to Principia two years after Marcella's death. Jerome's *Letter* 65 (an explanation of Psalm 45) and his commentary on Matthew's gospel are also addressed to Principia.

Jerome

Jerome was born at Stridon in what is now northern Croatia in about 340. He studied in Rome, and after some years spent in Trier, Aquileia and Antioch, he withdrew into the Syrian desert to lead a life of extreme asceticism and study. Unable to endure such a harsh existence he returned to Antioch where he was made a priest and then went to Constantinople and

Rome where he worked for Pope Damasus and began his work of producing a new Latin translation of the Bible. Jerome had many critics in Rome, who accused him among other things of having an improperly intimate relationship with Paula, one of the many aristocratic women with whom he was friendly, acting as a spiritual and intellectual mentor to them. Jerome consequently left Rome and went to Bethlehem where he settled in 386, in a monastery for men beside the women's monastery founded by Paula and Eustochium. Here he wrote vast numbers of works, particularly translations of and commentaries on books of the Bible, while also becoming involved in various theological controversies which impelled him to write polemical works defending his Christian beliefs, including his rather extreme views on the superiority of virginity over marriage. These, together with his biblical commentaries and his letters, were hugely influential in the Middle Ages; he was also very important as a transmitter of literary and cultural information concerning classical antiquity and early Christianity. His Latin version of the Bible, translated from Hebrew and Greek, became the standard version for Roman Catholics, known as the Vulgate. Many of the 154 extant letters by him are addressed to women whom he got to know during his three years in Rome. He died on 30 September 420.

This letter was written in 412.

1 You have often asked me, Principia, virgin of Christ, to compose a literary memoir for Marcella, that saintly woman, and to describe the goodness we long enjoyed so that others, too, may know of it and imitate it. I am very sorry that you have had to urge me to do something I was already keen to do and that you think that I have needed your entreaties, seeing that my love for her is greater than anyone else's, even yours. In recording her great virtues, I will benefit myself more than others. The fact that I have remained silent until now and said nothing for two years was due not to a lack of regard, as you wrongly suppose, but to an incredibly powerful grief. This caused me to go into such a deep depression that I considered it wiser to remain silent for the moment than to say something that failed to do her justice. I will not use any rhetorical tricks to praise your friend Marcella, or rather, my friend, or to be even more accurate, our friend, she who had the most glorious reputation of all the saints and particularly those of the city of Rome. I shall not give an account of her illustrious family, her famous ancestors and her family tree with its consuls and praetorian prefects. I will praise nothing in her except what was characteristic of her as an individual – she who in fact was all the more noble because by despising wealth and fame she became even more famous for poverty and humility.

2 Marcella's father had already died when she lost her husband after seven months of marriage. Then Cerealis, one of the more famous consuls, wanted to marry her – he was keen because she was young and a member of an ancient family, and as well as being of a modest demeanour, she was also strikingly beautiful

(a characteristic that men tend to find particularly attractive). As he was already an old man he could promise her his wealth, which he was willing to pass on to her as a daughter rather than as a wife. Marcella's mother Albina was eager to have such a distinguished man to protect her widowed daughter, but Marcella replied, 'If I wished to marry and had not decided to dedicate myself to permanent chastity, I would be looking for a husband, not an inheritance.' When Cerealis argued that even old men can live for a long time while young men can die young, she wittily retorted, 'A young man can certainly die young but an old man cannot live for long.' Cerealis realized that this statement signalled her rejection of him and others followed his lead in giving up the idea of marriage with her. We read in St Luke's gospel: 'And there was a prophetess called Anna, the daughter of Phanuel, of the tribe of Asher. She was of a great age, having lived with her husband seven years after her marriage, then as a widow to the age of eighty-four. She never left the temple but worshipped there with fasting and prayer night and day.'[1] It is not surprising that she was allowed to see the Saviour as a reward for having hoped for him for so long. Let us now compare the two cases: Anna's seven years with Marcella's seven months, Anna's hoping for Christ and Marcella's holding on to him, Anna's joyful acknowledgement of him at his birth and Marcella's belief in him when he was crucified, Anna's refusal to deny him when he was a baby and Marcella's joy in the man as king. I am not drawing a distinction between holy women as some people foolishly do with regard to holy men and church leaders, but I do draw the conclusion that those who make equal efforts should have an equal reward.

3 It is hard to avoid malicious gossip in a slander-loving community like Rome which was once so cosmopolitan. It was the city awarded the prize for vice, where good people are the object of calumny and where whatever is pure and clean is corrupted. That is why the prophet David hopes for, rather than expects to find, this most difficult thing, something that is almost impossible to attain, when he said, 'Blessed are the pure in the way who walk in the law of the Lord',[2] meaning by the pure in the way of this world those who are not the object of

the slightest slanderous rumour and who do not listen to anyone who speaks ill of others. It is of such people that the Saviour speaks when he says in the Gospel: 'Be kind (or 'well-meaning') to your enemy while he is with you on the journey.'[3] Was there ever anyone who heard anything unpleasant about Marcella to which they gave credence? Who did believe such a thing that did not make himself guilty of malice and slander? This woman caused confusion among non-Christians for she made them realize the nature of Christian widowhood, as revealed by her conscience and her appearance. Non-Christian women tend to paint their faces with rouge and white lead, to dress in flashy silk clothes, to wear sparkling jewels and gold necklaces and hang the most expensive Red Sea pearls from their pierced ears, and to give off a perfume of musk. Such women end up wishing to rid themselves of male domination, and they go in search of new husbands, not to serve them, as God wills, but to dominate them. So they go for men who are less well off but who have the advantage of being husbands in name only: these men know they have to put up with rivals for if they grumble, they will be kicked out immediately. But our widow Marcella dressed in clothes that would keep out the cold without being revealing; she would not even wear a signet ring of gold, choosing to store her money in the stomachs of the poor rather than in her purse. She did not go anywhere without her mother and would not interview any of the priests or monks (who were needed from time to time in a house as big as hers) without a chaperone. She was always accompanied by virgins and widows and serious women, knowing that a woman's behaviour is often judged by the frivolousness of her servant girls and a woman's character is known by the company she chooses.

4 Marcella's passion for Holy Scripture was incredible. She would often sing: 'I treasure your words in my heart so that I may not sin', and those words about the perfect man: 'He delights in the law of the Lord and he will meditate on his law night and day.'[4] She did not interpret the meditation of the law as referring to the written word, as the Jewish Pharisees believe, but applied it to actions, in accordance with the words of the

Apostle: 'So whether you eat or drink or whatever you do, do everything for the glory of God.'[5] She would also repeat the words of the prophet David: 'I gain understanding through your commands',[6] believing that only after she had fulfilled all this would she deserve to understand Scripture. In this sense we read in another passage about 'all that Jesus did and taught'.[7] For even an outstanding teacher is ashamed if he does not practise what he preaches, and it is useless if his tongue preaches poverty and encourages alms-giving when he is rolling in the riches of Croesus, and if despite being clothed in only a thin, shabby coat, he fights a constant battle to stop the moths destroying the silk clothes he keeps in his cupboards.

Marcella fasted in moderation, abstained from meat and was more familiar with the smell of wine than the taste, using it only for digestive purposes and as a tonic when she was ill, as she frequently was. She rarely went out in public and kept away from the homes of noble women in particular, so that she would not be forced to look upon what she had renounced. Instead she frequented the basilicas of the apostles and martyrs to pray there in secret, avoiding the crowds. So obedient was she to her mother that she sometimes did things of which she (Marcella) in fact disapproved. When her mother, out of love for her own relations, wanted to bequeath everything to her brother's children since she did not have any sons or grandsons of her own, Marcella wanted her to give it to the poor. However, she was unable to go against her mother's wishes and so Marcella allowed her jewellery and all her perishable belongings to be given to those who were already rich, preferring to throw away her money rather than upset her mother.

5 At that time no high-ranking Roman woman knew anything of the monastic way of life and no one dared to go in for something that, because of its novelty, would be regarded with suspicion and contempt. Some priests from Alexandria (Bishop Athanasius and his successor Peter who fled to escape persecution by the Arian heretics[8] – they had come to Rome as a safe haven where they could find people with similar beliefs) had told Marcella of the life of the blessed Antony who was still living at the time,[9] of the Pachomian monasteries[10] in the

Thebaid and of the monastic rule for virgins and widows. She was not ashamed to adopt this way of life which she knew had been pleasing to Christ. Many years later Sophronia followed her example, as did other women to whom these words of Ennius applied perfectly: 'Would that the pine trees in Pelion's woods had never been felled!'[11] The much-respected Paula enjoyed Marcella's friendship and it was in Marcella's room that Eustochium, that paragon of virgins, was brought up – so it is easy to judge what the teacher must have been like if this is how her pupils turned out!

The sceptical reader may perhaps laugh at me for wasting so much time in praise of mere women. But if he remembers those holy women, the companions of our Lord and Saviour, who took care of him using their own possessions, and the three women called Mary who stood before the cross, and especially Mary known as Magdalene, who on account of her passionate commitment and the enthusiasm of her faith was known as 'the Tower' and was deemed worthy to be the first to see Christ after his resurrection, even before the disciples did, he will see that he is guilty of arrogance rather than I of foolishness. I judge a person's virtue by his or her character rather than by gender. Jesus loved John the Evangelist most of all, for John, who was known to the high priest because of the nobility of his family, had so little fear of the Jews' attacks that he brought Peter into the high priest's courtyard; in addition he was the only one of the apostles to stand at the cross and receive the Saviour's mother as his own so that as the virgin son he might welcome the virgin mother as a legacy from the virgin Lord.

6 So Marcella lived in this way for many years and found herself old before she had time to remember that she had once been young. She thought highly of Plato's saying that philosophy was a preparation for death; that is why our Apostle also says: 'Every day I die through your salvation', and the Lord, according to the ancient copies, says: 'Unless a person takes up his cross every day and follows me, he cannot be my disciple.'[12] Long ago the Holy Spirit spoke through the prophet saying: 'For your sake we are being killed all day long; we are counted as sheep for the slaughter', and from many generations later we

have the saying: 'Remember always the day of death and you will never sin', as well as that most eloquent advice from the satirist: 'Live without forgetting death, for time flies and what I am now saying is already a thing of the past.'[13] So, as I began to say, Marcella lived in such a way that she never forgot that she would soon die. She dressed in a way that reminded her of the tomb and offered herself as a living sacrifice, reasonable and pleasing to God.

7 Then urgent church business brought me to Rome, in the company of the saintly bishops Paulinus and Epiphanius, one of whom was in charge of the church of Antioch in Syria and the other the church of Salamis on Cyprus. Out of modesty I avoided drawing attention to myself among the aristocratic women, but Marcella was so insistent, 'in season and out of season'[14] to use the words of the Apostle, that she overcame my modesty. At the time I had a certain reputation for scriptural learning, and so every time we met she would ask me a question about the Scriptures and would not be satisfied with the first answer but would put forward counter-arguments, not in order to pick a quarrel but so that by asking she might learn what answers could be given to any objections that might be raised. I am afraid to mention the virtue, intelligence, saintliness and purity I encountered in her, in case I should exceed the limits of what is believable and cause you even more sorrow by reminding you of what a wonderful person you have lost. I will just say that all that I had gathered together by long study and which had become part of my nature, so to speak, as the result of lengthy meditation, she dipped into, understood and made her own. The result of this was that after I left Rome, if a dispute arose concerning the testimony of Scripture, people would consult her for a decision. And because she was very wise and understood what the philosophers called 'the appropriate thing', when she was asked she would reply as if the opinion was not her own but rather mine or somebody else's, thus making it clear that what she taught she had herself learned as a pupil – for she was well aware of the saying of the Apostle, 'I do not allow any woman to teach',[15] for she did not want to offend members of the

male sex – sometimes even the priests – who questioned her on obscure and difficult subjects.

8 I have heard that you immediately took my place beside her and never moved even a hair's breadth, so to speak, from her side, using the same house, the same bedroom, even the same bed, so that everyone in that famous city got to know that you had found a mother and she a daughter. Her estate at the edge of the city became a monastery for you both, for she had chosen the countryside for its solitude. You have lived like this for a long time and we are very pleased to hear that many women, in imitation of you, have adopted a way of life that has turned Rome into Jerusalem. There are now numerous monasteries for women and innumerable monks. As a result of this large number of people serving God, what had previously been regarded as despicable became an object of admiration.

Meanwhile we used to comfort each other in our absence by writing letters, giving spiritually what we could not give in person. Our letters would always cross in the post and we tried to outdo each other in little acts of kindness and to be the first to send greetings. Separation involved no great loss since we were linked to each other by a constant stream of letters.

9 In the midst of this peaceful service of the Lord, a storm of heresy blew up in these provinces which threw everything into confusion. It finally grew to such a fury that it spared neither itself nor any of the good. And as if it were not enough to have disturbed everything, it dispatched a ship loaded with blasphemies to the port at Rome where it immediately found a cover to match it and trampled its muddy feet in the pure waters of the Roman faith. It is not surprising that in the streets and marketplaces of the city a painted soothsayer can beat the buttocks of the foolish and knock out the teeth of objectors with his gnarled stick, seeing that this poisonous and filthy teaching could find people in Rome to lead astray. Then came the scandalous translation of Origen's book *On First Principles*;[16] then came the disciple Olbius who would have lived up to the meaning of his name which means 'Fortunate', if he had not fallen in with such a teacher; then came my supporters' fiery refutation which threw the whole school of the Pharisees into confusion. The saintly

Marcella had for a long time turned a blind eye in case people thought she was motivated by partisanship, but when she noticed that the faith of many people in Rome, as praised by the Apostle,[17] was being put in danger and that this heretic was winning priests, monks and, particularly, the lay people over to his side, taking advantage of the bishop's naivety (for he tended to judge others by his own character), she took a stand against him in public, preferring to please God rather than men.

10 In the Gospel the Saviour praises the dishonest manager because although he had acted against his master's interests, he had acted wisely for himself.[18] The heretics now saw that a small spark had given rise to an enormous fire and the flame that had for a long time lain hidden had now spread to the housetops. The deception they practised could no longer be concealed and so they asked for and obtained letters from the church at Rome, so that it would seem that they were in communion with the church when they departed from the city. A little while later there succeeded to the papacy a man of outstanding ability, called Anastasius, but Rome was not privileged to have him for long lest the head of the world should be chopped off while such a man was bishop. Indeed he was carried off to prevent him using his prayers to try to avert the sentence that had already been passed, as the Lord says to Jeremiah: 'Do not pray for the welfare of this people. Although they fast, I do not listen to their cry and although they offer burnt offerings and sacrifices I do not accept them; for by the sword, by famine and by pestilence I consume them.'[19] You may ask, 'How is this relevant?' It is relevant to my praise of Marcella for she was the one who instigated the condemnation of the heretics. It was she who brought forward as witnesses those who had first been instructed by the heretics but had then seen their error. It was she who revealed how many the heretics had deceived, she who brandished in their faces those dangerous volumes of the work *On First Principles*, on display after being 'emended' by the hand of the scorpion. It was she who sent frequent letters to the heretics calling on them to come and defend themselves. But they did not dare to come forward for they had such guilty consciences that they

preferred to be condemned in their absence than to be con-
victed to their faces. Marcella was the one who brought about
this victory and you, the head and cause of this blessing, know
that I speak the truth. You know, too, that I am only selecting
a few things out of many, as I do not want to bore the reader
or to make people think that I am giving vent to my rancour
while pretending to praise someone else. So let me now return
to the rest of my story.

11 The whirlwind moved across from west to east, threatening
many with shipwreck. Then were the words of Jesus fulfilled:
'Do you think that when the Son of Man comes he will find faith
on earth?'[20] The love of many had grown cold[21] and those few
who loved the true faith took our side, but others publicly sought
to kill them, using every means possible against them so that
even Barnabas was led astray by their hypocrisy; he even committed murder openly, in intention at any rate, if not in deed. But
the Lord blew and the storm passed away, thus fulfilling the
prophecy spoken by the prophet: 'When you take away their
breath, they die and return to the dust. On that very day all their
thoughts will perish', and these words of the Gospel: 'You fool,
this very night your life is being demanded of you. What about
the things you have prepared, who will they belong to?'[22]

12 While these things were happening in Jebus,[23] a terrible
rumour arrived from the west. We heard that Rome was under
siege and that the citizens were having to hand over their gold in
exchange for their safety, and even after they had been robbed
they were being rounded up again so that they finished by losing
their lives as well as their possessions. My voice sticks in my
throat and sobs interrupt my dictation of these words. The city
which captured the whole world has itself been captured. In fact
more people died of famine than by the sword and only a few
citizens were left to be captured. People were driven mad by
hunger and forced to eat things that are taboo: they ripped apart
each other's limbs, while the mother did not spare her suckling
baby, taking into her belly the child she had recently brought
forth from it. 'By night Moab was captured, by night its wall fell
down.'[24] 'O God, the pagans have come into your inheritance;
they have defiled your holy temple; they have made Jerusalem

an apple orchard, they have put your servants' bodies out as food for the birds of the air, the flesh of your faithful for the wild animals of the earth. They have shed their blood like water all around Jerusalem and there was no one to bury them.'[25]

> Who can describe the disaster of that night, who can describe
> Its murders and pour forth tears to equal the suffering?
> An ancient city is falling, after long years of power.
> So many motionless bodies are scattered
> Along the streets and in the houses, and every shape of death.[26]

13 Meanwhile, as was natural in all this terrible confusion, the bloody conqueror burst into Marcella's house, too – 'allow me to tell what I have heard'[27] or rather to tell what was seen by the holy men who were there at the time. They say you stayed with her even in extreme danger and that she confronted the intruders without betraying any fear. When they demanded gold and hidden treasure, she pointed to her shabby tunic but they would not believe that she had adopted poverty voluntarily. It is said that she was beaten with sticks and whips but felt no pain. She threw herself at their feet and begged them in tears not to take you away or force you to suffer what old age had no need to fear. Christ softened their hard hearts and compassion found a place among the bloody swords. When the barbarians had taken the two of you to the basilica of the Apostle Paul to provide you with safety, or at least a tomb, she is said to have burst out with cries of joy, thanking God for keeping you unharmed for her. She was grateful that she had already been poor and had not been made so by the destruction of the city; although she lacked a daily supply of food, she would not feel hunger because she was filled with Christ and could say with total sincerity, 'Naked I came from my mother's womb, and naked shall I return there. The Lord has done as he saw fit. Blessed be the name of the Lord.'[28]

14 Some months later, while of sound mind, in good health and still physically active if frail, she fell asleep in the Lord, making you the heir of her poverty, or rather making the poor her heirs through you. In your arms she closed her eyes and she breathed

her last as you kissed her, smiling despite your tears, for she knew she had lived a good life and that rewards awaited her. This letter I have dictated for you, respected Marcella, and for you, her daughter Principia, during a single short night. I have not attempted to write in an elegant style, for my sole wish has been to show my gratitude to the two of you and to please both God and my readers.

THE LIFE OF
PAULA THE ELDER

by Jerome

(Letter *108 to Eustochium*)

Paula the elder

Paula the elder was born into a noble Roman family in 347. She was the mother of four daughters and one son. Widowed in about 380, she decided to follow Marcella's example and lead an ascetic life, first in Rome and then, after coming under the influence of Jerome who acted as her spiritual advisor and intellectual mentor, in Palestine where she moved in 385 when he left Rome. Paula visited the desert monks in Egypt and the sites of many of the events of the Old and New Testaments in Palestine. Together with Jerome she settled with her daughter Eustochium at Bethlehem where they founded monasteries for men and women. She spent the rest of her life in supervising the women's monastery and in studying Hebrew and the Scriptures. She also used her wealth to finance Jerome's projects and supported him in his work. She was renowned for her great virtue and was regarded as particularly saintly for putting up with Jerome as he had a difficult personality: Palladius in the *Lausiac History* records the view of one holy man who commented that 'Paula who looks after Jerome will die first and be set free at last from his meanness. Because of him no holy person will live in those parts. His bad temper would drive out even his own brother.' She is mentioned by Palladius in chapters 36 and 41; and Jerome sent her his *Letters* 30, 33 and 39 (on the death of her daughter Blesilla) while they were in Rome, and she is mentioned in 32, 45, 47, 54, 60, 66 (on the death of Paula's daughter Paulina), 77, 99, 102, 107 and 127. She and Eustochium are the authors of *Letter* 46 in Jerome's correspondence. He also dedicated several of his commentaries on books of the Old Testament to her. Paula died on 26 January 404.

Jerome

See headnote to *The Life of Marcella*.

Jerome's *Letter* 108 was written after Paula's death in 404 to console her daughter Eustochium.

1 If all my bodily limbs were to turn into tongues and if every limb could speak with a human voice, I would still be unable to give a proper account of the virtues of the holy Paula. She was of noble birth but much more noble in her holiness. Now she is more distinguished by the poverty she adopted in imitation of Christ than she was by her wealth when young. She, who was a member of both the Gracchi and the Scipio families, the heir of Paulus whose name she bears, a true descendant of Maecia Papiria, the mother of Africanus, preferred Bethlehem to Rome and exchanged a house adorned with gold for a rough shack. We do not grieve that we have lost such a woman; instead we give thanks that we had her, or rather that we have her – for all things live in God and whatever is given to the Lord is still reckoned as part of the family. It is true that we have lost her but the heavenly home has gained her; as long as she remained in the body she was absent from the Lord, and with a voice full of grief she used to complain, saying, 'Woe is me, that my journey is prolonged, I have lived with the inhabitants of Cedar, my soul has travelled much.'[1] Is it surprising that she complained that she was living in the dark – for that is the meaning of Cedar – given that the world is mired in evil? 'And its light is like its darkness; and the light shines in darkness and the darkness did not overwhelm it.'[2] And so she would often repeat these words, 'I am a stranger and a traveller as were all my ancestors',[3] and also 'I long to be released and to be with Christ.'[4] Whenever she was suffering from the illness that ravaged her poor body, which she had brought on herself by her unbelievably austere lifestyle and by even more extreme fasting,

she would repeat these sayings: 'I punish my body and enslave it so that after proclaiming to others I myself should not be disqualified', and 'it is good not to eat meat or drink wine', and 'I humbled my soul in fasting', and 'You have turned my bed in my illness', and 'I have lived in misery while I was pierced by a thorn.'[5] When experiencing the pricks of pain which she endured with marvellous patience, she would say, as if looking up at the heavens opening for her, 'Who will give me the wings of a dove and I will fly and be at peace?'[6]

2 I call on Jesus as my witness as well as his holy angels and the particular angel who was this admirable woman's guardian and companion, that I am not being ingratiating or flattering: I was a witness to everything I tell you and anything I say is less than she deserves, she who is praised by the whole world, admired by priests, longed for by many virgins and wept for by large numbers of monks and poor people. Does the reader need a summary of her virtues? She left her friends and family poor, but she was even poorer. It is hardly surprising that she acted in this way with regard to her relatives and her small household – including those servants and serving maids whom she treated rather as brothers and sisters – given that she left the virgin Eustochium (for whose consolation this little book is written), her daughter, dedicated to Christ, far from her noble family and rich only in faith and grace.

3 Let us then hasten along the path of this narrative. I will leave others to delve into the past, back as far as her cradle and her baby toys, so to speak; I will leave them to talk about her mother Blesilla and her father Rogatus, of whom one is the descendant of the Scipios and the Gracchi, while the other is said to go back to Agamemnon from whom he traces his wealthy and noble family line, distinguished through all of Greece down to the present day – the same Agamemnon who destroyed Troy after a ten-year siege. But I will only praise what is peculiar to her, what pours forth from the purest spring of her holy mind. When the apostles asked our Lord and Saviour what he would give them, seeing that they had left everything for his name's sake, he told them they would receive a hundred times more in the present and eternal life in the future. This teaches us that there is

nothing admirable in possessing wealth but only in rejecting it for Christ's sake and that we should not be swollen with pride in the privileges we have acquired but should consider them of no value in comparison with faith in the Lord. Truly, the Saviour has given to his servants, both male and female, in the present what he promised. For the woman who despised the admiration of one city is now a world-famous celebrity; when she lived in Rome she was known to no one outside the city, but when she lived hidden away in Bethlehem she won the admiration of people in barbarian and Roman lands alike. Is there any country whose people do not visit the holy places? Who found anything more wonderful in the holy places than Paula? And just as the most precious stone sparkles among many jewels and as the sun's rays outshine and obscure the lesser fires of the stars, so Paula outdid the virtues and powers of all by her humility. She became the least among all so that she might be the greatest of all; the more she humbled herself, the more Christ raised her up. She hid but failed to conceal herself. By trying to escape admiration she won admiration which follows virtue like a shadow; abandoning those who seek it she sought those who despise it. But what am I doing? Allowing myself to get bogged down in details, I am failing to keep to the order of the narrative or observe the rules of writing.

4 Born into such an illustrious family, Paula married Toxotius whose family line goes back as far as Aeneas and the Julian family. That is why Toxotius' daughter, the virgin of Christ, is called Julia Eustochium after Julius whose name derives from the great Iulus. I mention this not because there is anything to admire in those who have such things but because it is admirable if people consider them of no value. People who are attached to the world look up to those who are powerful because they have such privileges, but we praise those who despise them for the sake of the Saviour. Rather perversely we despise people for having such things but praise the same people for rejecting them. Born from such ancestors, as I said, Paula gave birth to five children, thus proving her fertility and fidelity first to her husband, then to her closest relatives and to the whole city for whom her life was a spectacle. Her children

were Blesilla, on whose death I consoled her mother Paula at
Rome; Paulina, who left a saintly and admirable husband, Pam-
machius, both as the heir to her proposed way of life and to her
possessions, to whom we sent a small book to console him on
her death; Eustochium, who is now a most precious necklace of
virginity and of the church in the Holy Land; and Rufina, whose
premature death devastated her mother's loving heart; and
finally Toxotius. After he was born Paula stopped having children, thereby proving that she did not wish to continue for long
in her role as wife, but was just obeying her husband's wishes
because he wanted a male child.

5 When her husband died she herself nearly died of grief, and
yet she devoted herself to serving the Lord in such a way that
she almost seemed to have longed for her husband's death. How
can I mention all the riches of her large, aristocratic and once
wealthy household which were sold and given to the poor? How
can I describe that woman's heart which was so compassionate
to all, spreading kindness even to people she had never seen?
Was there a poor person who was not wrapped in her clothes as
he lay dying, was there any bedridden person whom she did not
support at her own expense? She would eagerly seek out such
people all over the city and would feel that she had lost out if
any weak and hungry person was living off someone else's food.
In effect she was robbing her children and when her relatives
rebuked her for doing so, she said that she was leaving them
Christ's mercy which was a better thing to inherit.

6 Being a member of a family that was high-ranking in worldly
terms and very aristocratic, she had to endure visits and
crowded receptions but she could not bear these for long. She
deplored the high esteem in which people held her and would
hurry to get away from those who wanted to pay her compliments. When the bishops had been summoned from east and
west by letters from the emperor to deal with certain disputes
between the churches, she was introduced to two admirable
men, both bishops of Christ: Paulinus, the bishop of Antioch,
and Epiphanius of Salamis (now called Constantia) in Cyprus.[7]
She offered Epiphanius hospitality in her own house and even
though Paulinus was staying in someone else's house, she

treated him as kindly as if he were staying with her. Inspired
by their virtues she began to spend every moment planning
to leave her country. Disregarding her home, her children,
her family, her possessions and everything connected with her
worldly life, she was keen to go alone (if that could ever be
said of her) and unaccompanied into the desert inhabited by
men like Antony and Paul.[8] And when winter was over at last
and the sea routes were open again, allowing the bishops to
return to their churches, she sailed with them in her prayers
and longing. To cut a long story short, she went down to the
harbour accompanied by her brother, her relatives and, what
is more significant, her children. The sails were already
stretched taut and the ship was being rowed out to deeper
waters, when little Toxotius, standing on the shore, stretched
his arms out to her, begging her to stay, while Rufina, who had
already reached a marriageable age, implored her mother with
tears rather than words to wait until she was married. But
Paula remained dry-eyed, her gaze fixed on heaven, and her
love of God was stronger than her love for her children. She
denied that she was a mother to prove herself Christ's servant.
She suffered profound torment and felt that she was being torn
limb from limb as she fought against the pain, proving herself
more admirable than everyone else because she overcame such
a powerful love. Among the cruel hardships suffered by prisoners of war at the hands of the enemy, there is nothing more
cruel than the separation of parents from their children.
Though it is against the laws of nature, she endured this with
complete faith – indeed she sought it out joyfully. No longer
considering her love for her children important in comparison
with her greater love for God, she was content to take Eustochium as her only companion on her voyage and in her new
way of life. As the ship ploughed a furrow through the sea, all
her fellow passengers were looking at the shore, but Paula
turned her gaze away so as not to see her family, the sight of
whom caused her great pain. No woman, it has to be admitted, has ever loved her children as much as she did. Before she
set off she had given them all she had, disinheriting herself on
earth so that she might gain her inheritance in heaven.

7 On the way she stopped at the island of Pontia which is well known as the place of exile of the celebrated lady Flavia Dom-itilla[9] who under the Emperor Domitian was banished for being a Christian. Here Paula went to visit the cells in which Flavia had spent a long period of martyrdom. Then she hurried swiftly on to Jerusalem, eager to visit the holy places. But the winds were not favourable and progress was slow. Between Scylla and Charybdis she entrusted herself to the Adriatic Sea and crossed over a still pond, so to speak, to Methone where she rested for a while and 'stretched her limbs, crusted with brine, on the shore, then past Malea and Cythera and the Cyclades dotted over the sea and those straits blossoming with many islands'.[10] After pass-ing Rhodes and Lycia she at last saw Cyprus where she knelt before the holy and venerable Epiphanius. She stayed with him for ten days not to rest, as he believed, but to serve God, as events proved. For she went around visiting all the monasteries in that region, and as far as her resources allowed she left sub-stantial provision for the brothers who had been drawn there from all over the world by their love for the holy Epiphanius. After this she made the short crossing over to Seleucia and from there she went up to Antioch, where she was detained for a while by the affection of the holy confessor Paulinus. Then, in the mid-dle of winter, this noble woman who used to be carried by eunuch litter-bearers now set out seated on an ass.

8 I will not give an account of her journey through southern Syria and Phoenicia – for I do not intend to write a travel guide – but will only mention those places recorded in Holy Scrip-ture. After leaving Beirut, a Roman colony, and the ancient city of Sidon, Paula entered Elijah's little tower on the shore at Zarephath, where she worshipped the Lord our Saviour, and then crossing the sands of Tyre on which Paul once knelt,[11] she arrived at Acco, now known as Ptolemais. Crossing the plains of Megiddo which witnessed the murder of Josiah,[12] she entered the land of the Philistines. After admiring the ruins of Dor, once a very powerful city, and the tower of Strato which had con-versely been an insignificant place until Herod, king of Judea, called it Caesarea in honour of Caesar Augustus, she saw Cornelius' house,[13] now a Christian church, and the little house

of Philip and the room of his daughters, the four virgins who had the gift of prophecy.[14] Next she came to Antipatris, a small town half in ruins which Herod named after his father, and then to Lydda (later Diospolis), famed as the place where Dorcas was restored to life and Aeneas was healed,[15] and not far from there Arimathea, the village Joseph came from[16] – the man who buried the Lord – and Nob, once a city of priests and now the tomb of those who were slain,[17] and also Joppa, the port to which Jonah fled[18] and (to mention something from the mythology of the poets) which witnessed the chaining of Andromeda to the rock.

Resuming her journey Paula visited Nicopolis – formerly Emmaus – where the Lord was recognized as he broke the bread and where he dedicated the house of Cleopas as a church.[19] Then she set off again and went up to Lower and Upper Beth-horon, cities founded by Solomon and later destroyed by several devastating wars. There she could see on her right Ajalon and Gibeon where Joshua, son of Nun, gave orders to the sun and moon when he was fighting against the five kings and where he condemned the Gibeonites to be hewers of wood and drawers of water because of the deceitful way they had obtained a treaty.[20] In the city of Gibeah, which had been razed to the ground, Paula stood for a while remembering its sin and the concubine torn to pieces and the six hundred men from the tribes of Benjamin saved for the sake of the Apostle Paul.[21]

9 To cut a long story short: with the abandoned mausoleum of Helen (who as the queen of Adiabene had helped the people with corn during a period of famine) on her left, she entered Jerusalem, a city with three names – Jebus, Salem and Jerusalem – which was restored by Aelius (later Emperor Hadrian) as Aelia, out of the ruins and ashes into which it had sunk. And although the proconsul of Palestine, who had been a close friend of Paula's family, had sent his attendants on ahead and told them to prepare his official residence for her, she chose to stay in a simple little room. She went round all the places with so much passion and enthusiasm that if she did not hurry on to the next one, she could not be dragged from the one she had just visited. Throwing herself down in front of the cross she

worshipped it as if she could see the Lord hanging here. Going into the tomb of the resurrection she kissed the stone the angel had removed from the entrance to the tomb and licked the very place where the Lord's body had lain,[22] as if she were thirsting for the waters she had longed for in faith. The whole of Jerusalem and the Lord to whom she prayed bear witness to all the tears she shed there, all the sorrowful sighs she uttered. Leaving Jerusalem she went up to Mount Sion, which is translated as 'citadel' or 'watch tower'. David had long ago taken this city by storm and rebuilt it.[23] Of the city that was stormed it is written: 'Woe to you, city of Ariel (in other words 'lion of God' for it was once the most powerful city) which David has taken by storm',[24] while of the city that had been rebuilt it is said: 'Its foundations are on the holy mountains; the Lord loves the gates of Sion more than all the dwellings of Jacob.'[25] He does not mean those gates we see today, smashed into dust and ashes, but the gates against which hell cannot prevail, through which the crowds of believers enter to reach Christ. There Paula was shown a column supporting the church portico, stained with the Lord's blood, to which it is said that Christ was tied and then whipped. She was also shown the place where the Holy Spirit came down upon more than a hundred and twenty souls, so that the prophecy of Joel might be fulfilled.[26]

10 Then after distributing her money to the poor and to her fellow servants as far as her limited resources allowed, she travelled on to Bethlehem. On the right-hand side of the road she stopped at the tomb of Rachel, where Rachel gave birth to Benjamin, not Benoni (in other words 'son of my sorrow') as his mother had called him as she lay dying,[27] but, as his father prophesied in the spirit, 'son of my right hand'. Then she entered the Saviour's cave. Here she saw the virgin's room and the stable in which the ox knew its owner and the donkey its master's crib, so that what is written by the same prophet might be fulfilled: 'happy is he who sows upon the waters where the ox and the donkey tread'.[28] There I myself heard her swear that she could see with the eyes of faith the baby wrapped in swaddling bands and crying in the manger, and the Magi worshipping God, and the star shining above them, as well as the virgin

mother, the attentive foster-father, the shepherds arriving at night to see the Word that was made: already at that moment they were realizing the opening words of St John's Gospel: 'In the beginning was the word and the word was made flesh.'[29] She was also convinced she could see the babies slaughtered, Herod in a rage, and Joseph and Mary fleeing to Egypt. Mingling tears with her happiness she said, 'Greetings, Bethlehem, house of bread, in which was born the bread that came down from heaven. Greetings, Ephrathah, most fertile and fruitful land, whose fertility is God. It is with regard to you that Micah once prophesied: "And you, Bethlehem, house of Ephrathah, are you not the least of the thousands of Judah? Out of you will come forth for me one who will be the leader of Israel whose origin is from the beginning, from the days of old. Therefore you will give them up until the time when she will give birth to them. She will give birth and the rest of his brothers will turn to the sons of Israel."[30] For in you the leader has been born, he who was conceived before Lucifer, whose birth from the Father was before all ages. David's line continued in you until a virgin should give birth and the rest of the people who believe in Christ should turn to the sons of Israel and gladly declare to them: "It was necessary to speak the word of God to you first but because you rejected it and judged yourselves unworthy of eternal life, we will now turn to the Gentiles."[31] For the Lord had said, "I have only come for the lost sheep of the house of Israel."[32] At that time the words of Jacob were fulfilled concerning him: "The prince from Judah will not fail nor the leader from his thighs, until he comes to whom it has been entrusted and he himself will be the expectation of the peoples."[33]

'David swore a good oath and fulfilled his vow correctly when he said, "I will not enter into the dwelling of my house, or go up to my bed, or grant sleep to my eyes and slumber to my eyelids and rest to the temples of my head, until I find a place for my Lord, a dwelling for the God of Jacob."[34] Immediately afterwards he explained what he wanted, seeing with the eyes of a prophet the one who would come and whom we now believe has come: "See, we heard of him in Ephrathah, we found him in the wide spaces of the forest."[35] "Zoth" is of course a Hebrew word as I learned from your teachings: it does not mean "her", in other words Mary, the mother of the Lord, but rather "him". And so he goes on confidently, "We will go in to his dwellings; we will worship him in the place where his feet rested."[36] Am I, wretched and sinful as I am, considered worthy to kiss the manger in which the Lord cried as a baby, to pray in the cave in which the virgin who gave birth brought forth the infant God? This is where I shall rest because this is the home of my Lord. Here I will live, because my Saviour chose it. "I have prepared a lamp for my Christ. My soul will live for him and my offspring will serve him."[37]

Then she went on a little further to the tower of Eder, in other words the tower of the flock, for close to it Jacob grazed his flocks, and the shepherds keeping their watch by night were privileged to hear: 'Glory to God in the highest and on earth peace to men of good will.'[38] While they were watching the sheep, they found the Lamb of God whose pure and spotless fleece was moistened with heavenly dew[39] in the dry places of the whole world and whose blood, when smeared on the doorposts,[40] forced the destroyer of Egypt to flee and who took away the sins of the world.

11 Without delay she continued her journey along the old road leading to Gaza, which means the 'power' or 'wealth' of God: there she meditated in silence on how the Ethiopian eunuch, who prefigured the Gentiles, changed his skin and, while reading the Old Testament, discovered the refreshing waters of the Gospel.[41] Then Paula turned to the right, and from Bethsur she came to Eshcol which can be translated as 'bunch of grapes':[42] it was from this place that the inspectors carried an amazingly large bunch of grapes, thereby indicating that it is a most fertile area and a type of him who said: 'I have trodden the winepress alone and of the people there was no one with me.'[43] A little further on she entered Sarah's little room and saw Isaac's cradle and the traces of Abraham's oak, under which he saw the day of Christ and was glad.[44] Then she rose and went up to Hebron, that is Kiriath-arba, in other words the town of the four men, Abraham, Isaac, Jacob and the great Adam, who the Hebrews believe were buried there according to the book of Joshua.[45]

But most people think that the fourth man was Caleb, and they point out his tomb on one side. She did not want to go to Kiriath-sepher, in other words the 'bond of letters', because she rejected the letter that kills and had found the spirit that gives life.[46] She chose instead to admire the upper and lower springs which Othniel, son of Kenaz, son of Jephunneh, received in exchange for the southern land and his arid estates:[47] from these streams he irrigated the field which was dry in the Old Testament, foreshadowing the fact that the people who had been sinners would find redemption in the waters of baptism. On the next day, soon after sunrise, she stood on the heights of Kiriath-barucha, in other words 'the town of blessing', to which Abraham followed the Lord. From there she looked down on the vast wilderness and the land that had once been Sodom and Gomorrah, Admah and Zaboiim. She looked long at the vineyards of balsam in Engedi and at Segor, 'the three-year-old heifer' (which was previously called Bala, translated as Zoar, in other words 'the little one' in the Syriac language). She was reminded of Lot's cave and with tears in her eyes she warned the young women who were with her to beware of wine which leads to debauchery,[48] and which caused the creation of the Moabites and Ammonites.

12 I take my time passing through the south where the betrothed woman found her fiancé resting and Joseph drank with his brothers.[49] I will return to Jerusalem, passing through Tekoa and Amos, and I will behold the shining cross of Mount Olivet from which the Saviour ascended to the father. Here every year a red cow was burned as a sacrifice to the Lord and its ashes were used to purify the people of Israel. Here, according to Ezekiel, the cherubim, after leaving the temple, founded the church of the Lord.[50] Then Paula visited the tomb of Lazarus and saw the house of Mary and Martha, as well as Bethany, which means 'the town of the priestly jawbones', and the place where the frisky foal that served as a type of the Gentiles accepted the bridle of the Lord and offered its back, covered with the apostles' soft garments, for him to sit on.[51] From there she took the direct route down to Jericho, thinking of the wounded man in the Gospel, of the cruelty of the priests and

Levites who passed him by, of the compassion of the Samaritan, that is the 'guardian', who placed the half-dead man on his mule and took him to the inn of the church.[52] She noticed the place called Adommim, which means 'the place of blood', because much blood was shed there during frequent attacks by robbers; she also saw Zaccheus' mulberry tree, representing the good works of penitence, which allowed him to trample on his former sins of bloodshed and theft, and from which he looked upon the high lord from the height of virtues.[53] Beside the road she saw the place where the blind men sat who in receiving their sight became types of the two peoples who should believe in the Lord. Entering Jericho she saw the city that Hiel founded at the cost of his first-born son Abiram and the gates of which he set up at the cost of Segub, his youngest son. She saw the camp of Gilgal and the pile of foreskins suggestive of the mystery of the second circumcision. She saw the twelve stones brought there from the bed of the river Jordan as firm foundations for the twelve apostles. She saw the spring that was once brackish and barren when it belonged to the law, but which the true Elisha seasoned with his wisdom, turning it into a well of sweet and life-giving water.[54] Night had hardly passed when Paula reached the Jordan in blazing heat. She stood on the riverbank and as the sun rose she recalled the sun of justice, while the river reminded her of how the priests' feet were dry as they stood in the middle of the river; how at the command of Elijah and Elisha the water stood still on both sides and the river offered a path; and how by his baptism the Lord cleaned the river polluted by the flood and stained by the destruction of the whole human race.[55]

13 It would take a long time to tell of the vale of Achor, in other words of 'tumult and crowds', where theft and greed were condemned,[56] and of Bethel, 'the house of God', where Jacob slept, naked and poor, on the bare earth with a stone beneath his head.[57] In Zechariah this stone is described as having seven eyes, while in Isaiah it is referred to as the cornerstone.[58] Here Jacob saw a ladder leading up to heaven and above it stood the Lord stretching a hand out to those who were climbing up, but hurling down from on high those who were careless. Paula also

went to Mount Ephraim to venerate the tombs of Joshua, son of Nun, and Eleazar, son of Aaron the priest. One of these tombs was built at Timnath-serah on the north side of Mount Gaash; the other at Gabaath, the town of his son Phinehas. She was quite amazed that the person who was in charge of allotting the estates had chosen for himself the rocky and rugged parts. What should I say about Shiloh where a ruined altar is still shown today and where the tribe of Benjamin anticipated Romulus' kidnapping of the Sabine women?[59] She passed through Shechem (not 'Sychar' as many wrongly read), now renamed Neapolis, and on the side of Mount Garizim she entered the church built at Jacob's well, beside which the Lord sat when he was hungry and thirsty and where he was refreshed by the Samaritan woman's faith,[60] who left her five husbands (representing the five books of Moses) and the sixth whom she boasted of (namely Dositheus the false teacher), when she found the true Messiah and the true Saviour.

Then Paula made a detour to see the tombs of the twelve patriarchs and Samaria, called Augusta by Herod in honour of Augustus, or Sebaste in Greek. There lie the prophets Elisha and Obadiah as well as the man who is the greatest of all those born of woman – John the Baptist. There she trembled at many amazing things. For she saw demons roar under various forms of torture, and in front of the tombs of the saints she saw men howling like wolves, barking like dogs, roaring like lions, hissing like serpents and bellowing like bulls. She saw others with their heads spinning round and bending backwards so that their heads touched the ground; she saw women hung upside down by their feet without their dresses falling over their faces. She pitied them all and prayed for Christ's mercy for each of them, as tears flowed down her cheeks. And although she was by this time weak with exhaustion, she climbed the mountain on foot to visit the two caves where, at a time of persecution and hunger, Obadiah the prophet fed one hundred prophets with bread and water.[61]

She made a brief trip to Nazareth, where the Lord spent his childhood, to Cana and Capernaum, familiar from the miracles he performed there, to the lake of Tiberias, which was sanctified by the Lord's boat trip on it, and to the desert wilderness where many thousands of people were fed with a few loaves and the twelve baskets of the tribes of Israel were filled with the leftover food. She climbed Mount Tabor where the Lord was transfigured.[62] She saw from a distance Mount Hermon and Mount Hermonim and the broad plains of Galilee, where Sisera and his whole army were destroyed when Barak won the battle,[63] and the torrent of Kishon running down the centre of the plain. She was shown the nearby town of Nain where the widow's son was brought back to life.[64] The day would come to an end sooner than my account if I were to run through all the places visited by Paula, who won great respect for her incredible faith.

14 I will pass on to Egypt, but first I will stop a while at Socoh and wet my dry lips at Samson's spring which he produced from the large tooth in the jaw.[65] Then I will feel refreshed when I visit Moresheth, which was once the tomb of the prophet Micah and is now a church. I will pass by the country of the Horites and Gittites, Mareshah, Edom and Lachish, and crossing the desert's vast wilderness over sands so soft that they cannot hold the imprint of one's footsteps, I will come to the Egyptian river Sior, a name that means 'turbid'. Then I shall pass through the five cities of Egypt where the Canaanite language is spoken and through the land of Goshen and the plains of Zoan where God performed miracles, to the city of No which later became Alexandria, and Nitria, the town of the Lord, where the nitre[66] of virtue washes away the dirt of large numbers of people. When Paula had seen this she was met by that holy and revered man, Bishop Isidore the Confessor, and by huge numbers of monks many of whom had been raised to the rank of priest or Levite. She was very pleased to behold the glory of God but admitted that she was unworthy of such great honour. What shall I say of men such as Macarius, Arsetes and Serapion and other pillars of Christ? Was there anyone whose cell she did not enter or at whose feet she did not kneel? She believed that in each of these holy men she was seeing Christ, and whatever she brought them she was pleased to have brought to the Lord. What wonderful passion and courage – it was hard

to believe that these virtues could be found in a woman! Taking
no account of her sex and her physical weakness she longed to
live with her female companions, surrounded by all these thousands of monks. Indeed she might have managed this for they
all welcomed her, had she not been pulled away by an even
stronger desire to see the holy places. Due to the extreme heat
she sailed from Pelusium to Maiuma, returning to Bethlehem
so quickly that you would have thought she was a bird. Shortly
afterwards she made the decision to live permanently in the
holy town of Bethlehem, and so she spent three years in cramped
hostel accommodation while she built cells and monasteries as
well as a roadside guest house for travellers, remembering how
Mary and Joseph had been unable to find a place to stay. At this
point I conclude my account of the travels she made in the company of her daughter and a large number of unmarried
women.

15 Now I will give a more detailed account of the goodness
peculiar to her. In describing it I promise, with God as my judge
and witness, that I will add nothing and exaggerate nothing as
do those who are intent on flattery. In fact I will play down
many things because I do not want the facts to seem incredible,
nor do I want my detractors and those who are always trying
to grind me down to think I am making things up or decking
Paula, like Aesop's crow, with bright feathers that belong to
someone else.

Paula behaved with such humility – which is the most important of Christian virtues – that anyone who saw her, who was
eager to set eyes on her because of her celebrity status, could
not believe that it was she but thought she was just a maid of
the lowest rank. Surrounded by a large group of young girls,
she was the least conspicuous of all in the way she dressed,
spoke and behaved. From the time of her husband's death until
the day she died she never ate with a man, even if she knew he
was holy and had attained the rank of bishop. She did not go to
the baths unless she was seriously ill. She did not have a soft
mattress to lie on even when suffering from a really serious
fever; but she would rest on the hard ground on a bristly mat,
if indeed it can be called rest when she spent days and nights in

almost continuous prayer, thereby fulfilling those words from
the Psalms: 'every night I will wash my bed, I will water my bed
with tears'.[67] You would think that she had springs of tears
inside her: she would weep for her trivial faults in such a way
that you might believe her guilty of the most serious crimes.
When we advised her, as we often did, to spare her eyes and to
preserve them for reading the Gospels, she would say, 'I must
defile my face for I frequently used to apply make-up to it,
using rouge, white lead and antimony, in contravention of
God's commands; I must mortify my body which I over-indulged;
I must compensate for the years of laughter with perpetual
weeping; I must exchange soft linens and expensive silk garments for the roughness of the hairshirt. I who used to please
my husband and the world, now wish to please Christ.'

If among her virtues – and there were many of them – I wished
to praise her chastity, my words might seem superfluous. With
regard to this virtue, she was the paragon of all the married
women in Rome while she lived in the world. She behaved in
such a way that not even the most malicious person ever dared
to make up gossip about her. No one was more compassionate
than she, no one kinder towards those who lacked self-esteem.
She did not seek out the powerful but neither did she despise
them with an attitude of arrogant scorn, as if she herself were
seeking admiration. If she saw a poor person, she would offer
him support; if she saw a rich person, she would encourage him
to be generous to others. Her own generosity knew no bounds:
she would often borrow money to give away, so that she need
not refuse anyone who asked her for a sum of money. I was
wrong, I admit: I rebuked her for being excessively generous,
citing these words of the Apostle Paul: 'I do not mean that there
should be relief for others and pressure for you, but it is a question of a fair balance so that your present abundance should
help them and their abundance help your need', and the words
of our Saviour from the Gospel: 'whoever has two coats must
share with anyone who has none'.[68] I told her that she had to be
careful for she might not always have the means to do as she
wished. I put forward many similar arguments but she under-
mined them all, concisely and with admirable tact, calling the

Lord to witness that everything she did was done for his sake. She said that she wanted to die a beggar, leaving not a single penny to her daughter; at her funeral she expected to be buried in someone else's shroud. Finally she added, 'If I look I can find many people who will give me things, but if that beggar were to die without receiving from me what I can give him even if I have to borrow money to do so, from whom would his soul be required?' I wanted her to be more careful in her domestic economy, but she was more ardent in her faith than I was and clung to her Saviour with her whole soul. Poor in spirit herself she followed her Lord in his poverty, giving back to him what she had received. In the end she achieved what she wanted and left her daughter deep in debts which are still owing – in fact Eustochium will only manage to pay them back by Christ's faith and mercy rather than by her own efforts.

16 Most women like to bestow their gifts on people who will blow their trumpet for them: giving generously to a few, they refuse to offer anything to the rest. Paula was completely free from this fault, for she distributed her money to individuals according to each individual's need, not in order to indulge them. No poor person came away from her empty-handed. All this she was able to do not because her wealth was so huge but because of the sensible way she distributed it, always repeating these words: 'Blessed are the merciful for they will receive mercy', and 'Just as water puts out a fire, so mercy extinguishes sins', and 'Make friends for yourself by means of dishonest wealth so that they will welcome you into the eternal homes', and 'Give alms and everything will be clean', as well as the words of Daniel warning King Nebuchadnezzar to atone for his sins by giving away his money.[69] Paula did not want to waste her money on stones that will pass away with earth and this age, but on living stones which roll over the earth: these are the stones from which the great king's city is built in the book of Revelation and which, according to Scripture, will be turned into sapphire, emerald, jasper and other precious stones.[70]

17 But she may well share these virtues with a number of others and the devil knows that it is not in these that the highest virtue lies. That is why the devil says to the Lord after the loss of Job's

wealth, after his house has been destroyed, after his children have been killed: 'Skin for skin, a man will give everything he has for his life. But stretch out your hand and touch his bones and flesh if he has not blessed you to your face.'[71] We know that many have given to charity but refuse to give up any of their bodily comforts; they have stretched out their hand to the poor but they remain mired in the pleasures of the flesh. They whitewash the outside but inside they are filled with the bones of the dead. But Paula was not like this: she was almost excessively self-restrained and she weakened her body by severe fasting and hard work. She would use hardly any oil on her food except on feast days – this fact alone gives one an indication of her views on wine, sauce, fish, milk, honey and lamb and other tasty things. In eating these things some people believe that they are very abstemious: if they eat such things, they still believe their chastity is safe.

18 Envy is always hunting down virtues and lightning strikes the mountain tops.[72] Does it surprise you if I say that this is true of human life when even our Lord was crucified as a result of the Pharisees' jealousy? Even holy people are the object of jealousy and even in Paradise the serpent's jealousy caused death to come into the world. The Lord had roused Adar the Edomite[73] against Paula to beat her so that she would not grow proud, and he often warned her with the thorn of the flesh not to think too highly of herself because of her great virtues, as this might lead her to believe that she had attained the summit of perfection, leaving other women far behind. I used to say that it was better for her to give way before the envy of others and withdraw in the face of their madness. That was how Jacob dealt with his brother Esau and David with the unrelenting persecution of Saul.[74] I reminded her of how Jacob fled to Mesopotamia, while David handed himself over to a foreign tribe, preferring to be subject to his enemies than to envy. But Paula replied, 'What you say would be fair enough if the devil were not constantly fighting against God's servants, both male and female, and beating them to whatever place they fled to. It would be fair enough if I were not held back by my love for the holy places and if I could find my beloved Bethlehem in another part of the world.

For why should I not overcome envy by means of patience? Why should I not crush arrogance with humility and when struck on the cheek turn the other cheek? As St Paul says, "Overcome evil with good."[75] Were not the apostles proud to suffer abuse for the Lord's sake? Did not the Saviour himself act with humility when he took the form of a servant and became obedient to his father to the point of death, death on the cross, so that he might save us through his suffering? If Job had not put up a struggle and been triumphant in battle, he would not have received the crown of justice and been told by the Lord: "Do you think that I would have talked to you for any other reason than that you might appear just?"[76] In the Gospel it is said, "Blessed are those who suffer persecution for the sake of justice."[77] Keep a clear conscience so that you can be sure that it is not because of our sins that we are suffering; affliction in this life provides the opportunity for reward.'

When the enemy persisted and tried to hurl abuse at her, she would recite these words from the Psalm: 'When the sinner stood firm against me, I fell silent and was humiliated and I refrained from saying good things', and also 'Like a deaf person I did not hear and like a dumb person I did not open my mouth. And I became like a man who could not hear and who has no rebukes on his lips.'[78] In moments of temptation she would repeat the words from Deuteronomy, 'The Lord your God tests you, so that he may know whether you love the Lord your God with all your heart and with all your soul.'[79] When tempted she would repeat what Isaiah had said, 'You who have been weaned off milk and removed from the breast, expect one tribulation after another, one hope after another, here a little, there a little because of the malice of lips, because of another person's tongue.'[80] She consoled herself by interpreting this scriptural passage in this way: to be one of the weaned ones – of those who have reached maturity – we must endure one tribulation after another, so that we might deserve to receive one hope after another, knowing that suffering produces endurance and endurance produces experience and experience hope but hope does not disappoint us,[81] because 'if our outer nature wastes away, our inner nature is renewed. Temporary tribulation which is easy to bear is preparing us for eternal glory: we do not look at what can be seen but at what cannot be seen. For things that are seen do not last while those that cannot be seen are eternal.'[82] Even if one felt, with all the impatience typical of humans, that God's help was a long time coming, it would not really be long for God has said: 'I heard you at the right moment and on the day of salvation I helped you.'[83] Paula believed that one should not be daunted by what deceitful or malicious people said, for we will be happy with God's help. We ought to listen to him when he gives us the following advice: 'Through your patience you will possess your souls', and 'the sufferings of the present life cannot be compared with the future glory which will be revealed in us',[84] while in the passage where it is said: 'The patient person is very sensible; but the one who is impatient is extremely foolish',[85] the aim of the words is to make us patient in all things that happen to us.

19 In her frequent periods of ill health and weakness, Paula would say, 'when I am weak, then I am strong', and 'we have this treasure in clay jars' until 'this mortal body puts on immortality and this perishable body puts on imperishability', and also 'just as the sufferings of Christ abound in us, so also our consolation is abundant in Christ', and a little further on in the same passage, 'as you share in his sufferings, so also you will share in his consolation'.[86] In times of grief she would sing, 'Why are you sad, my soul, and why are you upset within me? Hope in God, for I shall again praise him, the salvation of my countenance and my God.'[87] In times of danger she would say, 'Anyone who wishes to follow me let him deny himself and take up his cross and follow me'; and also 'Anyone who wishes to save his life will lose it', and 'He who loses his life for my sake will save it.'[88]

When news came that her family wealth was used up and that all her inheritance had been lost, her response was, 'What does it benefit a man if he gains the whole world but loses his life? Or what will he give in return for his life?'[89] 'Naked I came from my mother's womb and naked shall I return. As it pleased the Lord, so it has come to pass; may the Lord's name be praised',[90] and these words: 'Do not love this world nor the things of the world, for everything that is in the world is desire of the flesh, and desire of the eyes, and pride in this life which do not come from the Father but are of this world. And the world and its desire will pass away.'[91] I know that when she received letters telling her of the serious illnesses of her children and especially of her son Toxotius whom she loved very much, she would keep a tight grip on herself, thereby fulfilling these words: 'I was upset but I did not speak.'[92] Then she would cry out, 'Anyone who loves his son or daughter more than [he loves] me is not worthy of me.'[93] She prayed to the Lord saying, 'Possess the children of those who have been put to death',[94] who mortify their bodies every day for your sake.

I am aware that some telltale (the worst kind of person) had told her (pretending to do so out of kindness!) that some people thought her insane because of what they considered her excessive zeal for virtue; they thought she needed counselling. To these she replied, 'We have been made a spectacle to the world, to angels and to mortals; we are fools for Christ's sake but the foolishness of God is wiser than men.'[95] That is why the Saviour also said to the Father: 'You know my weakness.'[96] In the Gospel we read that even his relatives wanted to have him restrained on the grounds that he was mentally ill, while his opponents reviled him, saying: 'He has a demon and is a Samaritan',[97] and 'He casts out devils in the name of Beelzebub, prince of devils.'[98] But let us listen to the Apostle who encourages us by saying: 'This is our boast, the testimony of our conscience, that we have behaved in the world with holiness and sincerity and by the grace of God'; let us listen to the Lord when he says to the disciples: 'The world hates you because you are not of this world; for if you were of the world, the world would love you as its own.'[99] And Paula would turn her words to the Lord himself, saying: 'You know the secrets of our heart', and 'All these things have come upon us and we have not forgotten you nor have we been false to your covenant. Our heart has not turned back', and 'We face death for your sake all day long; we are counted as sheep for the slaughter', but 'The Lord supports me; I will not fear what man can do to me.'[100] For I have read: 'My son, honour the Lord and you shall be made strong; do not fear anyone apart from him.'[101] She used these and other similar passages from Scripture to arm herself with the armour of Christ, so to speak, to protect herself against all sins but especially against raging envy. By refusing to take offence she calmed the fury of her heart though it was fit to burst. Until the day of her death her patience was obvious to all, as was the envy of others. But envy gnaws at its source and while it strives to harm the object it envies, it only manages to turn its insane rage on itself.

20 I must also describe the organization of her monastery and the way she turned the chastity of holy people to her own profit. She sowed material things so that she might reap spiritual things; she distributed worldly things so that she might receive heavenly things; she gave up what lasts only a short while so that she could exchange it for what is eternal. First, she established a monastery for men, handing it over to the men to administer it. Then the many women, whom she had gathered together from different provinces, she divided up, aristocratic as well as those from the middle and lower classes, into three groups and three monasteries, in such a way that they worked and ate their meals separately but assembled to pray and sing psalms. After the singing of the Alleluia (this being the signal summoning them to the collect), no one was allowed to remain behind. The first one or the first group who arrived would wait for the others. It was her modesty and good example, rather than fear, that inspired them to work.

At dawn, at the third, sixth and ninth hours, at nightfall and in the middle of the night they would sing through the psalms in order. Each of the sisters had to know the psalms and each day learn a certain passage from the Holy Scriptures. Only on Sundays did they process to the church beside which they lived, each group following its own mother superior; and when they left the church in the same way, they would devote themselves to some task in a disciplined manner, making clothes for themselves or for others. For any of them of noble birth, she was not allowed to have a companion from her own home, in case memories of past behaviour might revive the old mistakes of a frivolous childhood or renew them through frequent chats. There was one form of dress for all: they used linen cloth only to wipe their hands. There was such complete separation from the men that Paula even kept the women apart from the eunuchs, so as not to encourage malicious gossip, which tends to find fault with holy people in order to make those who behave less well feel better.

If one of the women happened to arrive late for the psalms or was slow at her work, Paula would deal with her in differ-ent ways. If the woman was irritable, Paula would speak soothingly; if she was apathetic, she would rebuke her, thereby imitating the words of the Apostle when he said: 'What do you want? Shall I come to you with a stick or in a spirit of gentle-ness and mildness?'[102] She allowed no woman to have anything apart from food and clothing, for St Paul had said: 'If we have food and clothing that is enough.'[103] She did not want them to get used to having things which might engender covetousness which no amount of possessions can satisfy: indeed, the more someone has, the more he wants, for neither abundance nor need causes desire to diminish. When people were arguing, she would speak gently to them and make them come to an agree-ment. If the young girls became frisky with thoughts of sex, Paula would crush these tendencies by prescribing frequent and redoubled fasts, preferring the girls to have stomach pains rather than mental troubles. If she saw one of them rather ele-gantly dressed, she would rebuke the girl who was at fault with a frown and an expression of displeasure, pointing out to her that elegance of appearance and dress were indications of spiritual ugliness. A foul or dirty word should never be uttered by a virgin for these were signs of a lewd mind, and a person's external characteristics revealed the faults of the inner person. When she found someone talkative or frivolous or insolent and this girl refused to correct her behaviour even after several warnings, Paula would make her pray among the younger ones, separated from the others, outside the dining-room doors, and eat her meal apart so that if she could not be cor-rected by rebuke, shame might force her to amend her ways. She detested theft as a form of sacrilege and she used to say that an act that was considered by people in secular society as something trivial or of no importance was in fact a very serious crime inside a monastery. Do I need to describe her compassion and committed care of the sick and the extraordinary devotion and concern with which she looked after them? Although she generously offered everything to others when they were ill, even allowing them to eat meat, if ever she herself fell ill, she refused to be self-indulgent and so appeared inconsistent, in that the compassion she showed to others turned into strictness towards herself.

21 Not a single one of the young girls, with a healthy and vigorous body, made as strong a commitment to self-restraint as Paula with her broken and frail body, weakened by age. I admit that in this matter she was too determined not to spare herself nor to yield to anyone's advice. I will tell you something from my own experience. There was a period of very great heat one July when Paula succumbed to a fever and we despaired of her life. But by God's mercy she recovered a little and the doctors urged her to drink a little light wine as a tonic for they feared that if she drank water she might suffer from dropsy. I asked Bishop Epiphanius to advise her, or rather to compel her to drink the wine, but being as sharp and alert as ever, she immediately perceived our stratagem, and with a smile she said that it was no doubt my idea that the bishop should speak to her. What more need I say? After trying repeatedly to persuade her, the bishop came outside and I asked him what he had managed to do, to which he replied, 'Only that, old as I am, I have almost been persuaded to give up wine.' I relate this episode not because I approve of people taking on burdens recklessly or beyond their ability (for Scripture warns us: 'Do not take upon yourself a burden'[104]), but so that I might use this instance of her stubbornness to show her passion of spirit and the longing of her faithful soul, for she would say, 'My soul has thirsted for you and how many times also has my body?'[105] It is hard to maintain moderation in all things. And it is true what the philosophers say: 'moderation is considered a virtue, while excess is something bad' (which can be expressed more succinctly as 'nothing in excess').[106]

But she who was so obstinate when it came to contempt for food was easily moved in sorrow and was devastated by the death of family members, particularly those of her children. When her husband and children died one after another, she herself almost died of grief, and although she made the sign of the cross over her mouth and stomach, trying in this way to lessen a mother's suffering with the sign of the cross, her maternal feelings got the better of her and caused her faith to falter. Although her reason remained in control, she was overcome by physical weakness, for once sickness seized her she remained in its grip for a long time, endangering her life and causing us much anxiety. But even then she was happy, constantly repeating to herself St Paul's words: 'What a miserable human being I am! Who will free me from the body of this death?'[107]

The perceptive reader may say that I am being critical rather than laudatory. I call Jesus as my witness, he whom she served and whom I desire to serve, that I am inventing nothing whether of praise or criticism, but as a Christian man writing about a Christian woman, I put down what is true, in other words I am writing history not eulogy. What were faults in her might well be considered virtues in other people. I mention her faults to satisfy my own feelings and the longing of all the sisters and brothers who love her and miss her.

22 However, she has completed her life's course and kept her faith, and now she is enjoying the crown of justice. She followed the Lamb wherever he went and she who was hungry is now filled. Joyfully she sings, 'As we have heard, so we have seen, in the city of our lord of virtues, in the city of our God.'[108] What a fortunate exchange! She wept and now she can laugh for ever, she looked with scorn at the broken cisterns but now she has found the Lord, her fountain; before she wore the hairshirt and now she can be dressed in white and say, 'You have torn my sackcloth and you have clothed me in happiness.'[109] She ate ashes as if they were bread and she mixed her drink with tears, saying, 'My tears were to me bread day and night;'[110] now she can feed on the bread of angels for ever and can sing, 'Taste and see, for the Lord is gracious', and 'My heart has uttered a good word; I tell my deeds to the king.'[111] She sees

fulfilled in herself the words of Isaiah, or rather the words of
the Lord speaking through Isaiah: 'Behold my servants will eat
but you will be hungry, my servants will drink but you will be
thirsty; my servants will rejoice but you will be put to shame;
my servants will exult with joy, but you will cry out with pain
of heart and will wail for anguish of spirit.'[112] I have said that
she always avoided the broken cisterns so that she might find
her Lord, the fountain, and be able to sing joyfully, 'As the deer
longs for flowing streams, so my soul longs for you, O God.
My soul thirsts for the strong and living God: when will I come
and appear before the face of God?'[113]

23 I shall briefly describe how she avoided the filthy pools of the
heretics whom she considered as no better than non-Christians.
Some cunning old man who thought himself both learned and
clever began, without my knowledge, to question her, saying,
'What sin has a baby committed that it should be seized by the
devil? At what age will we be resurrected? At the same age as
we are when we die? If so there will be need of foster-mothers
after the resurrection! Or at a different age? Then it will not be
a resurrection of the dead but rather a transformation into new
people. Will there still be differences of gender, male and female?
If there will be, then there will be marriages and sexual union
and reproduction; if not, it will not be the same bodies being
resurrected.' For he argued that 'the earthly habitation weighs
down the mind which muses on many things'[114] – but our bodies will be subtle and spiritual according to the words of the
Apostle: 'it is sown a natural body; it is raised a spiritual
body'.[115] With all this the man sought to prove that rational
creatures have through their faults and previous sins fallen into
the bodily condition; and that their state in life depends on the
nature and guilt of their transgressions. Some enjoy physical
health and a noble and wealthy family, while others get sent
into sickly bodies and poor homes so that they might pay the
penalty of former sins by being as it were imprisoned in a body
in the present life.

When Paula heard this and reported it, pointing out the man
to me, I was forced to take a stand against this wicked snake,
this deadly beast, the sort of person to whom the writer of the

Psalms refers when he says: 'Do not hand over to the beasts the souls confessing to you', and 'Rebuke, O Lord, the beasts of the reeds',[116] who when they write nasty things tell a lie against God and raise up their voice to the heights. So I went to see the man and by means of a few questions I managed to put a stop to his talk with which he was attempting to lead Paula astray. I asked him whether he believed that there would be a resurrection of the dead or not. When he replied that he did believe that there would be one, I said, 'Will they be resurrected with the same bodies or different ones?' He replied, 'The same', so I asked him, 'And the same gender as before or not?' He refused to answer my question and like a snake he moved his head this way and that to avoid being struck. So I said to him, 'Since you refuse to say anything, I will answer my question for you and tell you what follows.

'If one is resurrected as neither male nor female, there will be no resurrection of the dead because gender involves having limbs and it is the limbs that make the body complete. If there will be neither gender nor limbs, how can there be a resurrection of bodies that cannot exist without gender and limbs? Furthermore, if there is to be no resurrection of the body, there will certainly be no resurrection of the dead. But your objection concerning marriage, that if they were the same limbs, there would have to be marriage, is dismissed by the Saviour when he says: "You are wrong because you know neither the Scriptures nor the power of God; for in the resurrection of the dead they will be like the angels."[117] When it is said "they neither marry nor are given in marriage", it clearly implies that there is to be a distinction between the sexes. After all, no one would say of stone or wood that they neither marry nor are given in marriage, for it is not in their nature to marry. It is only said of those who can marry but who do not do so by the grace of Christ and by their own virtue. But if you put forward the objection "How then will we be like the angels since there is no male or female among the angels?", listen briefly: Christ does not promise us angelic substance but their way of life and their blessedness, which is why John the Baptist, too, before he was beheaded, was called an angel and all the saints and virgins of

God manifest, even in this world, the life of the angels within them. For when it is said: "You will be like the angels", Christ is promising likeness, not a change of nature.

24 'And now answer me, how do you interpret the fact that Thomas touched the hand of the risen Lord and saw the side wounded by the spear?[118] How about the fact that Peter saw the Lord standing on the shore, eating honeycomb and a piece of roasted fish?[119] If he was standing, he must have had feet; if he showed his wounded side, he must have had a chest and stomach, too, for otherwise there could be no side which is joined to the stomach and chest; if he spoke, he did so with a tongue and palate and teeth, for just as the plectrum strikes the strings so the tongue strikes the teeth producing a vocal sound; and if his hands were touched, it follows that he must have had arms as well. And so, as he is said to have had all his limbs, he must have had a complete body which is made up of limbs, and not of course a female body but a male one, in other words, of the same gender as he was when he died. But if you object to this by replying with a sneer, "Oh, so we too will eat after our resurrection? How come Christ could walk through closed doors,[120] which would be impossible for solid bodies made of flesh and blood?", you will receive this reply: "Do not use the question of food to undermine belief in the resurrection." For Jesus ordered the daughter of the chief of the synagogue to be given food after she had been raised from the dead, and Lazarus, after being dead for three days, is said to have attended a party with Jesus so that their resurrection should not be considered a mere illusion.[121]

'But if you use the fact that Christ walked through closed doors to try to prove that his body was spiritual and ethereal, he must then have had a spiritual body even before he suffered because he was able to walk on water, which is unnatural since bodies are too heavy to do so. The Apostle Peter must also have had a spiritual body because he too walked on water, as his feet skimmed the surface.[122] When something occurs which is against nature, it demonstrates the great power and virtue of God. To prove to you that in these great miracles there was no change of nature but rather a demonstration of God's omnipotence, he who by faith had walked on water began to sink through lack of faith, and would have done so if the Lord's hand had not lifted him up, with the words: "Why do you doubt, you of little faith?"[123] I am amazed that you are so obstinate when the Lord says: "Put your finger in here and touch my hands. Stretch out your hand and put it into my side and do not be faithless, but trusting",[124] and elsewhere it says: "Look at my hands and my feet, that it is I myself. Feel them and see, for a spirit does not have flesh and bones as you see that I have. And when he had said this, he showed them his hands and feet."[125] You hear him speak of bones and flesh, feet and hands, and you present me with the Stoics' delusions, as fragile and vacuous as bubbles!

25 'You also ask how a baby, that has no sins of its own, can be seized by the devil, and how old we will be at the resurrection, given that we die at different ages. No doubt my answer will not be welcome: "the Lord's judgements are a great abyss", and "O the depth of the riches and wisdom and knowledge of God! How unsearchable are his judgements and how inscrutable his ways! For who has known the mind of the Lord? Or who has been his counsellor?"[126] The difference in ages does not alter the reality of the bodies. For since our bodies change every day and either grow or shrink, are we to suppose that we will be all the people we have been through our daily changes? Was I one person when I was ten years old and a different one when I was thirty, another at fifty and a different one now that I am grey-haired? And so according to the traditions of the churches and the Apostle Paul, the answer must be that we will rise again as a perfect person attaining to the whole measure of the fullness of Christ.[127] The Jews believe that Adam was created at this age and we read that the Lord our Saviour rose again at this age.'

I put forward many other arguments from both the Old and New Testaments to stifle this heretic. From that day on Paula began to detest the man and all who shared his opinions so much that she would publicly proclaim them to be enemies of the Lord. I have related this not in order to give a brief refutation of a heresy – that would require many volumes – but to demonstrate this woman's faith in that she preferred to be exposed to the lasting hostility of men than to provoke God's anger by means of friendships that could harm her.

26 Now I shall continue with my description of Paula's virtues. No mind was more docile than hers. She was slow to speak and ready to listen, mindful of those words of advice: 'Be silent, Israel, and listen.'[128] She knew the Scriptures by heart and although she loved the historical facts, referring to them as the foundation of truth, she preferred to follow the spiritual meaning and used this as the roof to protect the edification of her soul. She persuaded me to allow her to read through both the Old Testament and the New with her daughter, while I commented on it. I refused to do so because I did not think I was up to it, but she insisted and so I agreed to teach what I had learned, not from myself (for over-confidence is the worst possible teacher) but from the outstanding men of the church. When I hesitated and openly admitted that there was something I did not know, she absolutely refused to give up but by constant questioning she forced me to tell her which of the many powerful arguments seemed to me the most compelling. I will mention something else which may perhaps seem incredible to those who envy her: she expressed a desire to learn the Hebrew language which I had been studying since my teenage years and in which I had gained a partial competence, tirelessly continuing with my studies so as not to forget what I had learned. And in fact she persisted with it to the point where she could sing the Psalms in Hebrew and read the language aloud without any trace of a Latin accent. Indeed, this degree of accomplishment is also to be found now in her holy daughter Eustochium, who always stayed close to her mother's side, obeying her so completely that she never slept apart from her, never went out or took her meals without her, did not have even a penny of her own but was happy that her mother gave away her family's wealth, such as it was, to the poor. Eustochium firmly believed that her love for her mother was the greatest wealth and the best inheritance she could receive. I must not fail to mention with what joy she heard her granddaughter Paula,[129] the child of Laeta and Toxotius (or rather

conceived as a result of her mother's vow and the dedication to virginity of the child that had not yet been born), singing the Alleluia with babyish pronunciation while still in her cradle and playing with rattles, and coming out with distorted attempts to pronounce her grandmother's and aunt's names. Paula's homesickness revealed itself only in the fact that she wanted to hear that her son, her daughter-in-law and her granddaughter had withdrawn from the world to serve Christ. In this she was partially successful, for her granddaughter is being preserved to take the veil of Christ, while her daughter-in-law has committed herself to everlasting chastity, imitating her mother-in-law's deeds of faith and alms-giving and trying to carry out in Rome what Paula achieved in Jerusalem.

27 What is the matter, my soul? Why are you afraid to approach her death? I have already made this work longer than it should be because I am afraid to reach the end, as if by not mentioning it and by concentrating on praising her we could postpone her death. Thus far we have sailed with favourable winds and the gliding ship has ploughed a furrow through the rippling waves of the sea; now my words have hit rocks and both monasteries are threatened by shipwreck on waves as high as mountains. We are forced to cry out, 'Save us master, for we are dying', and 'Get up, Lord, why are you asleep?'[130] For who could tell of Paula's death without crying? She fell seriously ill, or rather, she found what she wanted, which was to leave us and be joined more fully to the Lord. During her illness Eustochium's love for her mother which had already been tried and tested became clear to everybody. Eustochium sat beside her bed, held the fan, raised her head to put a pillow under her, massaged her feet, saw to the needs of her stomach, arranged soft bedclothes for her, cooled the hot water and brought her towels. In fact she did all the maids' duties before they had time to do them, and if one of the maids did something, she felt she had been robbed. She ran sobbing and sighing back and forth between her mother's bedside and the Lord's cave, praying that she would not be deprived of her company, that she would not have to live without her, that she might be carried to burial on the same bier! But alas for frail and fleeting human nature! Except that faith

in Christ raises us up to heaven and promises eternity to the soul, we share the same physical condition as wild animals and beasts of burden! The same death affects both the just and the unjust, the good and the bad, the clean and the unclean, someone who sacrifices and one who does not. There is no difference between the good person and the sinner; or between the one who swears and the one who fears an oath. Man and beast alike will dissolve into dust and ashes.

28 Why do I still delay, prolonging my grief by dwelling on other matters? The wisest of women sensed that death was close. While the rest of her body and limbs grew cold, only in her holy breast did her warm heart continue to beat. As if she were leaving strangers to go to meet her dearest ones, she whispered the following verses, 'O Lord I have loved the beauty of your house and the place where your glory abides', and 'how lovely is your dwelling place, O Lord of virtues. My soul longs, indeed it faints for the courts of the Lord', and 'I would rather be an outcast in the house of my God than dwell in the tents of the wicked.'[131] When I asked her why she was silent, why she refused to answer me when I asked whether she was in any pain, she replied in Greek that she was not at all uncomfortable, and that everything seemed peaceful and quiet to her. After this she fell silent and closed her eyes, as if she had already lost interest in human affairs. Until she breathed her last she continued to repeat the same verses so quietly that I could hardly hear what she was saying; and bringing her finger up to her mouth she made the sign of the cross on her lips. Her spirit was failing and she longed for death; but even though her soul was keen to break free, she managed to turn her death rattle into praise of the Lord. The bishops of Jerusalem and other cities were present as well as innumerable members of the lower clergy, both priests and Levites. The whole monastery was filled with virgins and monks. As soon as she heard the bridegroom calling, 'Arise, my love, my fair one, my dove, and come away, for now the winter is past, the rain is over and gone', she responded cheerfully, 'The flowers have appeared on the earth and the time of reaping has come', and 'I believe I can see the good things of the Lord in the land of the living.'[132]

29 After her death there was no weeping or wailing as usually happens; instead the psalms rang out from the crowds of monks. Paula's body was lifted up by the bishops and the stronger ones supported her bier on their shoulders; some walked in front carrying the lamps and candles while others led the choirs who were singing psalms. They laid her down in the middle of the church of the Saviour's cave. A huge crowd of people from the towns of Palestine had turned up for her funeral. Not a single monk living in the remote desert remained in his cell. Not a single virgin stayed in her room. Everyone regarded it as sacrilege if they failed to pay their final respects to such a woman. As in the case of Dorcas,[133] widows and poor women showed off the dresses she had given them; all the poor people, large numbers of them, cried out that they had lost their mother and nurse. And what is amazing is that her face did not lose its colour – in fact, she maintained such a dignified and serious expression that you would not have thought she was dead but rather asleep. The Psalms were sung, one after the other, in Greek, Latin and Syriac, not only for the three-day period until she was buried beneath the church and next to the Lord's cave but throughout the week. All who had come behaved as if it was their own funeral and the tears were for themselves. That remarkable virgin, her daughter Eustochium, could not be torn from her parent, like a child being weaned from its mother: she kept kissing Paula's eyes, putting her cheek close to her mother's, embracing her whole body, insisting that she wanted to be buried beside her.

30 Jesus will testify to the fact that Paula has left not a single penny to her daughter – in fact, as I have already mentioned, she has left her with a huge debt and (what makes it all the more difficult) a large number of monastic brothers and sisters whom it is hard for her to support but whom she cannot reject. Is there any more remarkable instance of virtue than that of this noble woman who had such strong faith that she gave away so much of what had once been a massive fortune that she was almost reduced to extreme poverty? Others may boast of how much money they have piled high in God's treasury and hung up as votive offerings with cords of gold: no one gave

more to the poor than this woman who left nothing for herself. Now she can enjoy the wealth and good things which neither eye has seen nor ear heard nor have they gone up into the heart of man.[134] We may mourn for our situation but if we continue to weep for one who reigns with Christ, we shall seem to be begrudging her the glory she has won.

31 Be confident, Eustochium: you are endowed with a great inheritance. Your share is the Lord and – a source of even greater joy to you – your mother has been crowned for her long martyrdom. It is not only the shedding of blood that is considered a confession: the service performed by a devout mind is also a daily martyrdom. Both are rewarded with a crown – a crown of roses and violets for the former, for the latter a crown of lilies. That is why it is written in the Song of Songs, 'My lover is white and red',[135] for whether in peace or in war God gives the same prizes to the winners. Like Abraham, your mother heard the words: 'Go forth from your land and your family and come to the land that I will show you', and the Lord's command given through Jeremiah: 'Flee from the midst of Babylon and save your souls.'[136] Till the day of her death she never returned to Chaldaea nor did she long for the fleshpots of Egypt and its juicy meats, but accompanied by her group of virgins she became a fellow citizen of the Saviour. From tiny Bethlehem she has gone up to the kingdom of heaven and can say to the true Naomi, 'Your people shall be my people and your God my God.'[137]

32 I have spent two nights of hard work dictating this book for you and suffering the same grief as you. Whenever I wanted to put pen to paper and start writing the work I had promised you, I would find my fingers grow stiff, my hand would fall to my side and my mind lose concentration. The rough style, devoid of any elegance or charm, will give an indication of the writer's feelings.

33 Farewell, Paula: please pray for me in my final years, I who idolize you. Your faith and your works unite you with Christ and so, face to face with him, you will easily gain what you ask for. I have raised a monument more lasting than bronze[138] which the passing of time cannot destroy. I have inscribed a

eulogy on your tomb which I include below so that wherever
my words go, the reader may see that you have been praised
and that you are buried in Bethlehem.

On the tomb is inscribed:

A woman descended from Scipio, whose parents belonged to the
    Pauli,
A descendant of the Gracchi, the famous offspring of Agamemnon
Lies in this tomb, to whom her parents gave the name Paula.
Mother of Eustochium, leading lady of the Roman senate,
She went to live in rural Bethlehem to follow Christ in poverty.

And on the doors of the cave:

Have you noticed this narrow tomb cut into the rock?
It is the resting place of Paula who dwells in heaven.
Leaving her brother, relations, Rome and her country,
Her wealth and her child, she is buried in a cave in Bethlehem.
Here was your manger, Christ; here the kings
Brought their mystical gifts to him who was king and God.

34 The saintly and blessed Paula died on Tuesday 26 January,
after sunset. She was buried on 28 January, during the sixth
consulship of the Emperor Honorius and the first of Aristaenetus.
She lived the life of holiness she had chosen for five years in
Rome and then for twenty years at Bethlehem. She lived for a
total of fifty-six years, eight months and twenty-one days.

ON CHOOSING A LIFE
OF VIRGINITY

by Jerome

(Letter *22 to Eustochium*)

Eustochium

Eustochium was born around 368, the daughter of Paula and Toxotius the elder. Her mother was widowed and her family came under the influence of Jerome when he came to Rome, and she followed her mother in refusing marriage and adopting an ascetic life (see also *The Life of Paula the Elder*). When her mother followed Jerome to Bethlehem, she, alone of Paula's surviving children, accompanied her, and spent the rest of her life as her mother's companion, taking over the running of the women's monastery there after her mother's death, until her own death in 419. Jerome addressed his *Letters* 22, 31 and 108 to her, and many of his biblical commentaries on books of the Old and New Testaments. She is mentioned in his *Letters* 30, 32, 39, 45, 52, 66, 99, 107, 123, 127, 134, 137, 142–3, 151 and 153–4.

Jerome

See headnote to *The Life of Marcella*.
    This letter was written in 384.

1 'Listen, my daughter, consider and incline your ear; forget your people and your father's house and the king will desire your beauty.'[1] In Psalm 45 God tells the human soul to follow Abraham's example and go out from its country and its relatives, leaving the people of Chaldaea, who are interpreted as 'like demons', to live in the region of the living which the prophet longs for when he says in another passage: 'I believe I will see the good things of the Lord in the land of the living.'[2] But it is not enough for you to leave your country: you must also forget your people and the home of your father; scorning the flesh, you must be embraced by the Bridegroom. 'Do not look back,' he says, 'or stop anywhere in the surrounding area; find safety in the hills so that you cannot be caught.'[3] Once you have grasped the plough it is not a good idea to look behind you or to go home from the field or to enter the house to fetch another garment, once you have Christ's tunic. This is something completely amazing: the father urges his daughter, 'Forget your father.' It is said to the Jews: 'Your father is the devil and you wish to carry out the desires of your father', and in another passage, 'Anyone who commits sin is of the devil.' Born in the first instance of such a parent we are naturally black and even after we have repented, but before we have climbed the hill of virtue, we say, 'I am black and beautiful, daughter of Jerusalem.' But you will say, 'I have gone out from the home of my childhood, I have forgotten my father, I am reborn in Christ. What is my reward for this?' The passage from the Psalm continues: 'The king will desire your beauty.' This, then, is that great sacrament: 'for this reason a man will leave his father and

mother and will be joined to his wife and the two will become one flesh',[4] but now not one flesh, as in that verse, but one spirit. Your bridegroom is not arrogant, not proud: he has married an Ethiopian wife. As soon as you are willing to listen to the wisdom of the true Solomon and come to him, he will tell you everything he knows. Then he will lead you into his bedroom and now that the colour of your complexion has miraculously changed, these words will apply to you: 'Who is this woman who goes up and has been made white?'[5]

2 I write this, my lady Eustochium (for it is right that I address the Lord's bride as 'lady'), to show you, from the very outset, that I do not intend to write in praise of virginity which you have most commendably approved by adopting it, nor am I going to enumerate the unpleasant aspects of marriage – the swollen belly, the crying baby, the pain caused by your husband's mistress, the anxieties involved in running a household and all those imagined advantages which death at last cuts short – for even married women can have a certain status if they have an honourable marriage and an untainted marriage bed. But I want you to understand that you are fleeing from Sodom and must take the example of Lot's wife as a warning. This letter of mine, such as it is, will contain no flattery – for a smooth-tongued flatterer is no better than an enemy – or pompous rhetoric to persuade you that you are already among the angels and have trampled the world beneath your feet now that the blessedness of chastity has been set before you.

3 I do not want your decision to choose this way of life to make you proud but rather fearful. You are walking laden with gold so you must steer clear of robbers. This mortal life is like a stadium: this is where we compete but we are awarded our prize elsewhere. No one is safe when he walks among snakes and scorpions. 'My sword has drunk its fill in heaven,'[6] says the Lord. Do you expect there to be peace on earth when the earth only produces weeds and thorns as food for snakes? 'Our struggle is not against flesh and blood but against the princes and powers of this world and of the present darkness, against the spiritual forces of evil in the heavenly places.'[7] We are surrounded by huge hostile forces and our enemies are everywhere. Our flesh is

weak and will soon turn to dust; it is fighting against tremend-
ous odds. You will not be safe until it has been dissolved and the
prince of the world comes and finds nothing in it; then you will
be safe and you will hear the words of the prophet: 'You shall
not fear the terror of the night or the arrow that flies by day or
the trouble that stalks through the darkness or the demons'
attack at midday. A thousand may fall at your side, ten thousand at your right hand but it will not come near you.'[8] But if a
hostile crowd harasses you and you get upset at all their attempts
to lead you astray and make you sin, and you say to yourself,
'What should I do?' Elisha will reply, 'Do not fear, for there are
more on our side than on theirs.'[9] He will pray and say, 'Lord,
open the eyes of your daughter and let her see.' And when you
open your eyes you will see a fiery chariot that will take you up
to heaven as it did Elijah, and then you will rejoice and sing,
'Our soul has escaped like a sparrow from the snare of the fowl-
ers; the snare is broken and we have escaped.'[10]

4 As long as we are trapped in this frail little body, as long as
we have this treasure in clay jars,[11] as long as what the spirit
desires is opposed to the flesh and what the flesh desires is
opposed to the spirit,[12] there is no definitive victory. Our enemy
the devil prowls around like a roaring lion looking for someone
to devour.[13] David said, 'You made darkness and it became
night when all the animals of the forest creep about, the lion
cubs roaring for their prey to find food from God.'[14] The devil
does not look for unbelievers or for those who are outside and
whose flesh the Assyrian king roasted in the fire: he is keen to
snatch people from the church of Christ. According to Habakkuk,
his foods are of the choicest kind.[15] He wishes to overthrow Job
and when he has destroyed Judas he seeks power to sift the
apostles.[16] The Saviour does not come to bring peace on earth,
but a sword.[17] Lucifer fell, he who rose at dawn and he who
was brought up in the garden of delights deserved to be told: 'If
you are carried up on high like an eagle, I will tear you down,
says the Lord',[18] for he had said in his heart, 'I will set my seat
above the stars of heaven', and 'I will be like the Almighty.'[19]
And so every day God says to the angels who climb down the
ladder of Jacob's dream, 'I have said, you are gods and all sons

of the almighty. But you will die like men and you will fall like one of the princes.'[20] The devil fell first, and since God has taken his place in the divine council and gives his judgement among the gods, the Apostle writes to those who cease to be gods: 'As long as there is jealousy and quarrelling among you, are you not of the flesh and do you not behave according to human inclinations?'[21]

5 If the Apostle Paul, the vessel of election who was prepared for the good news of Christ,[22] kept his body in subjection on account of the pricks of the flesh and the attractions of vice so that he would be seen to practise what he preached, and yet he could see another law in his body at war with the law of his mind and it held him captive in the law of sin; if after naked-ness, fasting, hunger, prison, whippings, tortures, he turned to himself and exclaimed, 'Wretched man that I am, who will res-cue me from this body of death?',[23] do you think that you are safe? Take care, I beg you, that God does not say to you at some point, 'The virgin Israel has fallen and there is no one who can raise her up.'[24] I say boldly, 'Although God can do everything, he cannot raise up the virgin once she has fallen.' He can save the girl who has been defiled from punishment but he cannot crown her. Let us fear lest that prophecy be fulfilled in our case, too: even the good virgins will fail[25] because there are also bad virgins. The Lord says, 'Anyone who looks at a woman with lust, has already committed adultery in his heart.'[26] So virginity can be lost even by a thought. These are the bad virgins, who are virgins in the flesh but not in the spirit, the foolish virgins who have no oil in their lamps and are shut out by the bridegroom.

6 If bodily virginity is not enough to save even real virgins if they have other faults, what will happen to those who have prostituted the members of Christ and have turned the temple of the Holy Spirit into a brothel? They will immediately be told: 'Come down, sit on the ground, virgin daughter of Baby-lon, sit on the ground; there is no throne for the daughter of the Chaldaeans; you will not be called soft and delicate any more. Take this millstone and grind flour, take off your veil, bare your legs, cross the rivers, and your shame will be revealed and

your shameful behaviour will be evident.'[27] Is this what she is reduced to after she has experienced the wedding chambers of the son of God, after the kisses of her brother and bridegroom? She is the girl of whom the prophet once said: 'The queen stood at your right hand in a golden robe, covered in many colours',[28] but she will be stripped naked and her skirts lifted up over her face; she will sit beside the waters of loneliness, and having laid aside her pitcher she will spread her legs to every passer-by and will be defiled head to toe.[29] It would have been better for her to marry and to have walked in level places than to try to reach the heights and then to fall into the depths of hell. I beg you, do not let the faithful city of Sion become a prostitute; do not let the demons dance there and beasts and sirens make their nests where the Trinity has lived.[30] Do not untie the bands that bind your breasts. As soon as lust stimulates your senses and the soothing fire of pleasure caresses you with its sweet heat, cry out, 'God my helper, I will not be afraid of what the flesh can do to me.'[31] When for a little while the inner person shows signs of wavering between vice and virtue, you must say, 'Why are you sad, my soul, and why are you upset within me? Hope in the Lord, for I shall again praise him, the salvation of my countenance and my God.'[32] I do not want you to let foul thoughts develop; do not let the shameful chaos of Babylon gain strength in you. Kill the enemy before it is strong; nip evil in the bud. Listen to the words of the psalmist: 'Unhappy daughter of Babylon. Happy shall they be who pay you back for what you have done to us! Happy shall they be who take your little ones, and dash them against the rock!'[33] Because it is impossible to prevent the natural heat of our senses kindling our passions, he is praised and considered fortunate who, as soon as he begins to have foul thoughts, kills them by dashing them against the rock; for the rock is Christ.[34]

7 When I was living in the desert, in that vast wilderness which is parched by the blazing heat of the sun and provides a harsh home for hermits, how often I imagined myself among the pleasures of Rome. I used to sit alone because I was filled with bitterness. I looked awful: my limbs clothed in shabby sackcloth, my filthy skin making me look like an Ethiopian. Every

day I wept, every day I groaned, and if from time to time sleep overcame me though I struggled to resist, my bones which scarcely held together would knock against the bare earth. I will not talk about my food and drink: even when they are sick hermits only have cold water, and cooked food is regarded as self-indulgence. And so I who had condemned myself to such a prison out of fear of hell, with only scorpions and wild animals as my companions, often imagined myself being tended to by lots of young women. My face was pale and my body cold from fasting, but my mind was aflame with desire, and now that my flesh was as good as dead only the fires of lust boiled before me. Totally helpless I lay down at Jesus' feet, I washed them with my tears, I wiped them with my hair and by means of week-long fasts I subjugated my body. I am not ashamed of my misery; rather I lament that I am not now what I was then. I remember how I cried out all night and all day and did not cease from beating my breast until tranquillity returned when the Lord rebuked me. I used to dread my tiny cell as if it knew my thoughts; angry with myself and grim-faced I went deep into the desert on my own. Wherever I saw hollow valleys, rocky mountains, steep cliffs, I would go there to pray, finding there a prison for my wretched flesh. And as the Lord himself will testify, after shedding many tears, after riveting my eyes to the sky, I sometimes felt myself to be among hosts of angels. Exultant with joy I would sing, 'We run after you for the fragrance of your perfumes.'[35]

8 If people whose bodies are so emaciated with fasting that the only thing they have to fear is foul thoughts have to endure such things, what temptations will be experienced by a girl who is surrounded by luxury? Do not the Apostle's words apply to her: 'she is dead even while she lives'.[36] And so if I have the right to advise and if my experiences make me credible, my first piece of advice is this: the bride of Christ should avoid wine as if it were poison, for this is the devil's primary weapon against young people. Greed does not shake you, nor pride puff you up nor ambition infatuate as much as this. It is easy to avoid other vices, but this enemy is shut up within us and wherever we go we carry him with us. The combination of alcohol and youth is

bound to make sensuality explode. Why do we add oil to the flames? Why do we add kindling to a body that is already on fire? Paul writes to Timothy: 'Do not just drink water, but drink a little wine for the sake of your stomach and your frequent ailments.'[37] Notice the reasons he gives for allowing the drinking of wine: stomach pains and frequent ailments are only just a sufficient reason. And in case we perhaps start to indulge every little ailment, he says that only a little wine should be taken, speaking more like a doctor than an apostle – although an apostle is also a spiritual doctor. He was anxious that Timothy should not succumb to this weakness and be unable to travel around as was necessary when preaching the Gospel. Besides, he remembered that he had said: 'Wine is a cause of debauchery', and 'It is a good idea for people not to drink wine and not to eat meat.'[38] Noah drank wine and got drunk in the earliest period of history; and then he was the first to plant the vine, so perhaps he did not know that wine caused drunkenness. To help you understand that Scripture is sacramental in every respect – for the word of God is a pearl and can be pierced in every part – after his drunkenness Noah went on to lie down naked and so lust was added to self-indulgence.[39] First the stomach and then the rest followed. For the people ate and drank and rose up to revel.[40] Lot was the friend of God: he was saved on the mountain and of all the thousands of people he was the only one found to be good, yet he was made drunk by his daughters. And even if they did this out of a desire for children – for they thought the human race was in danger of extinction – rather than out of lust, yet they knew that a good man would not have done this unless he was drunk. Although he did not know what he was doing and was not a willing participant in the crime, his error was a serious one for as a result of it the Moabites and Ammonites were born, those enemies of Israel who down to the fourteenth generation and for ever may not enter into the church of God.[41]

9 Elijah, when he fled from Jezebel and lay exhausted beneath the oak tree, was roused by the arrival of the angel who said to him, 'Get up and eat', and he looked and saw at his head a loaf of bread and a jug of water.[42] Surely God could have sent him

spiced wine and food flavoured with oil and meat tenderized by beating? Elisha invited the sons of the prophets for a meal and fed them with wild herbs, and then he heard his guests shouting, 'There is death in the pot, man of God': he was not angry with the cooks – for he was not accustomed to more luxurious food – but he sweetened the bitterness by sprinkling flour on it; in the same way Moses used his spiritual power to sweeten the waters of Marah.[43] Similarly when those who had come to arrest Elisha were struck blind both physically and mentally so that he could lead them into Samaria without their knowledge, notice what food he ordered for their refreshment: 'Put before them bread and water; let them eat and drink and then be sent back to their master.'[44] A more sumptuous meal could have been brought to Daniel from the king's banquet, but he preferred the ploughman's lunch brought to him by Habakkuk.[45] Daniel was called the 'greatly beloved',[46] because he did not eat the bread of desire or drink the wine of concupiscence.

10 There are numerous passages scattered throughout Holy Scripture where greed is condemned and simple food approved; but because it is not my intention at this point to discuss fasting – and to deal with these matters adequately would require a book in itself – these few points must suffice. These should enable you to understand why the first man, pandering to his stomach rather than being obedient to God, was expelled from Paradise and sent into this vale of tears, and why Satan used hunger to tempt the Lord in the desert, and why the Apostle exclaims, 'Food for the stomach and the stomach for food, but God will destroy both',[47] and why he said of the self-indulgent, 'God is their stomach.'[48] Each person worships what he loves. And so one must make sure that hunger brings back to paradise those whom a full stomach once expelled.

11 You may reply that you are born of a noble family and brought up among delicacies and soft beds, and so you are unable to abstain from wine and rich foods or to live according to strict laws like this, and I will answer, 'Go on then, live according to your law since you cannot live according to God's.' Not because God, the creator and lord of the universe, enjoys it when our intestines rumble, our stomach is empty and our

lungs seem to be burning, but because it is impossible to preserve chastity in any other way. Job was dear to God and in his
eyes pure and innocent, but listen to what he says about the
devil: 'His strength is in his loins and his power in the muscles
of his belly'.[49] (For the sake of decency the names have been
changed but it is the male and female genitals that are being
referred to.) Thus the descendant of David who, it is promised,
is to sit upon his throne is said to come from his loins; and the
seventy-five souls descended from Jacob who entered into Egypt
were said to come from his thigh. So also after Jacob wrestled
with God his strong thigh withered away and he ceased to produce children; and those who were going to celebrate the Passover were told to gird their loins and mortify them. God said to
Job, 'Gird your loins like a man',[50] while John [the Baptist]
wore a leather belt round his waist.[51] The apostles were told to
gird their loins so that they could carry the lamps of the Gospel.[52] In Ezekiel Jerusalem which, sprinkled with blood, is
found on the field of wandering is told: 'Your navel cord was
not cut.'[53] All the devil's power against men is in the loins, all
his strength against women is in the navel.

12 Do you want proof of my assertions? Here are some examples: Samson was stronger than a lion, tougher than a rock, and
alone and unprotected he could fight against armed men, but
he grew weak in Delilah's embraces; David was chosen according to the Lord's heart and with his holy lips he often sang of
the coming of Christ, but after he walked on the roof of his
house, he was seduced by the beauty of the naked Bathsheba,
and committed not only adultery but murder. Notice how a
person cannot use his eyes without danger even in his own
house. Then David repented and said to God, 'I have sinned
against you alone and I have done wrong in your sight.'[54] Being
a king he feared no one else. Solomon, through whom Wisdom
sang her own praise, Solomon, who discoursed on all plants
from the cedar of Lebanon to the hyssop which grows out by
the wall, withdrew from the Lord because he was a lover of
women.[55] And as if to show that even close blood-ties provide
no safeguard, Tamar's brother Amnon was fired with illicit passion for his sister.[56]

13 I cannot bear to tell how many virgins fall every day and are lost to the bosom of mother church – stars over whom the proud enemy places his throne, rocks which the serpent hollows out so he can live in their cracks. You may see many women dressed as widows before they are married to disguise their guilty conscience. Unless they are betrayed by their swelling bellies or crying babies, they walk with heads held high and with tripping feet. Some take medication to ensure sterility and so commit murder of a child that is not yet conceived. Others when they realize they have conceived in sin use drugs to procure an abortion and when (as often happens) they die with their foetus, they go down to hell laden with the guilt of three crimes, namely their own suicide, adultery against Christ and murder of their unborn child. These are the women who are heard to say, 'To the pure all things are pure.[57] My conscience is enough for me. What God wants is a pure heart. Why should I abstain from food which God has created for our use?' And if occasionally they wish to be charming and entertaining, they drink strong wine in abundance, then adding sacrilege to drunkenness when they say, 'Far be it from me to abstain from the blood of Christ.' If they see some other woman sad and pale, they call her 'a wretch' and 'a Manichee',[58] quite logically for according to their principles fasting is a heresy. These are the women who when they go out in public try to draw attention to themselves, and with nods and winks they attract a crowd of young men who follow them. To them the words of the prophet will always apply: 'You have the face of a whore, you are shameless.'[59] It may be that they are content with only a narrow purple stripe on their dress and their hair is tied only loosely to allow it to hang down, that their shoes are cheap and they only have a short cape over their shoulders, that their sleeves are tight and their gait lacks confidence: that is the sum total of their virginity. Let women of this kind have their own admirers and let them go to hell under the pretext of virginity. I have no desire to be respected by such people.

14 It makes me ashamed to speak of this next point, so shocking is it, but it is true, though sad. What is this plague of 'dearly beloved sisters' that has entered the churches? Where do these

women come from who are wives without being married, a new kind of concubine? Indeed I will go further and say, where do these monogamous prostitutes come from? They share the same house, the same bedroom, even the same bed – and then they call us suspicious if we think something is wrong. A brother deserts his virgin sister, a virgin rejects her celibate brother, and although they pretend to be committed to the same way of life, they seek the spiritual solace of people who are not related to them while their real aim is to have sexual intercourse at home. In the Proverbs of Solomon God rebukes people like this, saying: 'Can fire be carried in the bosom without setting one's clothes on fire? Can one walk on hot coals without scorching one's feet?'[60]

15 These women who do not want to be but only to seem to be virgins must be exposed and driven away. Then everything I say will be directed to you. Since you are the first noble woman in the city of Rome to adopt the life of a virgin, you must work all the harder not to lose your present benefits as well as future ones. Certainly you have learnt of the difficulties and uncertainties of marriage from the example of your own family, since your sister Blesilla, older than you but less mature in regard to her commitment, was widowed in the seventh month after taking a husband. How wretched is our human condition, ignorant of what lies in store for it! Blesilla has lost both the crown of virginity and the pleasure of marriage. Although as a widow she holds the second degree of chastity, imagine how painful it is for her every day to see in you, her sister, what she herself has lost. She finds it more difficult to be without the pleasure of marriage that she has experienced, and yet she also gets a lesser reward than you for her chastity. Yet she should feel secure and happy: the fruit that is a hundredfold and that which is sixtyfold both spring from the same seed which is chastity.[61]

16 I do not want you to spend time with married women, I do not want you to go to the homes of noble women, I do not want you to get frequent opportunities to see the things you rejected when you decided to be a virgin. Just because foolish women are in the habit of congratulating themselves if their husbands are judges or appointed to some high position, just

because ambitious people rush to pay their respects to the emperor's wife, does that mean that you should insult your Husband? Why should you who are the bride of God hasten to visit the wife of a mere mortal? In this regard you should learn a holy pride and be aware that you are better than they. But I want you not only to avoid meeting these women who have been made proud by their husbands' successes, who are surrounded by crowds of eunuchs and whose clothes have fine threads of gold woven into them; I want you also to avoid anyone whom necessity has made a widow. It is not that they ought to have desired their husbands' death but that they ought to have taken the opportunity for chastity of their own free will by not marrying in the first place. As it is, their former ambition remains unchanged: it is only their clothes they have changed. Rows of eunuchs walk in front of their enclosed litters, and their skin is so plump and their lips so red that you would think they were looking for a husband rather than that they had lost one. Their homes are full of admirers, full of guests. Even the clergy, whom they ought to respect and learn from, kiss the heads of their patronesses and stretch out their hands so you would think they wanted to confer a blessing, if you did not know that they were receiving the fee for their visit. These women, meanwhile, seeing that the priests need their support, become inflated with pride and, knowing what it is like to be under a husband's authority, they prefer the freedom of widowhood. People call them chaste nuns but after a dubious dinner they fall asleep and dream of the apostles.

17 Choose as your friends those whom you can see have grown thin by fasting, whose faces are pale, who are of a suitable age and way of life and who every day sing in their hearts: 'Where do you pasture your flock? Where do you let them rest at noon?'[62] Such women say, 'I long to depart and to be with Christ',[63] as if they really meant it. Be obedient to your parents; imitate your Bridegroom. Only go out in public very occasionally, seek out the martyrs in your bedroom. If you go out whenever it is necessary, you will never lack a pretext for doing so. Do not eat large amounts and never let your stomach get full. There are in fact many women who, although they do not drink

wine, overdo things by eating too much. When you get up at
night to pray, you should not burp from indigestion; no, your
stomach should rumble as the result of hunger. Spend much of
your time reading and learn as much as possible. Let sleep steal
up on you with the book in your hands and let the sacred page
catch your head as it droops. Practise fasting every day and do
not eat so much that you get full. It is no good going around
with an empty stomach for two or three days, if you then compensate by overeating. If you are full up, your mind immediately becomes sluggish and the watered ground produces thorns
of lust. If ever you feel that the outer person is sighing for the
flower of youth and if as you lie on your bed after a meal a
delightful procession of erotic images excites you, seize the
shield of faith which alone can destroy the devil's fiery arrows.
'They are all adulterers, their hearts are like an oven.'[64] Follow
closely in Christ's footsteps and pay close attention to his
words, saying: 'Were not our hearts burning within us when he
was opening the Scriptures to us?'[65] and 'Your words were fiery
and your servant loved that.'[66] It is difficult for the human soul
to avoid loving something and our mind must necessarily be
drawn towards some kind of affection. Spiritual love is superior to physical love; desire is quenched by desire. As the one
diminishes, so the other increases. So always repeat these words:
'On my bed at night I have sought him whom my soul loves.'[67]
The Apostle says, 'Mortify your body on earth',[68] as he himself
used to do so he could say confidently, 'I live, yet not I, but
Christ who lives in me.'[69] The person who mortifies his body
and walks through this world as through an illusion is not
afraid to say: 'I have become like a leather bottle in the frost;[70]
whatever moisture I contained has evaporated', and 'My knees
are weak from fasting',[71] and 'I forgot to eat my bread; because
of my loud groaning my bones stick to my flesh.'[72]

18 Be the grasshopper of the night-time. Wash your bed and
sprinkle your couch each night with tears. Stay awake and
become like the sparrow in your solitude. Sing with your spirit,
sing with your mind: 'Bless the Lord, my soul, and do not forget all his benefits, he who looks with mercy on all the wicked
things you have done, who heals all your weaknesses and

redeems your life from corruption.'[73] Which of us can say sincerely: 'Because I have eaten ash as bread and I have mixed my drink with tears'?[74] Should I not cry and sigh when the serpent invites me again to partake of forbidden foods? When, after driving us out from the paradise of virginity, he wishes to clothe us in garments of skin such as Elijah on his return to paradise threw to the ground? What have I to do with pleasure which will soon pass? What have I to do with this sweet but deadly siren song? I do not want you to be subject to that sentence imposed on man when he was condemned: 'in pain and sorrow, woman, you will give birth' – that law does not apply to me – 'and your yearning will be for your husband'. Let the woman who does not have Christ as her husband yearn for her husband. When God finished his condemnation by saying, 'You will die',[75] that is the end of marriage. My rule for life has no place for sex. Let marriage have its place and its status; for me virginity is consecrated in Mary and in Christ.

19 Someone may say, 'Do you dare to devalue marriage which has been blessed by the Lord?' You do not devalue marriage by preferring virginity. No one compares a bad thing to something good. Married women should take pride in being the next best thing to virgins. 'Be fruitful and multiply and fill the earth.'[76] Anyone who wants to fill the earth can be fruitful and multiply, but the company to which you belong is in heaven. The commandment to be fruitful and multiply was originally meant to refer to the period after Paradise, after the nakedness and the fig leaves signifying sexual passion. Let him marry and be married who eats his bread in the sweat of his brow, and whose land produces weeds and thorns, whose plants are choked by brambles. My seed is fruitful and brings forth a hundredfold. Not everybody can accept the word of God but only those to whom it is given.[77] Some people may be eunuchs out of necessity; I am one of my own free will. There is a time to embrace and a time to keep from embracing; there is a time to throw stones and a time to gather them up.[78] Now that the harshness of the Gentiles has given birth to sons of Abraham, they begin to be holy stones rolling on the ground. They blow through this world like whirlwinds and in the chariot of God they roll by on

spinning wheels. Let those people sew tunics who have lost the tunic woven from the top in one piece, who delight in the crying of babies who, as soon as they see the light, lament that they were born. Eve was a virgin in Paradise; it was only after they got their tunics of skin that she began her married life. Paradise is your home. Keep yourself as you were at birth and say, 'Return, my soul, to your rest.'[79] To help you understand that virginity is natural and that marriage follows sin: a virgin is born as flesh from marriage, giving back as fruit what it lost in the root. The branch will go forth from the root of Jesse and the flower will spring from the root.[80] The branch is the mother of the Lord, simple, pure, and untainted, with no shoot imported from another plant but fruitful in singleness like God himself. The flower of the branch is Christ who says: 'I am the flower of the field and the lily of the valleys.'[81] In another passage he is spoken of as a stone cut from the mountain without hands,[82] a prophecy signifying that a virgin will be born from a virgin. For the hands are interpreted as the effects of marriage, as when it says, 'His left hand is under my head and his right hand will caress me.'[83] This also agrees with the interpretation that the animals taken into the ark by Noah two by two were unclean, for it is odd numbers that are regarded as clean. Similarly Moses and Joshua were told to walk on holy ground with bare feet while the disciples were sent out to preach the Gospel unburdened by shoes or leather shoelaces; and the soldiers who divided Jesus' garments by lot found no shoes they could take away. For it was impossible for the Lord to possess anything he had forbidden his servants to have.

20 I am in favour of marriage, I am in favour of wedlock, but only because they produce virgins. I gather roses from a thorn bush, I find gold in the earth and pearls in shells. Surely the ploughman will not plough all day? Will he not also enjoy the fruits of his hard work? Marriage is more highly valued when what it produces is loved more. Why do you envy your daughter, you who are a mother? She is nourished with your milk, she was pulled from your womb, grew in your arms and you have kept her safe with your devoted affection. Are you angry that she does not want to be the wife of a soldier but

of a king? She is offering you a great advantage: you are about to become God's mother-in-law. 'Concerning virgins,' says the Apostle, 'I have no command from the Lord.'[84] Why not? Because his own virginity was not the result of a command but of his own free choice. One should not listen to people who claim St Paul had a wife, seeing that when he speaks about continence and tries to persuade them to perpetual chastity, he said, 'I wish that all were as I myself am. To the unmarried and the widows I say, "It is good for them if they remain as I am"', and in another passage he says, 'Do we not have the right to be accompanied by wives like the other apostles?'[85] Why, then, does he not have a commandment from the Lord on virginity? Because the reward is greater when virginity is not compulsory but voluntary. If virginity had been obligatory, it would appear to detract from marriage. It would have been hard to compel them to something unnatural and to demand that men lead the life of the angels; this would somehow have been to condemn something given as a rule.

21 The old law had a different ideal of blessedness. 'Blessed is the man who has his seed in Sion and domestic servants in Jerusalem, and cursed be the sterile woman who did not give birth', and 'Your sons are like the new crop of olives around your table.'[86] There was also the promise of riches and we are told that 'there will be no one weak in your tribes'.[87] Now it is said, 'do not think that you are a dry tree',[88] for you have an everlasting place in heaven instead of sons and daughters. Now the poor are blessed and Lazarus is preferred to the rich man dressed in purple; now a weak person is regarded as strong. In those days the world was empty and (passing over examples of childlessness that were meant to be interpreted typologically) children were considered the sole source of happiness. That is why Abraham, when he was already an old man, married Keturah and Jacob was redeemed by mandrakes, and the beautiful Rachel, a type of the church, bewailed the closing of her womb.

But gradually the crop grew and the reaper was sent in. Elisha was a virgin, and so was Elijah and many of the sons of the prophets. To Jeremiah it was said: 'You must not take a wife.'[89] He had been sanctified in the womb and was not allowed to take a wife because captivity was at hand. The Apostle expresses the same thing differently: 'I think that in view of the impending crisis, it is better for you to remain as you are.'[90] What is this impending crisis that takes away the joy of marriage? 'The time is short; even those who have wives must be as if they did not.'[91] Next comes Nebuchadnezzar: a lion has stirred from its lair.[92] What good is a wife to me if she will become the slave of a proud king? What good are children, whom the prophet deplores when he says: 'Thirst causes the tongue of the suckling child to stick to his throat. The little ones demanded bread and there was no one to break it for them.'[93] And so, as I said, the virtue of continence was at that time only found in men; Eve continued to give birth in pain. But after a virgin conceived in her womb and gave birth to a boy for us, and the government is on his shoulders,[94] a strong God, a father of a future age, the curse was broken. Through Eve came death, through Mary, life. And so the gift of virginity flowed more richly into women because it started with a woman. As soon as the son of God walked on this earth, he established for himself a new family in order that the one who was adored by the angels in heaven might be served by angels on earth as well. Then chaste Judith once more cut off the head of Holofernes; then Haman, whose name means iniquity, was burned by his own fire; then James and John left their father, their nets and the boat and followed the Saviour, leaving behind their family responsibilities and their ties to the world and their care of their homes; then for the first time were heard the words: 'If anyone wants to become my follower, let him deny himself and take up his cross and follow me.'[95] No soldier takes his wife into battle. The disciple who wanted to bury his father was not allowed to do so.[96] The foxes have holes and the birds of the sky have nests, but the Son of Man has nowhere to lay his head.[97] So do not complain if you do not have spacious accommodation. 'The unmarried man worries about the affairs of the Lord and how he can please God; but the married man worries about the affairs of the world and how to please his wife. The married woman and the virgin are also different: the one who is not married thinks about the things of the Lord, so that she might be holy in body and spirit;

while the married woman thinks of worldly things and how she might please her husband.'[98]

22 As for the inconveniences of the married life and the worries involved, I think I have summed them up in the treatise that I wrote against Helvidius on the perpetual virginity of the blessed Mary. It would take too long to list them all here and if anyone wishes to, he can draw them from that little spring of mine. But in case I should seem to have failed altogether to mention them, I will now point out that the Apostle tells us to pray without ceasing and that the person who is doing his duty within marriage is unable to pray. Either we pray constantly and are virgins or we give up praying so that we can perform our marital duties. 'If a virgin marries,' St Paul says, 'she does not sin; however, those who marry will experience trouble in this life.'[99] At the beginning of my letter I stated that I would say little or nothing about the problems of marriage and now I say it again. But if you wish to know how many troubles the virgin escapes and how many the married woman suffers, read Tertullian's work To a Philosophic Friend and his other treatises on virginity, as well as the outstanding volume by St Cyprian and those both in prose and verse composed by Pope Damasus and those by our friend Ambrose that he recently wrote for his sister.[100] In these last works he expresses himself with such eloquence that he has sought out and set forth in a coherent fashion everything relevant to the praise of virginity.

23 I must proceed by a different path for it is not my intention to praise virginity but to preserve it. To know that it is a good thing is not enough: we must protect what we have chosen with great care. To choose it is a matter of judgement – and many people can do this, but to protect it requires great effort, and only a few can manage that. The former we share with most people, but the latter with just a few. Jesus says, 'The one who endures to the end will be saved', and 'Many are called but few are chosen.'[101] So I entreat you before God and Christ Jesus and his chosen angels not to bring out of the temple vessels which may only be seen by priests, in case some profane person should look upon God's sanctuary. Uzziah touched the ark although it was not permitted to do so and as a result he was suddenly

struck dead.[102] But no gold or silver vessel was ever as dear to God as the temple of a virgin's body. First came the foreshadowing, now the reality is here. You may speak sincerely and treat strangers kindly, not despising them, but the shameless see things differently. They cannot appreciate spiritual beauty, only physical beauty. Hezekiah showed God's treasure to the Assyrians but they only saw something to covet.[103] As a result Judea was torn apart by a series of wars, and the first things to be captured and carried off were the vessels of the Lord. Belshazzar, surrounded by concubines at his feast, used the vessels as drinking cups,[104] because the most wicked thing one can do is to defile what is noble.

24 Do not listen to harmful talk. Those who say something indecent are trying to test your commitment. If you listen with pleasure to what is said or if you burst out laughing at every funny thing, they approve of everything you say, and deny whatever you deny. They call you witty and good, a woman in whom there is no guile. They say, 'Here is a real servant of Christ! Look how utterly open she is, not like that ugly, repulsive and scary woman, totally lacking in charm, who probably could not find a husband for that reason.' We are easily seduced by our natural inclination to what is bad: we willingly agree with those who flatter us, and although we may reply that we do not deserve such compliments and a warm blush may spread over our face, yet secretly our soul is pleased to hear them.

The bride of Christ is like the ark of the covenant, covered in gold both inside and out, and a guardian of the Lord's law. Just as in the ark there was nothing except the tablets of the law, so in you there should be no thought of anything that is outside. The Lord wishes to sit on this mercy seat as he sat upon the cherubim. He sends his disciples so that they may free you from the cares of this world, as they freed the foal of the ass, and so that you may leave the straw and bricks of Egypt and thereby follow Moses into the wilderness and enter the promised land. Do not let anyone stop you, not your mother, not your sister or any female relative nor your brother: your closest relative is the Lord. But if they want to make difficulties for you, let them fear the scourges that afflicted Pharaoh, as is recorded in the Bible, when he refused to let the people of God go so that they could worship God. When Jesus entered the Temple he cast out everything that did not belong to the Temple. For God is jealous and will not allow the Father's house to become a den of thieves. Otherwise if the place is used to count money, if cages of doves are kept there and simplicity is put to death, in other words if the virgin's heart is troubled by worldly business, the veil of the Temple is immediately torn, and the Bridegroom gets up in anger and says, 'Your house is left to you, desolate.'[105]

Read the Gospel and notice how Mary sitting at the Lord's feet is preferred to the busy Martha, even though Martha, eager to be hospitable, was preparing a meal for the Lord and his disciples. 'Martha,' said Christ, 'Martha, you are worried and distracted by many things; but there are few things that are really necessary, or in fact only one. Mary has chosen the better part which will not be taken from her.'[106] You should be like Mary, and prefer spiritual learning to physical food. Let your sisters run round thinking of ways to offer hospitality to Christ. Now that you have put aside the burden of worldly worries, you must sit down at the Lord's feet and say, 'I have found him whom my soul was seeking; I will hold on to him and not let him go.'[107] And he will reply, 'My dove, my perfect one, is my only one; she is the darling of her mother, chosen by the one who gave birth to her',[108] in other words the heavenly Jerusalem.

25 Always remain secluded in your room where you will be safe, always let your Bridegroom play with you inside. If you pray, you are talking to your Bridegroom; if you read, he is talking to you; and when sleep weighs down your eyelids, he will come behind the wall and put his hand through the opening[109] and touch your stomach. Then you will get up, trembling, and say, 'I am wounded by love', and he will say to you, 'A garden enclosed is my sister, my bride; a garden enclosed, a sealed fountain.'[110] Take care not to leave the house and do not express an interest in seeing the daughters of a foreign country, when you have the patriarchs as your brothers, and rejoice in Israel as your father: when Dinah went out she was raped.[111] I do not want you to go into the streets to look for your Bridegroom; I do not want you to go round all the corners of the city.

You may say, 'I will rise and go round the city, to the market square and through the streets, and I will try to find the object of my soul's love.'[112] You may inquire, 'Have you not seen the one whom my soul loves?'[113] but no one will bother to reply. The Bridegroom cannot be found in the streets. 'Strait and narrow is the path that leads to life.'[114] Then this passage continues: 'I looked for him but I did not find him; I called him but he did not reply to me.'[115] If only it were simply a question of not finding him! But you will be wounded, stripped naked, and then you will sob, saying, 'The guards found me as they went round the city;[116] they beat me, they wounded me, they took my cloak.' If the girl who said, 'I sleep but my heart is awake',[117] and 'My cousin is a bunch of myrrh lying between my breasts',[118] suffers such things when she leaves her house, what will happen to us, we who are still young girls and who remain outside when the bride goes in with the Bridegroom? Jesus is jealous. He does not want your face to be seen by others. You may try to make excuses and argue, 'I did cover my face with my veil. I went out to look for you and said to you, "Tell me, you whom my soul loves, where do you pasture your flock, where do you let it lie down at midday, for why should I be like one who is veiled beside the flocks of your companions?"'[119] But he will get angry and say, 'If you do not know yourself, fairest of women, follow the tracks of the flock and pasture your young goats beside the shepherds' tents.[120] Though you are beautiful and your bridegroom loves your beauty more than that of any other woman, unless you know yourself and keep a watch over your heart to keep it safe, unless you avoid the looks of young men, you will leave my bedchamber to pasture your goats which will be set on the left hand.'

26 And so, my dear Eustochium, daughter, lady, fellow servant, sister – for the first term suits your age, the second your rank, the third your devotion to God and the last our affection – listen to what Isaiah says: 'My people, enter into your bedrooms, close your doors and hide yourselves for a while until the Lord's anger has passed.'[121] The foolish virgins can wander around outside, but you must stay inside with your Bridegroom because if you shut your door and pray to your father in secret, in accordance

with the Gospel precept,[122] he will come and knock on your
door and say, 'Listen, I am standing at your door, knocking; if
someone will open for me, I will come in and eat with him and
he with me.' Then you will at once reply eagerly: 'It is the voice
of my lover who is knocking; open for me, my sister, my dearest,
my dove, my perfect one.'[123] You must not say, 'I have taken off
my dress, how can I put it back on? I have washed my feet –
I cannot get them dirty.'[124] Get up at once and open the door for
if you delay he may go away, and then you will be sorry and say,
'I opened the door for my lover but he had gone away.'[125] For
why should the door of your heart be closed to your Bridegroom? Let it open for Christ and close it to the devil, according
to the saying: 'If the spirit of the one who has power should rise
up against you, do not leave your place.'[126] When Daniel could
no longer stay on the lower floor, he kept the windows in his
room open towards Jerusalem:[127] you too should have your
windows open to let the light in so that you can see the city of
God. Do not open those windows of which it is said: 'Death has
come in through your windows.'[128]

27 You must also be very careful to avoid being seduced by a
desire for the admiration of others. Jesus said, 'How can you
believe when you accept glory from one another?'[129] Consider
how bad the thing must be that prevents the one who has it
from believing. We must say, 'You are my glory', and 'Let anyone who takes pride, take pride in the Lord',[130] and 'If I were
still pleasing people, I would not be Christ's servant',[131] and
'May I never boast of anything except the cross of our Lord
Jesus Christ by which the world has been crucified to me and I
to the world',[132] and 'In you we will be praised all day and my
soul will be praised in the Lord.'[133] When you give to charity,
let God be the only one who sees you. When you fast, your face
should be cheerful. Your clothes should not be too smart but
not too shabby either and should not attract attention by being
too distinctive, which might cause passers-by to stop and point
at you. Maybe your brother has died or your little sister's body
is to be buried: take care that you yourself do not die if you
attend such funerals too often. Do not try to appear very devout
or more humble than necessary, in case you win admiration by

pretending to shun it. There are many people who hide their poverty, compassion or fasting from others, but in fact they are trying to gain approval by apparently despising it, and perversely they win praise while trying to avoid it. I find many who are free from the other disturbing influences that cause people to experience joy, sickness, hope or fear; but this is a fault that few are free of, and the best person is the one whose character, like a beautiful body, has the fewest blemishes. I am not going to warn you against being proud of your wealth or boasting that you are from an upper-class family or feeling superior to others: I know your humility, I know that you can sincerely say, 'O Lord, my heart is not lifted up, my eyes are not raised too high.'[134] I know that the pride which caused the devil to fall has absolutely no place in you or your mother. So it is unnecessary for me to write to you on this subject, for it is the height of folly to teach somebody something he already knows. But now that you have come to despise the boastfulness of the world, do not let this in itself make you boastful. Do not harbour a secret thought that because you have ceased to be admired for clothes of gold, you might be admired for your shabby clothes. When you are in a room full of brothers or sisters, do not take a seat at the far end, pleading that you are not worthy to sit anywhere else. Do not speak quietly on purpose as if your voice were weakened by fasting, and do not lean on someone else's shoulder as if you were feeling faint. There are some women who disfigure their faces so that men will think that they are fasting; as soon as such women see someone, they groan and look down and cover their faces, just allowing one eye to peep out; they wear dingy clothes and a belt of sackcloth; their hands and feet are unwashed but their stomachs, because they cannot be seen, churn with food. It is with reference to people like this that the following psalm is sung every day: 'God has scattered the bones of men who please themselves.'[135] Other women change their way of dressing and adopt men's clothes; ashamed to be women as they were born to be, they cut their hair short and shamelessly choose to look like eunuchs. There are other women who put on clothes of sackcloth and dress in childish styles with hooded tunics which make them look like some kind of owl.

28 But it is not only women I should criticize. You should also avoid men whom you see wearing lots of chains or with long hair worn in a feminine style, contrary to the Apostle's precept, or those sporting a goatee beard, or wearing a black cloak and going around with bare feet, despite the cold. All these things are evidence of the devil. Some time ago Rome groaned over Antimus who was just such a person, and more recently there was Sofronius. When once such people gain access to the houses of the nobility and manage to deceive silly women overwhelmed by their sins, who are always being instructed but never arriving at a knowledge of the truth,[136] they put on a martyred look and pretend to practise long fasts while secretly eating at night; I am ashamed to say any more in case I appear to be attacking rather than warning. There are others – I am talking of men of my own order – who are keen to become priests and deacons only so that they may visit women without restriction. All they care about is their clothes and whether they smell nice and whether their feet are bulging out of their shoes. Their hair is curled and still shows traces of the tongs, their fingers are covered in glittering rings and they walk along on tiptoe so that their feet do not get splashed in the wet streets. When you see men like this, think of them as husbands rather than clergy. Some of them devote their whole life and all their efforts to knowing the names, houses and characters of married women.

I will briefly and cursorily describe one of these men, a prime example of this kind of behaviour, so that once you know the master, you may more easily recognize his disciples. He hastens to rise with the sun; he knows exactly in what order to make his morning calls; this old man takes a short cut and barges more or less straight into the bedrooms of women who are still asleep. If he sees a cushion or an elegant tablecloth or any other piece of furniture, he admires and praises it as he handles it, lamenting that he has nothing like this. In this way he does not so much ask for it as extort it from the owner, because all the women are afraid to offend this cunning old fox. He cannot bear chastity or fasting; what he likes is a tasty meal with a plump chicken, usually known as a 'cheeper'. He has a rude and impertinent way of talking and is always armed with abuse.

Wherever you go, he is the first person you see. Whatever piece of news is going around, he is the one either who first reported it or who exaggerated the story. He changes horses every hour – in fact, his horses are so sleek, so spirited that you might think he was the brother of the king of Thrace.

29 That cunning enemy, the devil, uses many different strata-gems to deceive us. The serpent was cleverer than any other animal created by the Lord God on this earth. That is why the Apostle says, 'We are not ignorant of his tricks.'[137] But a Chris-tian ought not to affect shabbiness nor dress with elaborate elegance. If there is something you do not know, if you have some doubt about a passage of Scripture, ask someone whose life commends him, whose age puts him above suspicion, whose reputation no one questions and who can say, 'I gave you in marriage to one man, a chaste virgin to present to Christ.'[138] Or if there is no one who can explain the passage, it is better to be safe but ignorant than to expose oneself to danger for the sake of knowledge. Remember that you are walking over a series of traps and that many women who remained virgins for a long time, right at the end of their lives lost the chance to win the crown of chastity which they thought was guaranteed to them.

If any of your servants wish to share your commitment to this way of life, do not treat them with contempt like an arro-gant employer. You have all chosen one Bridegroom: together you sing psalms to Christ, together you receive his body, so why should you eat at separate tables? You must challenge other women. The respect you show your virgins will serve as an invitation to others to do the same. But if you notice that one of them is a little weaker in her faith, give her support and comfort, speak kindly to her; make it clear that you value her chastity. If one of them pretends to a vocation so as to escape her servant status, read out to her the words of the Apostle: 'It is better to marry than to burn with passion.'[139] But those idle and gossiping virgins and widows who are constantly doing the rounds of married women's homes and who in their unblushing effrontery outdo the hangers-on in the comedy plays, these you must flee like the plague. 'Bad company ruins good morals.'[140] They only care about their stomachs and what lies just below their stomachs. This is the kind of advice they tend to give: 'My pet, make the most of what you have and enjoy life while you can', and 'Surely you are not saving your money for your children?' Tipsy and flirtatious they make mischievous suggestions and encourage even those who are strict with themselves to become self-indulgent, and 'when their sensual desires alienate them from Christ they want to marry, and so they incur damnation for having violated their original commitment'.[141] Do not try to appear too eloquent or to compose popular songs in verse. Do not be overly refined, imitating the affected pronunciation of those married women who speak sometimes with teeth clenched, sometimes with their mouths wide open, or clip their words with lisping tongues. They seem to think that anything natural is uncivilized! Such pleasure they derive from adultery, even of the tongue. What can light and darkness have in common? What agreement does Christ have with Belial?[142] What has Horace got to do with the Psalter? Or Virgil with the Gospels? Or Cicero with St Paul? Is not your brother scandalized if he sees you sitting in a temple full of idols? Although all things are pure to the pure and one should reject nothing that is received with gratitude,[143] we still ought not to drink from the cup of Christ and the cup of demons at the same time. Let me tell you of my unfortunate past.

30 Many years ago I cut myself off from home, parents, sister, relatives and (what was far more difficult) from the sumptuous food I was used to, for the sake of the kingdom of heaven. I set off for Jerusalem to serve as God's soldier there, but found I could not do without the books I had collected with great care and dedication while I was in Rome. And so, pathetic creature that I was, I would fast while planning to read Cicero. After staying awake for several nights, after all the tears that welled up from deep within me when I remembered my past sins, I would pick up my copy of Plautus. If I ever came to my senses and began to read one of the prophets, I was put off by the inelegant style and (because my spiritual blindness prevented me from seeing the light) I blamed the sun rather than my eyes. While the old serpent was mocking me in this manner, about halfway through Lent my exhausted body succumbed to a fever

which crept deep within me. My poor body became so emaciated that my skin – and this may sound incredible – hung loosely
from my bones. Preparations were being made for my funeral
for I was hardly breathing, my heart had almost stopped beating
and my whole body was growing cold, when suddenly I was
snatched up in the spirit and dragged before the judge's tribunal.
Here the light was so bright and those standing around so radiant that I threw myself on the ground and did not dare look up.
When asked who and what I was I replied that I was a Christian. But the judge seated there said, 'You are lying. You are a
Ciceronian, not a Christian. Where your treasure is, there is
your heart also.'[144] I was completely dumbfounded and the
flames of my conscience caused me more pain than the strokes
of the lash (for he had given orders that I should be beaten). I
kept thinking to myself of that verse: 'Who will praise you in
hell?'[145] I began to wail and cry out, 'Have mercy on me, Lord,
have mercy on me.'[146] These words echoed amid the sound of
the whip's lashes. At last those who were standing by fell at the
feet of the judge, begging him to have pity on my youth and to
give me a chance to repent of my error. Let him inflict a painful
punishment if I ever read any books of pagan literature again. I
would have been willing to make even greater promises under
such pressure at that terrible moment, and so I began to swear
an oath, calling on his name: 'Lord, if ever I possess or read non-
biblical books I have denied you.' After swearing this oath I was
dismissed and I returned to the upper world. To everyone's surprise I opened my eyes, so full of tears that even the sceptical
were convinced by my suffering. But this was not sleep nor one
of those idle dreams that often delude us. I call to witness the
judgement seat in front of which I lay, and I call to witness the
judgement that terrified me – may I never again have to submit
to such an interrogation! – that I had bruised shoulders and that
I could feel the effects of the beating after I woke up. After that
I read the books of God much more enthusiastically than I had
previously read the books written by men.

31 You must also avoid the sin of covetousness: it is not just a
question of not seizing what belongs to others – for this is pun-
ishable by the laws of the state – but of not keeping what was

yours but now belongs to others. 'If you have not been faithful with what belongs to someone else, who will give you what is your own?'[147] The property of others is a pile of gold and silver, while our own property is a spiritual possession of which it is said elsewhere: 'The ransom of a man's life is his wealth.'[148] No one can serve two masters; either he will hate the one and love the other or he will endure the one and despise the other. You cannot serve God and mammon[149] (in other words wealth, for in the Syriac language mammon is the word for wealth). Our obsessive concerns about our food are like thorns that choke our faith; our desire for what the Gentiles have is the root of covetousness. But you may say, 'I am a delicate girl – you cannot expect me to do manual work. When I am old and if I begin to be ill, who will have pity on me?' Listen to what Jesus says to the disciples: 'Do not worry in your heart about what you are going to eat or wear. Is not life more than food and your body more than clothing? Look at the birds of the sky; they neither sow nor reap nor gather the harvest into the barns and yet your father in heaven feeds them.'[150] If you are without clothes, the lilies can provide you with a model; if you are hungry, remember how blessed are the poor and hungry; if you are suffering from some pain, read these words: 'This is why I take pleasure in my infirmities', and 'I was given a thorn in the flesh, a messenger of Satan, who will beat me to prevent me becoming arrogant.'[151] Rejoice in all God's judgements; for the daughters of Judah exult in all your judgements, Lord.[152] Let these words always be heard on your lips: 'Naked I came from my mother's womb and naked shall I return', and 'we brought nothing into the world and we can take nothing from it'.[153]

32 But nowadays you see many women filling their wardrobes with clothes, wearing new dresses every day, but they still cannot get the better of the moths. A more devout woman wears one dress till it is threadbare, but her cupboards are full of clothes. Parchment is dyed purple, liquid gold is used as ink, books are covered in jewels, but Christ lies naked and dying outside their door. Even if they do hold their hand out to give something, they cannot help blowing their own trumpet at the same time. When they invite people to a fellowship meal, they

publish the fact all round the city. I recently saw – well, I had better not mention any names in case you think I am writing a satire – one of the most aristocratic of Roman women in St Peter's church, preceded by a group of effeminate men, handing out the odd coin to the poor with her own hand, so that she might be thought more holy. While this was happening, an elderly woman, marked by wrinkles and rags, ran on ahead so that she could receive another coin – an occurrence that is not unusual – but when it was her turn, she got a punch instead of a penny and paid with her blood for the wrong she had committed.

The love of money is the root of all kinds of evil[154] and so the Apostle refers to it as idolatry. 'Seek first the kingdom of God and all these things will be added to you.'[155] The Lord will not let the soul of a good person die of hunger: 'I was young and now I am old, and I have never seen a good man abandoned nor his children begging for bread.'[156] Elijah was fed by ravens that ministered to him,[157] the widow of Zarephath who expected to die that night together with her sons went without food so she could feed the prophet: by a miracle the jar of flour filled up and so he who had come to eat food became the one who provided it.[158] The Apostle Peter said, 'I have no silver and gold but I will give you what I have. In the name of the Lord Jesus Christ get up and walk.'[159] Now there are many whose deeds speak volumes even though they do not actually say, 'I have neither faith nor mercy, and the gold and silver I do possess I will not give you.' Let us be content if we have food and clothing. Listen to what Jacob asks for in his prayer: 'If the Lord God will be with me and will keep me safe on the path along which I travel, and will give me bread to eat and clothes to wear [then shall the Lord be my God].'[160] Jacob only asked for what was necessary and yet, twenty years later, he returned to the land of Canaan, a wealthy master and an even wealthier father. There are numerous other examples in Scripture that teach us to avoid covetousness.

33 Having touched on this subject in passing – and if Christ allows, I will devote a separate volume to it – I will mention what happened at Nitria a few years ago. One of the brothers who could be described as thrifty rather than covetous, unaware

that the Lord was sold for thirty pieces of silver, on his death left one hundred shillings, earned by weaving linen. The brothers (and there were about five thousand of them living there in separate cells) held a meeting to decide what they should do. Some suggested the money be distributed to the poor, others that it should be given to the church, while some said that it should be sent back to the man's relatives. But Macarius, Pambo, Isidore and the others whom they called fathers, inspired by the Holy Spirit, decided that it should be buried with the man it belonged to, quoting the words: 'May your money perish with you.'[161] Let no one consider their decision too harsh: all the monks in Egypt are now in the grip of such fear that it is regarded as a crime to leave behind a single piece of gold.

34 Since I have mentioned the monks and I know that you enjoy hearing about what is holy, listen to me for a few moments. There are three types of monks in Egypt: the coenobium which they call 'sauhes' in their local language and which we can call 'those who live in common'; the anchorites who live on their own in the desert and are so called from the fact that they withdraw far from other people; the third kind, known as 'remnuoth', is the worst of all and is much despised – though in the province where I live it is the only or at least the dominant kind. These last live in groups of two or three or just a few more, living autonomously. They pool the proceeds of their work, using the money to buy food. Most often they live in towns and villages and everything they sell is extremely expensive, as if it were their craft rather than their way of life that was holy. They often quarrel among themselves because living as they do off their own produce they refuse to be subordinate to anyone else. It is true that they vie with each other in their fasting, making something that should be secret into a cause for boasting. Everything about them is an affectation: their loose sleeves, shoes puffed up like bellows, coarse clothes; the way they are always sighing, going round to visit virgins, criticizing the clergy and eating so much that they vomit whenever there is a feast day.

35 And so once we have got rid of these pests, let us consider the many men who live together in community, in other words those whom we said were called cenobites. They have a fundamental

agreement that they will obey the superiors and do whatever these men tell them. They are divided into groups of tens and hundreds in such a way that every tenth person is in charge of nine others and then every hundredth is in charge of ten leaders. They live separately but their cells are close together. Until three in the afternoon there is a kind of cessation of business: no one is allowed to visit anyone else apart from those whom we referred to as deans or leaders of ten, so that if someone happens to be upset or disturbed, they can calm him by talking to him. After three in the afternoon they all meet together to sing psalms and read passages from Scripture out loud, according to custom. After finishing their prayers, they all sit down while one of them whom they call father stands up in the middle and gives a talk. While he is speaking there is such complete silence that no one dares to look at anyone else or even clear his throat. The power of the speaker's words is proved by the fact that his audience is in tears. The tears roll silently down their cheeks but they restrain their emotion from breaking out in sobs. When he begins to speak about the kingdom of Christ, about future blessedness and the coming glory, you can see them all sigh gently as they raise their eyes to heaven, saying to themselves, 'Who will give me wings like a dove and I will fly away and be at rest?'[162] The gathering then disperses and they go off in groups of ten, each with its own leader, to the meal at which they take it in turns, week by week, to serve each other. There is no noise at the meal, no one speaks while he is eating. They live on bread, beans and vegetables, seasoned with salt and oil. Wine is only given to the old men who also often have the same food as the children: in this way the older ones who are a bit weak get the sustenance they need, while the little ones who are only just starting out are not harmed by a harsh regime. Then they all rise from the table at the same time and after singing a hymn they return to their accommodation. There they can talk with the others in their group until evening. They might exclaim, 'Did you see so-and-so, how filled with grace, how calm and self-controlled he is!' If they notice that someone is ill, they comfort him; if someone is fervent in their love of God, they encourage him in his enthusiasm. And because apart from the communal prayers, each of them stays awake in his own cell at night, they go round to all the different cells, trying carefully, by listening at the door, to ascertain what the person inside is doing. If they find that a monk is being a bit lazy, they do not rebuke him; instead they keep their discovery to themselves but visit him frequently and by starting the prayers they inspire rather than force him to pray.

There is a task allotted to each day: this is given to the dean who takes it to the steward who must, in fear and trembling, give an account each month to the father of the whole community. This man also tastes the food when it is cooked and because no one is allowed to say, 'I have no tunic or cloak or rush mat', the steward must arrange everything in such a way that no one has to ask for anything or be in need. But if anyone falls ill, he is moved to a larger room and is looked after so attentively by the older monks that he misses neither the luxuries of city life nor his mother's loving care. On Sundays they spend all their time praying and reading – in fact this is what they do every day when they have finished their tasks. Every day they learn a passage of Scripture. The regime of fasting is the same all the year round except during Lent – that is the only period when they are allowed to live more austerely. At Whitsun dinner is replaced by a meal at midday which serves to satisfy church tradition and ensures that the monks do not overload their stomachs with two meals. According to Philo, the imitator of Plato's dialogues, and Josephus, the Greek Livy, in the second book of his *Jewish Captivity*,[163] the Essenes had similar practices.

36 What I have said about the monks may seem irrelevant given that I am supposed to be writing about virgins, so I will now move on to the third type of monks, namely those known as anchorites, who leave the monastic community and move further into the desert, taking only bread and salt with them. The founder of this way of life was Paul, but it was made famous by Antony and (to go further back in time) its first example was John the Baptist. The prophet Jeremiah also gives a description of this kind of person when he says, 'It is good for a man to bear the yoke from his youth. He will sit alone in silence because he

has lifted the yoke on to himself, and he will offer his cheek to the one who hits him and will be overwhelmed by insults because the Lord will not cast him away for ever.'[164] I will give an account of their hardships and their way of life that is in the flesh but not of it, on another occasion if you like. Now I will return to my subject, for it was while I was discussing love of money that I mentioned the monks. If you hold them up before you as examples, you will despise not only gold and silver and other forms of wealth but even earth and heaven themselves. United to Christ you will sing, 'The Lord is my portion.'[165]

37 Although the Apostle tells us to pray without ceasing[166] and although holy people ought to consider even sleep as prayer, it is nevertheless a good idea to have fixed hours for prayer so that if we happen to be absorbed in some task, the time may remind us of our duty: everyone should know that he or she ought to pray at the third hour, the sixth, the ninth, as well as at dawn and in the evening. You must not start on a meal without having prayed first nor should you leave the table before you have given thanks to the Creator. You should get up two or three times a night to meditate on passages of Scripture you know by heart. When you leave your home, you should be armed with prayer, and when you return from the streets you should pray before you sit down, nourishing your soul before you allow your poor body to relax. Make the sign of the cross before doing anything and before going anywhere. Do not speak disparagingly about anyone and do not spread scandal about your mother's son. Who are you that you should judge someone else's servant? It is in front of his own master that he stands or falls. And he will stand for God is able to make him stand.[167] If you fast for two days, do not think that you are better than someone who does not fast. You fast and yet you get angry, while another person may eat but perhaps speaks kindly; you work off your irritation and your hunger by picking a fight, while the other person eats in moderation and gives thanks to God. That is why Isaiah proclaims every day: 'This was not the kind of fast that I chose, says the Lord.'[168] And again, 'For in the days of fasting you do as you please and you oppress all who are under your power. If you fast among judgements and

quarrels and you punch anyone who is weak, why do you fast for me?'[169] What kind of fast can that be when not only has his anger not evaporated by nightfall but it is just as violent by the time of the full moon? It is yourself you should look carefully at; do not take pleasure in other people's failure but only in your own achievements.

38 Do not set before yourself examples of women who are concerned with their bodies and who are always reckoning up their income and daily household expenditure. For the eleven apostles were not crushed by Judas' betrayal, and when Phygelus and Alexander were shipwrecked this did not mean that the others faltered in the race of faith.[170] Do not say, 'So-and-so enjoys her own property; she is respected by everyone; her brothers and sisters come to visit her: surely this does not mean that she is no longer a virgin?' First of all, it is doubtful whether such a woman really is a virgin. For the Lord will not see as man sees; man sees the outward appearance but God sees into the heart.[171] So even if she is a virgin physically, I am not sure whether she is a virgin from a spiritual point of view. The Apostle gave the following definition of a virgin: 'Let her be holy both in body and spirit.'[172] Finally, let her have her own glory. Let her dispute St Paul's statement – let her enjoy her good things and let her live. It is for us to follow better examples.

Keep the blessed Mary before your eyes. She was of such purity that she was chosen to be the mother of the Lord. When the angel Gabriel came down to her in the guise of a man, saying, 'Hail, you who are full of grace, the Lord is with you',[173] she was troubled and could not reply; for she had never been greeted by a man. Soon she found out who the messenger was and spoke to him. She spoke without fear to an angel even though she had been afraid to talk to a man. You too could be the mother of the Lord. 'Take a long new roll and write on it with the pen of a man who is quickly carrying off the spoils, and when you approach the prophetess and you conceive in your womb and give birth to a boy, say, "Lord we have conceived from your fear and we have suffered and have given birth; we have made the spirit of your salvation on earth." Then your son will reply to you and say, "Here are my mother and my brothers.'''[174] And he whose name you just recently inscribed in your heart, whose name you wrote hurriedly on its new surface, after he takes the spoils from the enemy and after he has stripped the principalities and powers, nailing them to the cross, after conception he grows up into an adult and when he reaches maturity, he takes you as his bride rather than his mother. To be as the martyrs, to be as the apostles or to be as Christ is a difficult task but the reward is great. All such efforts are only useful when they are made within the church, when we celebrate the Passover in one house, if we go into the ark with Noah, and if at the fall of Jericho we stay inside with Rahab who was declared innocent.[175] Such virgins as are said to exist among the various heretical sects or to be followers of Mani who was completely devoid of purity, must be regarded as prostitutes rather than virgins. For if the devil is responsible for their bodies, how can they honour something made by their enemy? But because they know that the term 'virgin' gives one an enviable reputation, they go about like wolves in sheep's clothing. The Antichrist pretends to be Christ and these women conceal their shameful lives beneath a false cloak of respect. Rejoice, sister, rejoice, daughter, rejoice my virgin: what others pretend to be, you have really begun to be.

39 All the things I have set out in this letter will seem hard to someone who does not love Christ. But anyone who considers the attractions of this world to be rubbish and who thinks everything beneath the sun is worthless if only he can gain Christ,[176] anyone who has died with his Lord and risen with him and crucified his flesh with its sins and desires, will openly proclaim, 'Who will separate us from the love of Christ? Will hardship or distress or persecution or hunger or lack of clothes or danger or the sword?'[177] And further on, 'For I am convinced that neither death, nor life, nor angels, nor rulers, nor things present nor things to come nor strength nor height nor depth nor anything else in all creation can separate us from the love of God which exists in Christ Jesus our Lord.'[178] For our salvation the son of God became the Son of Man; for ten months he waited in the womb to be born, he endured distress, he came forth covered in blood, he was wrapped in swaddling clothes, he was comforted

with kind words and he who has the whole world in his hand was confined in a narrow manger. I say nothing of the fact that until the age of thirty he was content to live in humble poverty with his parents; he was beaten and remained silent; he was crucified and prayed for those who were crucifying him. 'How shall I repay the Lord for all that he gives me? I will take the cup of salvation and I will call on the name of salvation. Precious in the sight of the Lord is the death of his faithful ones.'[179] This is the only suitable return, that blood should be paid for with blood and those who have been redeemed by Christ's blood should willingly die for their redeemer. Which saint has won the crown without a struggle? Abel who was a good man was murdered; Abraham was in danger of losing his wife and (as I do not want to make this work too long) you can find many examples of those who suffered in various ways. Solomon alone lived in luxury and perhaps that is the reason why disaster befell him. 'For the Lord disciplines those he loves; he rebukes every child he accepts.'[180] Is it not better to fight for a short while, to carry a stake, weapons, food rations, to grow weary while wearing a breastplate but then to experience the joy of victory – rather than to be perpetually enslaved because you could not endure for one hour?

40 Those who love find nothing hard; no hardship is difficult if you desire something. Look at what Jacob put up with for Rachel, his promised bride. 'So Jacob served seven years for Rachel', as it says in Scripture. 'And they seemed to him just a few days because he loved her.'[181] That is why he says later, 'By day the heat consumed me and the frost by night.'[182] Let us love Christ, too, and always seek his embraces and then all our difficulties will seem easy. We will think everything long is short; and wounded by his spear, we will say at each hour of the day, 'Woe is me that I have prolonged my journey. The sufferings of this present time are not worth comparing with the glory that is to be revealed in us;[183] for suffering produces endurance and endurance produces experience and experience hope but hope does not disappoint us.'[184] When what you endure seems harsh to you read St Paul's second letter to the Corinthians: 'In more labours, in more imprisonments, with unlimited beatings, in

frequent deaths – five times from the Jews I received thirty-nine floggings, three times I was beaten with a rod, once I was stoned, three times I suffered shipwreck – day and night I was in the depths of the sea, in frequent travels, in danger of rivers, in danger of bandits, in danger from the Gentiles, danger in the city, danger in the desert, danger at sea, danger from false brothers, in hardships, in wretchedness, in many sleepless nights, in hunger and thirst, in frequent fasting, in cold and lack of clothes.'[185] Which of us can claim even the smallest part of this catalogue of virtues for himself? In fact St Paul then goes on confidently, 'I have finished the race, I have kept the faith. From now on there is reserved for me the crown of righteousness which the Lord will award to me.'[186] If our food lacks salt we put on a martyred look and imagine we are doing God a favour; when our drink is a little too diluted we smash the cup, knock the table over, beat the servant loudly and claim that if the water is not cold enough he ought to pay with his blood. 'The kingdom of heaven suffers violence and the violent take it by force.'[187] Unless you use violence, you will not capture the kingdom of heaven. Unless you knock urgently, you will not be given the bread of the sacrament.[188] Do you not think that it is violence when the flesh desires to be what God is and to climb up to the place from which the angels fell, in order to judge the angels?[189]

41 Come out from your body for a while, I beg you, and picture before your eyes the reward for your present hardships, a reward which eye has not seen nor ear heard nor the human heart conceived.[190] What will that day be like when Mary, the mother of the Lord, will come to meet you accompanied by her company of virgins, when the Red Sea has been crossed and Pharaoh and his army drowned, when Miriam will take the tambourine in her hand and will lead the song to which they will sing in response, 'Let us sing to the Lord, for he has triumphed gloriously; horse and rider he has thrown into the sea'?[191] Then Thecla will rush in joy to embrace you. Then your Bridegroom himself will come to meet you and say, 'Rise, come, my love, my fair one, my dove, for look, the winter has past, the rain is over and gone.'[192] Then the angels will be amazed and will say, 'Who is this who looks out like the dawn, fair as the moon, bright as the sun?'[193] The daughters will see you and the queens and concubines will praise and proclaim you. Then another group of chaste women will meet you: Sarah will come with the married women, Anna the daughter of Phanuel with the widows. In different groups there will be your natural mother and your spiritual mother: the former will be happy that she gave birth to you, the latter that she taught you. Then the Lord will truly get up on the ass and enter the heavenly Jerusalem. Then the little ones, about whom the Saviour speaks in Isaiah, 'See, I and the children whom the Lord has given me',[194] raising up the palms of victory will sing in harmony, 'Hosanna in the highest; blessed is he who comes in the name of the Lord, hosanna in the highest.'[195] Then one hundred and forty-four thousand hold their harps in front of the throne and the elders and will sing a new song and no one will be able to know that song apart from the appointed group: these are the ones who have not defiled themselves with women,[196] for they have remained virgins; these are the ones who follow the Lamb wherever he goes. Whenever you are tempted by this world's empty ambition, whenever you see anything showy in this world, transport yourself to paradise in your thoughts; begin to be what you will be and you will hear from your Bridegroom: 'Set me as a seal on your heart, as a seal on your arm', and protected equally by deed and thought, you will cry, 'Many waters cannot quench love, neither can floods drown it.'[197]

ON THE EDUCATION OF
LITTLE PAULA

by Jerome

(Letter *107 to Laeta*)

Laeta

Laeta married Paula the elder's son Toxotius and was the mother of little Paula. According to *Letter* 108 Laeta vowed herself to perpetual chastity after her husband died in 403 and remained in Rome until her death before 419. She is mentioned in Jerome's *Letters* 108 and 153.

Paula

Paula the younger was born around 400, the granddaughter of Paula the elder and the daughter of Toxotius and Laeta. According to Jerome's *Letter* 108, she was dedicated to a life of chastity. She seems to have been in Palestine during 416–19, probably with her aunt Eustochium, and again in the 430s when she visited Melania the younger, who is said to have shown Paula the way to God. Paula is mentioned in Jerome's *Letters* 108, 134, 137, 142, 143 and 153.

Jerome

See headnote to *The Life of Marcella*.
The letter was written in about 403.

1 When St Paul the Apostle writes to the Corinthians, instructing Christ's novice church in the sacred teachings, among other commands he gives the following one: 'If any woman has a husband who is an unbeliever and he consents to live with her, she should not divorce him. For the unbelieving husband is made holy through his wife and the unbelieving wife is made holy in her husband. Otherwise your children will be unclean, but as it is they are holy.'¹ In case anyone should think that the chains of discipline have perhaps been too loose up till now and the teacher over-indulgent, he should consider the household of your father – a most noble and learned man but one who is as yet walking in darkness – and he will see that as the result of the Apostle's advice the sweetness of the fruits compensates for the bitterness of the root, while the thin twigs exude precious balsam. You are born of a mixed marriage, but from you and my dear Toxotius Paula has been born. Who would believe that the granddaughter of the priest Albinus would be born as a consequence of her mother's promise? As a result her delighted grandfather will hear the little girl, who cannot yet pronounce the words clearly, say 'Alleluia' and the old man will hold the virgin of Christ in his arms. We have done well to wait; our patience has paid off. A holy and faithful house makes the single unbeliever holy. He is as good as Christian now, surrounded by all his children and grandchildren who are believers. I think that even Jupiter might have believed in Christ if he had had such a family. Although he may reject my letter and pour scorn on it, calling me either stupid or insane, this is what his son-in-law used to do before he became a Christian. People are not

born Christians but become Christians. The gilded Capitol is looking dingy, all Rome's temples are covered in soot and cobwebs, the city is shaken to its foundations and people flock to the martyrs' tombs without stopping at the dilapidated shrines. If good sense does not induce one to believe, then let shame at least do so.

2 I say this, Laeta, most devout daughter in Christ, to prevent you despairing of your parent's salvation. I trust that the same faith that won you your daughter may win you your father, too, and that you may enjoy your whole family's blessing. You know that this has been promised by the Lord who said, 'What is impossible for humans is possible for God.'² It is never too late for conversion. The thief passed straight from the cross to paradise.³ Nebuchadnezzar, the king of Babylon, recovered his reason even after he had been turned into a wild beast in body and mind and had lived in the desert with the wild animals.⁴ And not to mention examples from the past which non-believers might regard as fantastic, a few years ago did not your close relative Gracchus, whose name is synonymous with a noble family, destroy the grotto of Mithras while he was in charge of the urban prefecture? Did he not overturn, smash up and burn all the dreadful statues by which people were initiated as raven, bridegroom, soldier, lion, Persian, sun-runner or father? Did he not send these before him as hostages, so to speak, so that he could obtain the baptism of Christ? Even in Rome itself paganism has now been abandoned and those who were once the gods of the pagans remain beneath their deserted pinnacles in the company of owls and night birds; the army standards bear the sign of the cross, the royal purple and the sparkling crown jewels are adorned with the image of the gibbet that brings salvation. Now even the Egyptian Serapis has become a Christian while Marnas of Gaza mourns in his prison, in constant fear that his temple will be overthrown.⁵ Every day we welcome large numbers from India, Persia and Ethiopia; the Armenians have put away their arrows, the Huns are learning the Psalms, the freezing Scythians are on fire with the ardour of faith; the blond and red-haired armies of the Getae carry their tents around with them, and the reason they fight with us

on equal terms is perhaps that their religious beliefs are the same as ours.

3 I have almost wandered off into another subject and while trying to make a pitcher on my spinning potter's wheel, my hands have made a flagon.[6] I was planning, in response to your request and that of the holy Marcella, to direct my speech to a mother, in other words to you. I intended to instruct you as to how you ought to bring up our little Paula who was consecrated to Christ before she was born and who was in your prayers before she was in your womb. We have seen in our own times an event recorded by the prophets: Hannah exchanged infertility for fertility, while you have exchanged the fertility that causes sorrow for children who will live for ever. I can confidently predict that having given your first-born to the Lord you will produce sons. It is the first-born that is offered under the Law: so it was with Samuel, so it was with Samson, so it was with the prophet John (the Baptist) who leapt with joy when Mary came in.[7] For from the Virgin's lips he heard the thundering words of the Lord and was eager to burst forth from his mother's womb to meet him. And so little Paula who was born as the result of a promise should be given by her parents an education that is worthy of her birth. Samuel was brought up in the temple, John was trained in the wilderness. Samuel inspired veneration for his hair that had been consecrated; he drank neither wine nor strong drink and conversed with God while he was still a little boy. John the Baptist avoided cities, wore a belt made of animal skin, lived on locusts and wild honey and dressed in camel skin as a symbol of the repentance he preached.

4 If Paula's soul is to become a temple of the Lord it must be trained in the following way. She must learn to listen to and say only what is consistent with fear of the Lord. She should not learn any bad language or be familiar with popular songs. Her tongue should be steeped in the sweetness of the psalms while she is still a child. Boys with their wild behaviour should be kept away from her, and even her maids and attendants should have no contact with worldly companions so that they cannot teach her the bad habits they have learned. Arrange for a set of

letters of the alphabet to be made for her out of boxwood or
ivory and teach her the name of each letter. Let her play with
them so that she can learn through play: she should not only
get to know the alphabet by heart so that she can make a song
out of the names of the letters, but you should also jumble up
the order of the letters to ensure that she recognizes their shape
and is not simply familiar with their sounds. When she begins
to move a pen across the wax with wobbly fingers, someone
else should put their hand over hers to steady her little fingers.
Or you can have the letters engraved on a tablet so that her
writing can follow their outlines, keeping to their proper shapes
and not wandering outside the lines. Offer her a prize for spell-
ing and encourage her with little presents of the sort that will
delight a child of her age. She should have companions in her
lessons – this will introduce an element of competition and
make her jealous when her rivals receive praise. She should not
be rebuked if she is a bit slow – instead her abilities should be
brought out by means of praise: she should be pleased when
she comes top and disappointed when someone else does better.
Make sure she does not get put off learning at an early stage:
you do not want the dislike she experiences when little to continue beyond childhood. The very names she uses in forming
sentences should not be taken at random but chosen on purpose and deliberately arranged (namely those of the prophets
and apostles and the whole line of patriarchs from Adam as set
out by Matthew and Luke) so that she can learn them off by
heart while doing something else. You should select a teacher of
mature age whose lifestyle and learning are approved – I do not
think a learned man would be ashamed to take on this task for
a close relative or a virgin of an aristocratic family. After all,
this was the task that Aristotle performed, like some low-paid
clerk, for he taught Philip's son, Alexander, to read when he
was little. One should not despise as unimportant things that
are essential for higher achievements. Even the sound of the
letters and the first lessons sound differently if they are spoken
by an educated teacher rather than an uneducated one. So you
must take care not to let your daughter get into the habit of
speaking in a clipped manner in imitation of women's silly baby

talk or of wearing clothes of gold and purple while she plays, for the former harms her speech and the latter her character. We certainly do not want her to learn something as a child that she will later have to unlearn. The eloquence of the Gracchi is said to have been largely the result of their mother talking to them when they were children, while Hortensius became an outstanding orator by sitting on his father's lap. It is difficult to erase what has seared itself into a child's mind. Who can restore the wool to its original whiteness once it has been dyed purple?[8] A new jar retains the taste and smell of its original contents for a long time. Greek history records that Alexander, the most powerful king and the conqueror of the world, inevitably had the same idiosyncrasies of gait and manner as he had picked up as a child from his teacher Leonidas. For it is easy to copy bad habits and if you cannot imitate someone's good points, you will soon imitate their faults. Paula's nurse must not be talkative or prone to drink or dirty jokes. Her nurse should be modest and her tutor a serious man. When she sees her grandfather she should jump up on his lap, put her arms round his neck and insist on singing the 'Alleluia' to him whether he likes it or not. Her grandmother should pick her up and Paula should welcome her father with a smile and be charming to everybody so that all her relatives are happy that the family has brought forth this rosebud. She should be made aware at once that she has another grandmother, too, and an aunt for whose service she is being trained as if for the emperor's army. She should long to join them and threaten to leave you for them.

5 Paula's outward appearance and her clothes should also remind her to whom she has been promised. Make sure you do not pierce her ears or use rouge or white lead on those cheeks that are consecrated to Christ; do not hang necklaces of gold or pearls round her neck or adorn her head with heavy jewels; do not dye her hair red, thereby giving her a preview of the fires of hell. She has other pearls which she will later sell so that she can buy that most valuable pearl. There was once a woman called Praetextata from a very aristocratic family who at the request of her husband, Hymetius, the uncle of the virgin Eustochium, changed that girl's appearance and the way she dressed

and curled her dishevelled hair, hoping to overcome Eustochium's resolution as well as her mother's wishes.[9] But that
same night this woman saw an angel approach her with a terrifying look on his face, threatening punishments and barking
out these words, giving weight to each of them: 'Have you
dared to respect your husband's orders more than Christ? Did
you dare to touch the head of God's virgin with your sacrile-
gious hands? Those hands will wither this moment so that your
torment will make you realize what you have done. After five
months you will be carried off to hell. And if you persist in sin-
ning, you will lose both your husband and children.' All these
things happened just as the angel had said and a swift death
marked the poor woman's repentance which came too late.
This is how Christ takes vengeance on those who violate his
temple, this is how he protects his jewels and his most precious
decorations. I have told you this not because I want to take
pleasure in the sufferings of unfortunate people but to warn
you with what fear and care you must protect what you have
promised to give to the Lord.

6 The priest Eli annoyed the Lord as the result of his sons' bad
behaviour; a man cannot become a bishop if he has children
who are self-indulgent and insubordinate. On the other hand it
is written of the woman that 'she will be saved by child-bearing,
if she stands firm in her faith and love and holiness, together
with chastity'.[10] If parents are responsible for their children's
behaviour when they are grown up and have reached the age of
majority, how much more so when they are still babies, weak
and unable to distinguish between the right hand and the left,
as the Lord says?[11] You take care to protect your daughter from
poisonous snakes, so why do you not take as much care to prevent her being struck by the hammer of the whole earth, or
drinking from the golden goblet of Babylon, or going out with
Dinah and wanting to see the daughters of a foreign country, or
dancing or wearing dresses that trail behind her? The rim of the
cup is smeared with honey before poison is administered and a
cloak of virtues only allows vices to deceive. You may say,
'How come we read that the sins of the fathers do not count
against the children or those of the children against the parents,

but it is only the soul that has sinned that will die?'[12] This refers to those who are able to understand, of whom it is said in the Gospel: 'He is of age. He will speak for himself.'[13] But as for one who is still very young and has the understanding of a small child, until he reaches the age of wisdom and Pythagoras' letter leads him to the fork in the road, his parents will be considered responsible for his good behaviour as well as the bad. Unless of course you happen to consider that the children of Christians if they have not been baptized are themselves guilty of sin and that their wicked behaviour is not to be blamed on their parents who refused to have them baptized, especially since those who were going to receive baptism were at an age when they could offer no objection. Just as baptism ensures the children's salvation, so it is also of advantage to the parents. It was up to you to offer your daughter or not, although your situation is different for you promised to consecrate her before she was conceived. If you failed to care for her once you had consecrated her, it would be dangerous for you. Anyone who offers for sacrifice a victim that is lame or maimed or has any kind of blemish is guilty of sacrilege. Will not an even worse punishment befall someone who prepares a part of his own body and the purity of an untainted soul for the king's embraces, but then fails to protect his offering?

7 When Paula gets a little older and by following the example of her Bridegroom she begins to grow in wisdom, in age and in grace in the eyes of God and of men, she should go out with her parents to her true father's temple but she should not leave the temple in their company. Let them look for her on the world's highway, among the crowds and throng of relatives, and let them find her nowhere except in the inner sanctuary of the Scriptures, questioning the prophets and the apostles regarding her spiritual wedding. She should imitate Mary who was discovered by Gabriel alone in her room and who was, it seems, terrified at seeing a man there unexpectedly. She should imitate the woman of whom it is said: 'All the glory of the king's daughter is from within.'[14] Wounded by love's arrow, she should say to her chosen one, 'The king has brought me into his bedroom.'[15] She should never go out lest those who go round the city should

find her, lest they should strike her and wound her and take away the veil of her chastity and leave her naked and bleeding. No, instead, when someone knocks on the door she should say, 'I am a wall and my breasts are a tower; I have washed my feet, I cannot get them dirty.'[16]

8 She should not eat in public, in other words at her parents' dinner parties, nor should she see any food that might tempt her to try it. And although some might think that it is more commendable for a virgin to reject a pleasure that is available to her, I consider it safer for self-restraint to be unaware of something you might like. When I was a boy I once read: 'You cannot blame something once you have allowed it to become a habit.'[17] Let her learn already at this age not to drink wine for it leads to self-indulgence.[18] On the other hand, strict abstinence is dangerous for young children until they are a bit stronger. Until then, if necessity so demands, let her go to the baths and drink a small amount of wine for the sake of her digestion, and let her become strong by eating meat, so that her feet will not grow weary before she begins to run. I say this as a concession, rather than as a command, fearing to weaken her rather than showing her the way to self-indulgence. Why should a Christian virgin not practise in every detail what the superstitious Jews practise in part by rejecting certain foods and animals, or what the Brahmans of India and the gymnosophists of Egypt observe by subsisting on a diet of polenta, rice and fruit? If a glass bead is so valuable, is not a pearl even more precious? A girl who is born as the result of a promise should live the same kind of life as others who were born of promise. Equal grace should also have equal hardship. Do not let her listen to musical instruments; let her remain ignorant of why flutes, lyres and harps were made.

9 Every day she should prepare for you a set passage of Scripture. She should learn by heart a number of Greek verses and then immediately start studying Latin, for if she does not train her young lips from the very outset, the language will be tainted by a foreign pronunciation and her mother tongue will be corrupted by faults from a foreign language. Let her have you as a teacher, let her admire you from her earliest infancy. She should

see nothing in you or in her father which she would be wrong to imitate. Do not forget that you are the parents of a virgin and that you can teach her more effectively by example than by your words. Flowers soon wilt, and violets and lilies and crocuses are quickly laid low by a strong wind. She must never go out in public without you or visit the martyrs' shrines and the churches without her mother. Let no young man, his hair curled, flirt with her. Our little virgin should celebrate vigils and all-night services without moving an inch from her mother. I do not want her to have a favourite among her maid servants into whose ear she can keep whispering. Whatever she says to one, all of them ought to know. Let her choose as her companion not a girl who is pretty or graceful or who sings sweetly with a clear voice but one who is serious, pale, a bit shabby and not too cheerful. Arrange for her to be put in the charge of an elderly virgin of proven faith, good character and chastity, who will teach her and by her own example train her to rise at night for prayers and psalms, to sing hymns in the morning and to stand in the front line as Christ's soldier at the third, sixth and ninth hours and to perform the evening sacrifice when the lamps are lit. May the day be spent in this way, may the night find her devoted to these tasks. Let reading follow prayer and prayer follow reading. It will seem a short time if she is occupied in so many different ways.

10 Paula should learn to make wool, to hold the distaff, to put the basket in her lap, to spin the spindle, to draw the threads with her thumb. Let her despise silk fabrics, Chinese fleeces and gold turned into soft thread. She should wear the sort of clothes that protect from the cold, not those that expose the limbs they are supposed to cover. Her food should be vegetables and wheat bread and occasionally fish. I do not want to give a long list of dietary rules – I have discussed these matters at length elsewhere – but she should eat in such a way that she is always hungry, so that as soon as she has eaten she is able to read, pray and sing the psalms. I do not approve of lengthy and excessively strict fasts, especially for young people, fasts that go on week after week, without any fruit or oil in food being allowed. I have learnt from experience that when an ass on the road is

weary it makes for an inn. Leave such behaviour to those who worship Isis and Cybele, who in greedy abstinence gobble up pheasants and piping-hot turtle doves, to avoid touching the gifts of Ceres, of course. If you fast without a break, you must make sure that you have strength for the long journey, so that you do not run the first lap and then collapse halfway through the race. However, as I have written previously, in Lent one should spread the sails of abstinence wide and relax all the reins of your chariot as the horses gallop forward, although the rules for those who live in the world differ from those for virgins and monks. During Lent a layperson consumes what is already stored in his stomach and like a snail he lives off his own fat while preparing his belly for future feasts and rich food; the virgin and the monk give their horses free rein in Lent in such a way that they must remember that their race lasts for ever. The greater efforts are limited while more moderate efforts can last for longer; for in the former case we will have a breathing space, while in the latter there is no end.

11 When you go out into the country on the edge of the city, do not leave your daughter at home for she should not be able to live without you; when she is alone, she should tremble with fear. She must not talk to people of the world or associate with virgins who are unreliable; she should not attend the weddings of her servants or take part in noisy family games. I know that some people have advised that a virgin of Christ should not bathe along with eunuchs nor with married women, because the eunuchs are still men at heart while pregnant women with their swelling stomachs are revolting to look at. I am completely against the idea of a grown virgin going to the baths, for she ought to feel embarrassed to see herself naked. If she weakens her body by fasting and staying up all night and brings it into subjection, if she desires to extinguish the flame of lust and the hot desires of youth by means of chill chastity, if she is eager to spoil her natural beauty by deliberate neglect, then why should she go to the baths and thereby rekindle the fire that has died down?

12 Instead of jewels and silk dresses, let her prefer the Holy Scriptures in which it is not the illuminations, richly decorated

in gold on Babylonian parchment, that give her pleasure, but the text carefully set out to encourage her faith. Let her first learn the Psalms and amuse herself by singing them. The Proverbs of Solomon will give her advice about living. In Ecclesiastes she will learn to trample on the things of this world, in Job she will follow the examples of virtue and patience. When she moves over to the Gospels she should do so with the intention of never letting them out of her hands; let her eagerly absorb the Acts of the Apostles and the Epistles with all her heart. When she has filled her heart's cellar with these treasures, let her commit to memory the Prophets and the Heptateuch, the books of Kings and Chronicles, the rolls of Ezra and Esther. Finally, she will be able to study the Song of Songs without danger, for if she were to read them at the beginning she would not understand that it was a wedding song for a spiritual wedding disguised beneath the description of a physical wedding and that would harm her. She should steer clear of all the apocryphal books and if ever she wishes to read them not for the truth of the doctrines but out of respect for the miracles contained in them, she must be aware that they are not really written by those whose names are given in their titles and that many bad things have been mixed into them and that one must take great care in trying to sift the gold from the mud. She should have Cyprian's writings always in her hands, and she can run through Athanasius' letters and Hilary's works without fear of stumbling. She should take delight in the writings and the genius of those whose faith stands firm; she can read the works of other people but should not follow them uncritically.

13 You will answer: 'How can I, an ordinary woman living amidst the crowds of Rome, carry out all this advice?' Well then, you must not take on a burden you are unable to carry. Instead, once you have weaned her with Isaac and clothed her with Samuel, send her to her grandmother and aunt. Place the most precious jewel in Mary's chamber and lay her in the cradle where the baby Jesus cried. Let her be brought up in the monastery surrounded by virgins, let her learn not to swear and to consider it sacrilege to lie, let her be ignorant of the world and live like an angel, let her be in the flesh but not of the flesh,

and let her suppose that everybody is like her. In this way (not to mention other advantages) you will be released from the difficulties of looking after her and the risks involved in protecting her. It is better for you to long for her when she is far away than to worry about every little thing – whom she talks to, what she is saying, whom she nods to, whom she likes to see. Hand over to Eustochium the little girl whose cries are even now a prayer for you, hand her over so that she can become Eustochium's companion now and the heiress to her holiness in the future. Let Paula gaze upon and love her and admire her from her earliest childhood, for Eustochium's words and way of dressing and walking will teach Paula virtue. Let her sit on her grandmother's lap so that her grandmother can repeat to her what she used to tell her daughter. For the elder Paula has learned by long experience how to bring up and teach virgins and how to keep them safe. In her crown is woven each day the mystic number one hundred, signifying chastity. Happy the virgin, happy Paula, daughter of Toxotius – her grandmother's and her aunt's virtues make her more noble in holiness than in her family line. If only it were possible for you to see your mother-in-law and your sister-in-law and to observe the great souls inhabiting their spare frames, given your naturally chaste character I have no doubt that you would go to them even before your daughter and would exchange God's first decree, 'Go forth and multiply',[19] for his second law of the Gospel. You would be less concerned for what your other children want and you would rather offer yourself to God. But because there is a time to embrace and a time to refrain from embraces[20] and because a wife does not have power over her own body and each person should remain in the calling to which he was called in the Lord, and because someone who is beneath the yoke should run in such a way that he does not leave his companion stuck in the mud, pay back in full in your children what you meanwhile put off paying in yourself. Once Hannah had handed over to the tabernacle the son whom she had dedicated, she never took him back, thinking it wrong for a future prophet to grow up in the house of a person who still wanted to have more children.[21] So after she had conceived and given birth to him she did not dare to go to the temple or to appear before the Lord empty-handed until she had paid what she owed. When she had made this sacrifice she returned home and gave birth to five children for herself as a reward for giving her first-born to God. Are you amazed at this woman's happiness? Imitate her faith. If you send Paula here I promise that I will act as her teacher and guardian. Old as I am I will carry her on my shoulders and will teach her properly to form the words which she pronounces in her babyish way. I will be far prouder than that worldly philosopher Aristotle, for I will not be teaching the Macedonian king whose destiny it was to die from Babylonian poison but the handmaiden and bride of Christ who is destined to be offered to the kingdom of heaven.

ON VISITING JERUSALEM

by Paula the Elder and Eustochium to Marcella

(*Jerome*, Letter 46)

Marcella

This letter, which is preserved in the collection of Jerome's correspondence, purports to be written by Paula the elder and Eustochium in Bethlehem to Marcella in Rome. Its purpose is to persuade Marcella to travel to Jerusalem to visit the holy sites associated with events recorded in the Old and New Testaments. It is a learned letter, which in its biblical allusions and its survey of biblical places recalls Jerome's *Letter* 108 describing Paula's travels in the Holy Land (see *The Life of Paula the Elder*, 8–14), and it has traditionally been regarded as the work of Jerome himself, writing it on behalf of his women companions. But we know that Paula and Eustochium were themselves very learned, and as they had actually visited many of these places, it is not surprising that they could write about them in such an elegant manner. The letter is charged with an excitement which seems more likely to be characteristic of these two women, longing to see their dear friend again and to show her all these important places, than of Jerome. On Marcella, see headnote to *The Life of Marcella*.

Paula the elder, Eustochium and Jerome

See the headnotes to *The Life of Paula the Elder, On Choosing a Life of Virginity* and *The Life of Marcella*.

1 Love knows no measure, impatience knows no bounds and eagerness cannot endure a delay. That is why we, disregarding our weakness and thinking only of what we want rather than what we are able to do, want to teach our teacher, although we are only pupils, like the sow in the proverb that tries to teach the goddess Minerva.[1] You were the first to put a spark to our little piece of kindling, you were the first to encourage us, by your words and by your example, to adopt this way of life and like a mother hen you gathered your chicks under your wings. Will you now allow us to fly free without our mother? Will you abandon us to fear the terrifying hawk and tremble at every shadow cast by birds flying past? We must do the only thing people who are separated can do: we pour out our desperate entreaties, making you aware of our longing, not just with tears but with sobs, in the hope that you will give us back our dear Marcella and not allow that gentle lady, that kind lady sweeter than the sweetest honey, to be stern with us or frown at those who were inspired by her friendliness to try to live a life like hers.

2 If what we ask for is for the best, then we need not be ashamed of our eagerness to obtain it. If the whole of Scripture supports our desire, then we are not being too bold when we beg you to do what you have often urged us to do. God's first words to Abraham were: 'Go out from your country and your family to a land that I will show you.'[2] The patriarch, who was the first one given a promise of Christ, was told to leave the Chaldaeans, leave the city of confusion and Rehoboth (in other words the broad places) and the plains of Shinar, where the tower of

pride was erected to touch the heavens. After passing through the floods of this world, the rivers beside which the saints sat down and wept when they remembered Sion,[3] after passing the deep whirlpool of Chebar from which Ezekiel was lifted up by the hair on his head and carried over to Jerusalem,[4] Abraham was told he would live in the land of promise which is not irrigated from below, like Egypt, but from above and does not produce vegetables as the food of the weak but awaits the rain from the sky both early and late. This land is hilly and situated high above sea level. It is completely lacking in the pleasures of this world but contains all the more spiritual pleasures for that. Mary, the mother of our Lord, left the plains and went to the mountain regions when, after the angel had made a promise to her, she understood that her womb was the home of the Son of God.[5] When the enemy was overcome and the devil's arrogance given a thrashing and he fell on his face, it was from this city, Jerusalem, that once belonged to another race, that the crowd of exulting souls moved forward and a chorus of ten thousand singing in harmony predicted the victory of our David. In this city the angel took hold of the sword to destroy the whole wicked place, and he marked out the temple of God on the threshing floor of the king of the Jebusites. In this way he showed that the church of Christ would grow up among the Gentiles rather than in Israel. Go back to Genesis and you will find Melchizedek, the king of Jerusalem, the ruler of this city who as a type of Christ offered the bread and wine to Abraham, dedicating the Christian mystery in the body and blood of the Saviour.[6]

3 Perhaps you will tacitly rebuke us for not following the order of Scripture but letting our muddled account ramble this way and that, touching on whatever it happens to come across. At the beginning we asserted that love knows no order and impatience knows no measure: that is why also in the Song of Songs that difficult command is given: 'Order love in me.'[7] If we are doing wrong we do so not out of ignorance but from strong feeling. Indeed, we must go back even further into the past to mention something even more out of sequence. It was in this city, or rather on this spot, so it is said, that Adam lived and

died. That is why the place where our Lord was crucified is
called Calvary, undoubtedly because the skull of the first man
was buried there, so that the blood of the second Adam, in
other words of Christ, dripping from the cross, might wash
away the sins of the first Adam, the originator of our race who
lay buried there. In this way those words of the Apostle would
be fulfilled: 'Awake, you who sleep, and rise up from the dead
and Christ will give you light.'[8] It would take too long to enumerate all the prophets and all the saintly men this city has
produced. The whole mystery of our faith is everyday reality in
this province and this city. By its three names it proves the doc-
trine of the Trinity, for it is called Jebus, Salem and Jerusalem.
The first name means 'downtrodden', the second 'peace' and
the third 'vision of peace'. For it is only gradually that we reach
our goal and after being downtrodden we are raised up to the
vision of peace. Because of this peace Solomon (whose name
means 'the peaceful one') was born here and his place became
peaceful. His name 'Lord of Lords and King of Kings' and the
name of the city prove that he was a type of Christ. Need we
mention David and all his descendants, who reigned in this
city? This city is as far superior to Judea as Judea is superior to
other provinces. In short, the glory of the whole province
derives from its capital city and all that is praiseworthy in the
body is due to its head.

4 In this letter we are writing we realized some time ago that
you would wish to say something, and this piece of paper
knows the question you are going to put. You will reply by saying that this was all in the past, at a time when the Lord loved
the gates of Sion more than all the dwellings of Jacob and when
its foundations were on the holy mountains[9] (although even
these verses could be given a more profound interpretation),
but afterwards the voice of the risen Lord thundered out, 'Your
house is left desolate to you', and with tears he has prophesied
its destruction when he said, 'Jerusalem, Jerusalem, you who
kill prophets and stone those who are sent to you; how often
have I wanted to gather your sons like a hen gathering her
chickens under her wing, but you refused. Look, your house is
left desolate to you.'[10] You will point out that after the veil of

the temple had been torn and Jerusalem was surrounded by an army and stained by the Lord's blood, the angels ceased to protect it and it was abandoned by the grace of Christ; Josephus, who is one of the Jews' own writers, asserts that at the time when the Lord was crucified there burst forth from the temple the voices of the heavenly powers saying, 'Let us leave this place.'[11] This and other things show that where grace had existed in abundance, there sin existed even more plentifully;[12] and after the apostles were told, 'Go forth and teach all the peoples',[13] and they themselves said, 'It was necessary to announce the word first to you; but since you refused to accept it, we are going to the Gentiles',[14] then all the spiritual significance of Judea and its long-standing intimacy with God were transferred by the apostles to the Gentiles.

5 This is a strong argument which could shake even those who know something of the Scriptures, but it is very easy to deal with. For the Lord would not have wept for the fall of Jerusalem if he did not love it; he wept for Lazarus because he loved him. You have to realize that it was the people who sinned rather than the place. The killing of its inhabitants involves the capture of a city. If Jerusalem was destroyed it was in order that the people be punished, and the temple was demolished so that the sacrifices which were of typological significance might be abolished. However, as far as the site goes, the passing of time has made it even more venerable than it was before. The Jews used to venerate the Holy of Holies because it contained the cherubim and the mercy seat and the ark of the covenant and the manna and the rod of Aaron and the golden altar: do you not consider the Lord's tomb to be even more worthy of veneration? Whenever we enter it we see the Saviour in his shroud, and if we linger there we see once more the angel sitting at the Lord's feet and the cloth folded at his head. We know that long before his tomb was hewn out of the rock by Joseph of Arimathea, Isaiah prophesied that it would be venerated when he said, 'His rest will be glorious',[15] meaning that the place of the Lord's burial would be the object of universal veneration.

6 But you may say, 'How come we read in the Revelation of John: "The beast that ascends out of the abyss will kill them

(no doubt meaning the prophets) and their dead bodies will lie in the streets of the great city that spiritually is called Sodom and Egypt, where also their Lord was crucified"?[16] For if, you say, the great city in which the Lord was crucified is Jerusalem and if the place of his crucifixion is spiritually called Sodom and Egypt, then as the Lord was crucified at Jerusalem, Jerusalem must be Sodom and Egypt.' First of all, we want you to know that Holy Scripture as a whole cannot contradict itself, and particularly one book cannot be at variance with another and one verse cannot contradict the book it occurs in. About ten lines before the verse of Revelation you cited just now, it is written: 'Rise and measure the temple of God and the altar and the people who are worshipping there. But leave out of your reckoning the courtyard that is outside the temple, for it has been given to the Gentiles and they will tread the holy city under foot for forty-two months.'[17] If Revelation was written long after the Lord's passion and in it the holy city is called Jerusalem, how then can it be called spiritually Sodom and Egypt? For you cannot immediately say that the Jerusalem that is called holy is the heavenly one which is in the future, while the one that is called Sodom and Egypt is the one that has fallen down, for it is the Jerusalem to come that is referred to in the description of the beast that will ascend out of the abyss and will make war against two prophets and will kill them, and their bodies will lie in the streets of the great city. At the end of this book the city is described in the following way: 'The city is square and its length is the same as its height; and he measured the city with the reed, twelve thousand furlongs. Its length and the breadth and height are equal. He also measured its walls which were a hundred and forty-four cubits according to the measure of a man, which is that of an angel. And its wall was of jasper and the city was of pure gold',[18] and so on. Now where there is a square one cannot distinguish between length and breadth. And what kind of measurement is it to say that the length and breadth are equal to the height? How can there be walls of jasper or a whole city of pure gold and its foundations and streets made of precious stones, with twelve gates sparkling with pearls?

7 As these facts cannot be taken literally (for in fact it is absurd
to talk of a city having a height of twelve thousand furlongs as
well as being that long and wide), each fact must be given a
spiritual interpretation. The great city which Cain first built
and named after his son must be taken to represent this world
which the devil, that accuser of his own brothers, that fratricide
who is doomed to die, has constructed out of sin, founded on
crimes and filled with wickedness. This is why it is spiritually
called Sodom and Egypt. Of Sodom it is written, 'Sodom will
be restored as of old',[19] in other words the world has to be
restored to its former state. For we cannot believe that Sodom
and Gomorrah, Admah and Zeboim are to be rebuilt: they
must be left to lie among the ashes for ever. We never read that
Egypt represents Jerusalem – it always stands for this world.
And as it would take too long to collect all the innumerable
examples from the Scriptures, we will put forward just one
example where this world is very clearly called Egypt. In the
catholic epistle the Apostle Jude, the brother of James, writes:
'I want to remind you (though you once knew all this) that
Jesus, having saved the people out of the land of Egypt, afterwards destroyed those who did not believe.'[20] In case you think
he is talking of Joshua son of Nun, it immediately goes on:
'And the angels who did not keep their own kingdom but left
their home he has kept in everlasting chains, in darkness, until
the judgement of the great day.'[21] To convince you that whenever Egypt and Sodom and Gomorrah are mentioned together,
it is not the places but this world that is meant, he immediately
adds this example: 'Sodom and Gomorrah and the cities around
them have committed fornication in the same manner as they
and pursued unnatural lust, and so they have been made an
example, suffering the punishment of eternal fire.'[22] Is there any
need to collect more examples when after the Lord's passion
and resurrection Matthew the evangelist tells us: 'The rocks
split and the tombs opened and many bodies of the saints who
had fallen asleep were raised. After his resurrection they came
out of their tombs and entered the holy city and appeared to
many.'[23] We should not hasten to interpret this as the heavenly
Jerusalem, as many people absurdly do. If the bodies of the

saints were seen in the heavenly Jerusalem, this could in no way
be a sign to men of the Lord's resurrection. Since then the evan-
gelists and the whole of Scripture call Jerusalem the holy city and
the psalmist tells us to worship the Lord at his footstool,[24] do not
allow it to be called Sodom and Egypt, for the Lord forbids anyone to swear by it because it is the city of the great King.[25]

8 They call the land accursed because it has drunk in the blood
of the Lord, but then how can they think that the city, where
Peter and Paul, the leaders of the Christian army, shed their
blood for Christ, is blessed? If the confession of men and servants is glorious, why is the confession of the Lord and God not
glorious? Everywhere we venerate the tombs of the martyrs
and apply their holy ashes to our eyes and if possible to our
lips; do some people think we should neglect the tomb in which
the Lord was buried? If we do not believe ourselves, then let us
at least believe the devil and his angels who, when in front of
his tomb they are driven out from the bodies they have possessed, tremble and moan as if they were standing before
Christ's judgement seat, and they lament – too late – that they
crucified the one they now fear. If after the Lord's passion this
place is an abomination, as some wicked people maintain, why
did Paul want to hurry to Jerusalem to celebrate Pentecost
there? When people tried to hold him back, he said, 'What are
you doing, crying and breaking my heart? For I am ready not
only to be bound but also to die in Jerusalem in the name of our
Lord Jesus.'[26] What of the other holy and illustrious men who
after the preaching of Christ brought their vows and offerings
to the brothers who were in Jerusalem?

9 It would take too long to run through every period from the
Lord's ascension down to the present day, to give an account of
the bishops, martyrs and those men eloquent in church doc-
trine who have come to Jerusalem in the belief that their devotion and knowledge would be incomplete and that their virtues
would not have received the finishing touch, so to speak, unless
they had worshipped Christ in those places where the Gospel
first flashed from the cross. If a famous orator thinks that anyone who has studied Greek in Lilybaeum instead of in Athens,
or Latin in Sicily instead of in Rome deserves criticism on the

grounds that each province has its own unique strength, why should we think that a Christian's education is complete without coming to the Christian Athens?

10 When we say this we do not mean to deny that the kingdom of God is within us and that there are holy men elsewhere too, but we are keen to emphasize that those who are the leading lights throughout the world are gathered together here. We ourselves are among the last, not the first, but we came here to see those who were outstanding from every nation. All the monks and virgins here are like beautiful flowers or most precious jewels. All the most distinguished people of Gaul come here. The Briton, separated from our world,[27] no sooner makes progress in religion than he leaves the setting sun and seeks the place known to him only from hearsay and from the account in the Scriptures. Need I mention the Armenians, the Persians, the peoples of India and Ethiopia, and our neighbour Egypt which is teeming with monks? And Pontus and Cappadocia, southern Syria and Mesopotamia, and all the peoples of the east? In accordance with our Saviour's words: 'Wherever the corpse is, there the vultures will gather',[28] they all come there, providing us with examples of many different virtues. They speak in various languages but they share the same religion. There are almost as many choirs of people singing hymns as there are different nationalities. But among them all there is no arrogance, no contempt for self-restraint – in fact they compete with each other in humility, this being the outstanding Christian virtue.[29] Whoever is last is here regarded as the first. There is no distinction in dress, no admiration for what anyone is wearing. No one is either admired or criticized for his appearance. Fasting or refusing to eat does not win particular respect; neither is one condemned for eating in moderation. Each person stands or falls before his own master.[30] No one judges anyone else, for fear that he will be judged by the Lord,[31] and backbiting which is common in most places is unheard of here. We are free from any self-indulgence and excess.

11 There are so many places of prayer in this city that it would be impossible to visit them all in a day. But as each person praises what he has, let us pass on to Christ's little house, the

place where Mary found shelter. What words can we use to describe to you the Saviour's cave? The manger in which he cried as a tiny baby ought to be honoured in silence rather than with feeble words. Where are the broad porticoes? Where are the gilded ceilings? Where are the houses adorned by the efforts of poor creatures condemned to hard labour? Where are the halls constructed like palaces and funded by private individuals, so that men's wretched bodies can walk in them surrounded by great wealth and so that they can choose to gaze at their roofs rather than the sky, as if anything could be more beautiful than the world around us? It was in this little crevice in the earth that the creator of the heavens was born. Here he was wrapped in swaddling clothes, here he was visited by the shepherds, here he was pointed out by the star, here he was worshipped by the Magi. I believe that this place is more holy than the Tarpeian rock[32] which has shown itself displeasing to the Lord by the number of times it has been struck by lightning.

12 Read the Revelation of John and consider what is said there about the woman in purple and the blasphemy written on her forehead, about the seven mountains, the many waters and the destruction of Babylon. 'Come out from her, my people,' says the Lord, 'so that you do not share her sins or receive the same punishment.'[33] Turning back to Jeremiah, notice how it is written: 'Flee from the centre of Babylon and save your soul, each one of you.'[34] For 'Babylon has fallen, that great city has fallen and has become a habitation for demons and a haunt of every foul spirit.'[35] Certainly Rome has a holy church and monuments to the apostles and martyrs, the true confession of Christ exists there as does the faith preached by the apostles, and now that paganism has been crushed under foot, the word Christian becomes more exalted every day. On the other hand, ambition, power, the size of the city, the seeing and being seen, the visiting and being visited, the admiration and criticism, the listening and talking and having to put up with crowds of people – none of these is conducive to the monastic vision or the quiet that is necessary for it. Either we see those who come to visit us and have to relinquish our peace and quiet, or we refuse to see them and then we are accused of arrogance. Sometimes, too, when

we return those visits, we arrive at lofty gates and entering between gilded gateposts, we are greeted by rude servants. But in the place where Christ was born, as I said before, all is simplicity and silence apart from the singing of the psalms. Wherever you turn there is a farmer guiding his plough while singing the Alleluia, or a man harvesting the crops, sweating from his labours but keeping himself cheerful with the psalms, or a vineyard owner pruning his vines while singing one of David's compositions. It is these that are the folk songs of this region, these are its love songs, these its shepherds' lays, and it is these that assist the farmer in his work.

13 But what are we doing? Forgetting what is required of us, we see only what we want. Oh, when will that time come when a messenger, out of breath, will bring us news that our friend Marcella has reached the shores of Palestine and all the monks and virgins will clap with joy. In our excitement we are already rushing to meet you and without waiting for transport we hasten on foot. We will take hold of your hands, we will look eagerly at your face and find it difficult to tear ourselves from your longed-for embrace. When will the day come when we will be allowed to enter the cave of the Saviour, to weep with our sister in the Lord's tomb, to weep with our mother? When will the day come when we can kiss the wood of the cross and be exalted in prayer and spirit on the Mount of Olives with the Lord as he ascends to heaven? When will we be able to see Lazarus emerging, wrapped in grave cloths, and see the waters of the Jordan purified for the baptism of the Lord?[36] Then we will go to the shepherds' sheepfolds,[37] we will pray in David's mausoleum[38] and look upon the prophet Amos still playing his shepherd's horn on his rock.[39] We will hurry to the tents, or at least to the monuments of Abraham, Isaac and Jacob and of their three famous wives.[40] We will see the spring in which the eunuch was baptized by Philip,[41] and go to Samaria and venerate there the ashes of John the Baptist, of Elisha and of Obadiah. We will enter the caves in which the prophets were fed in the time of hunger and persecution,[42] and we will go to see Nazareth, the 'flower' (for this is what the name means) of Galilee. Nearby Cana can be seen, where water was turned into

wine.[43] We will go to Tabor and the tabernacles of the Saviour which he shares not with Moses and Elijah, as Peter once hoped, but with the Father and the Holy Ghost. Then we will come to the sea of Gennesareth and see where five loaves were enough to feed five thousand people and where seven loaves fed four thousand people.[44] The town of Nain will appear, at the gate of which the widow's son was raised to life.[45] Hermon, too, will be visible and the torrent of Endor where Sisera was beaten.[46] We will visit Capernaum, well known for the miracles that the Lord performed there – in fact, we will see the whole of Galilee. Then accompanied by Christ, we will return to our cave by way of Shiloh and Bethel and the other places where churches have been set up like standards to commemorate the Lord's victories, so to speak. Then we will sing without ceasing, weep often and pray all the time; wounded by Christ's spear we will say together, 'I have found him whom my soul was seeking; I will hold on to him and not let him go.'[47]

THE LIFE OF MELANIA THE YOUNGER

by Gerontius

Melania the younger

Melania the younger was born in about 383, the daughter of Albina and Publicola, and granddaughter of Melania the elder. At the age of about fourteen she was married to Pinianus and bore him a son and a daughter both of whom died in infancy. (Palladius (see p. 50) states that she had two sons.) She persuaded Pinianus to give up his hope of heirs and to live with her as her spiritual brother rather than as a husband, and gradually to dispose of their vast family wealth. In 408 they left Rome and spent two years in Sicily and seven in Africa before settling in Jerusalem, as Melania's grandmother had done before her. Melania visited the desert fathers in Egypt, and spent twelve years living on the Mount of Olives with Pinianus and her mother, both of whom died around 431. She then visited Constantinople to see her uncle, whom she persuaded to convert to Christianity. On her return to Jerusalem she was visited by the Empress Eudocia who was much influenced by her. Melania died on 31 December 439. The monasteries on the Mount of Olives that she founded survived until the Persian invasions in the sixth century. She was also an important collector of Greek and Roman Christian texts. Jerome mentions her in *Letter* 143 to Alypius and Augustine. Augustine, whom she met in Africa, dedicated *On Grace and Original Sin* to her, Pinianus and Albina.

Gerontius

Little is known about Gerontius apart from what we learn incidentally in the course of this account. It would seem that he composed it in Greek (still extant) and from this a Latin version, differing in various details, was made, though there is still controversy over which version came first. Gerontius came from Jerusalem and it has been suggested that he went to Rome as a boy and lived in the household of Melania and Pinianus, but he is also supposed to have been in charge of the monastery she founded in Jerusalem for forty-five years after her death. Certainly he was her constant companion for the long period of her life when she lived in Jerusalem. The Latin version of her life was written in about 452, and this is the first translation of it into English. Several suggestions have been made as to the identity of the addressee: it is likely to have been a bishop, possibly Theodosius of Jerusalem.

Prologue

Blessed be God who has inspired you, most holy priest of God, to write to my humble self, asking me to give an account of the life of our most holy mother Melania who lives with the angels. Earlier I refused you on the grounds that I was not capable of carrying out this task, but just as God did not give in to Moses when he refused to rule God's people but gave him Moses' brother to help him, so you, priest of Christ, granted us your prayers to help us to say something, although I was not up to it. I do not think that anyone could give an account of her virtues or her passionate commitment to the ascetic life or her faith, her great acts of generosity, her nights spent in prayer or lying on the bare earth, her patience in hardship, the degree of abstinence she practised, her gentleness, sobriety, humility and the poverty of her clothes. But if you grant an opportunity to one who is wise he will become wiser, as it says in Scripture.[1] However, I do fear that when I speak in praise of Melania, I might do more harm than good because my account is defective. But I compare myself to the young fishermen who cast their nets into the sea: they know that they cannot catch all the fish, and even if they all got together they would not be able to do so: each of them just brings in as much as he can according to his own means. Or again, those who go into a garden where there are all kinds of lovely different trees and the flowers smell sweet – can they gather the contents of the whole garden? I will follow these examples, supported by your prayers, and cast my net to make a spiritual catch of the good works of our most holy mother. In case anyone should think to criticize me for praising a woman, I would say that one should not refer to her as a woman but as a man because she behaved like a man. It was she whom the wise Solomon speaks of when he talks of precious jewels.[2] For it is inevitable that precious jewels pass away, but she who believed in the unity of the Trinity and by means of her faith adorned herself with the spiritual decoration of all the virtues, she who stood firm in God, living together with the choirs of angels and reigning with Christ in company with the martyrs, now rejoices to be crowned with the apostles. She reached the end of her course without stumbling, she received what the eye has not seen and the ear has not heard and has not ascended to the heart of man.[3] By God's grace many people have left to the world different accounts written at different periods for the edification of believers, to strengthen the faith and purpose of those who were interested. I thought it necessary to carry out my own purpose and provide this account for my own benefit and that of my contemporaries who would be fortified by the life of our holy mother: I am able to do this because I know certain facts that I witnessed myself while other things I learned from reliable souls.

And so, of her many achievements I will relate a few that I remember. The first one I will mention is my own salvation. For since I owe ten thousand talents,[4] I hasten to pay the debt for my lack of literary polish, even though it is only a small debt. How shall I begin, what phrases shall I use to praise this wonderful mother of mine, for my speech is hardly elegant and I feel tongue-tied? What can I offer her, uneducated as I am, apart from the tears that caused her to give me hope of salvation? I hope that she will accept thanks from her servant in the form of a gift of words. For how could I repay her love? I ask God's help, that he will be kind enough to use his powers to assist me for I wish to be able, through God's grace, to give at least a partial account of Melania, in all moderation and honesty, while remembering her without ceasing: to do so I will need the medication of truth to drive out all forgetfulness that comes from foolish ignorance in the soul, and faith to drive out all perverse doubt. For if I wanted to relate her whole life I would run out of time before I had finished. Besides, how can her virtues be known to us when she used to conceal them, mindful of the saying: 'Let not the left hand know what the right hand is doing'?[5] But since saints' virtues cannot always remain hidden, even if they wish to conceal them, God will reveal them for the sake of his servants' glory and for the edification of others. I am weaving this text out of those facts her followers were able to tell me, so that the wise people who get the opportunity may become wiser and we may weave a crown of virtues worthy of this blessed woman.

1 Melania, who was the heiress of a senatorial family in the city of Rome, was forced to marry at the age of about fourteen. Her husband was the most blessed Pinianus and he was seventeen at the time. When she had had experience of marriage and had come to hate the world utterly, she made a request of her husband: 'If you want to live with me according to the law of chastity and continence, I will acknowledge you as my master and will call you the guardian of my life; but if this seems difficult to you as a young man, take all my wealth and just give my body its freedom, so that I may do what I desire in accordance with God's will.' He replied to her, 'Allow us to have two children to be heirs to our wealth and then, with God's will, we will renounce this way of life.' And so a daughter was born to them and they immediately consecrated her to the life of a virgin.

2 When Melania was told to go to the baths by her parents, she was forced to go even against her will. Going into the hot room, she used to just wash her face and wipe it for the sake of appearances. She would call all her servants to her and give them money, begging them not to betray her or tell her parents that she had not bathed properly. Then she would return from the baths, pretending that she had bathed. This shows how deeply embedded in her was the desire for God.

3 After some time had elapsed Pinianus, who was still attached to this world, was again urged by the saintly Melania to give in to her desire for chastity. But he refused, on the grounds that he still wanted another child.

4 So Melania tried to please God by despising her wealth, by

secretly wearing coarse woollen underwear beneath her rich garments of linen and silk embroidered with gold. Later her aunt realized what she was doing, so she took Melania aside and began to reprimand her, telling her that she ought not to wear this kind of garment in any circumstances, in case her parents should find out and be cross with her and it put her at risk. Then Melania begged her aunt not to tell her parents what she had discovered.

5 Meanwhile, as the result of the saints' prayers and God's grace, it happened that a son was also born to them. This is how she came to give birth: it happened that the solemn feast day of the blessed martyr Laurence was being celebrated. Melania, in her spiritual enthusiasm, longed to go to the church of that holy martyr to hold a vigil there, but her parents would not allow her because she was too weak and delicate to be able to endure the strain it would put on her. So Melania, respecting her parents and wishing to please God, remained awake all night in the oratory in her house, on her knees, until morning, praying to God with many tears that he might fulfil her heart's desire. At dawn her father sent Melania's eunuch servants to check on his daughter, their mistress, asleep in her bedroom. When they got there they found her on her knees, engrossed in praying to the Lord. When she got up and looked round she saw them and got a terrible shock. She pleaded with them, promising them money not to tell her father what they had seen, but instead to tell him that they had found her asleep in her room. (Although she did this quite often, she still wanted to keep it secret.) Getting up early she went with her saintly mother to the church dedicated to the memory of the blessed Laurence, and there she prayed fervently with many tears to the Lord that she should be granted a desire for good in the service of God. On her way back from church she went into labour. In the grip of terrible pains she was in mortal danger. A baby boy was born prematurely and was baptized the same day, but the next day he migrated to the Lord.

6 When her husband Pinianus saw that she was in great pain and that her life was at risk, he suffered such anguish that he himself nearly died. He too hurried to the holy martyr, and

prostrating himself before the altar he prayed earnestly to the Lord, in floods of tears, for Melania's recovery, begging that he himself should die rather than see her die. Then Melania sent him a message saying, 'If you want me to live, promise the Lord that from now on you will remain in a state of chastity with me. Then the Lord will come to me straight away.' As soon as he heard these words, Pinianus made the promise as she had instructed. Immediately all pain ebbed away from her and Melania gave thanks to God, more for the self-control of her holy brother than for her own physical recovery. These things happened as the result of God's providence. Melania rejoiced greatly at the young man's promise and now that she was completely free she gave thanks to the Lord. Furthermore she took the opportunity offered by her baby's death to give up wearing silk clothes or any jewellery. But while her father was trying to put much pressure on her, their baby daughter passed away in the Lord. Melania was deeply upset by this, but when her parents tried to console her she said to them, 'I can only be consoled if you allow me to despise all worldly concerns.' They said to her, 'But how can we put up with criticism from unsympathetic people?' Melania and Pinianus were in a terrible quandary for they were not allowed to take up God's yoke openly. Every day Melania would discuss with her brother Pinianus the possibility of running away together and going into exile or at least leaving her parents' home. While they were still making plans, as she later related for our edification, it happened that one day, towards evening, she and Pinianus were sitting together in the same house, feeling depressed, when suddenly they noticed a fragrance of such loveliness that they marvelled at it. It caused them great joy for which they gave thanks. As a result their confidence started to grow.

7 Meanwhile Melania's father died. After his death they felt more secure and renounced their old way of life more openly. They began to welcome pilgrims to their home and to take care of the poor. Settled in their country house on the outskirts of Rome, they showed great generosity to bishops and priests and to all the pilgrims who arrived at their house. After they had given up their old way of life, they did not permit themselves to

go into Rome, thereby fulfilling what is written in the Bible: 'Listen, my daughter, look, and pay careful attention: forget your people and your father's house, for the king has desired your beauty', and also, 'It is good for a man to take the yoke in his youth; he will sit on his own.'[6] They stayed at their country house, living in accordance with these words: 'When Jesus wanted to pray he climbed up onto the Mount of Olives',[7] for they knew that it was impossible to offer a pure ministry unless they could trample on and reject everything that was tainted with worldly honours.

8 Although they were unable to practise extreme abstinence at the beginning, they did at least dress in shabby clothing. Melania was about twenty-one at the time, while Pinianus was about twenty-four. Melania dressed in an old tunic of very poor quality and little value, so as to deprive herself of her youthful beauty by means of the unflattering condition of her clothes. Her husband dressed in the same way for he was as virtuous as she and imitated her behaviour. Because he had led a life of great wealth and comfort, in the beginning he used to dress in clothes of the highest quality, in a beautiful garment from Cilicia, not out of self-indulgence, but to show people that God had noticed him. The saintly Melania was keen to fulfil what was written in the Bible, 'Love your neighbour as yourself',[8] so her husband's way of dressing saddened her but she did not dare rebuke the young man openly or question his behaviour for she understood that his youth, as well as the comforts and magnificent lifestyle he was used to, made him rather self-indulgent. One day she took him aside and asked him tactfully and with respect whether he did not have any feelings of lust or desire for her, seeing that she was his wife. He smiled, content as he was in the Lord, and readily replied, 'Blessed are you for loving your husband in this way. You can be confident of me in the Lord: since we gave our word to God I regard you just like your mother Albina.' When she heard this she kissed his chest and his hands and praised God for his firm resolution. A few days later, wanting him to make progress and achieve even greater things, she spoke to him again, 'My lord, listen to what I say as your spiritual mother and sister, so to speak. Please lay

aside that precious garment of Cilician fabric and put on one
that is a little less luxurious.' When he heard this he was upset,
young man as he was, but as he did not want to upset her and
he knew her advice was given in accordance with God's will
and that it would be beneficial for the eternal salvation of them
both, he willingly went along with her suggestion and began to
wear less expensive clothes from Antioch. Melania, like a busy
bee, brought him the nectar of the virtues every day, but she
still wanted him to wear even less expensive clothes. And he did
so, with the result that he was now wearing clothes worth only
a solidus or two-thirds of a solidus, while Melania herself made
him clothes of rough, undyed woollen cloth.

9 And so, when they had sorted out the clothing arrangements
in a manner acceptable to both of them, as they were living on
their own estates, they set about discussing what degree of
abstinence they should undertake. They said, 'We cannot go in
for excessive or severe abstinence in case we harm ourselves
physically at the outset and then have to go back to our more
luxurious ways. It is better to choose the following way of life:
to go round all the prisons, visit the weak, give money to the
poor, offer hospitality to pilgrims who come here, provide
money for their journey and be an open door, in the words of
Job, to all the sick and all the visitors who come to us.'⁹ So they
began to sell their possessions, knowing that the Lord had also
said, 'If you wish to be perfect, sell everything and give to the
poor and take up your cross and come and follow me.'¹⁰

10 But when they started to sell their possessions, the enemy,
who is always jealous of good people, immediately suggested to
Melania's servants who lived on her estates, or rather, he used
the brother of the saintly Pinianus to persuade the slaves to
refuse to be sold and sent away. If Melania and Pinianus wanted
to use their power to disperse their possessions, the slaves
insisted they should be sold to no one other than Pinianus'
brother, Severus. This put Melania and Pinianus in a difficult
position, which was inevitable, given the size of their wealth.
So while Honorius Augustus, a most pious and devoted man,
was emperor,¹¹ Melania made the following suggestion to her
brother Pinianus: 'If those who are settled as slaves on the

country estate here and who are dependent on us dare to oppose us, what is going to happen to those who live in different provinces – in Spain, Italy, Apulia, Campania, Sicily and Africa or Numidia or Britain, or further away in other countries? So I think we should perhaps go and see the most pious empress. I have faith in our Lord Jesus Christ, whom they also recognize as their king and lord, that they will allow us to carry out God's will and our wishes.' Her brother replied to her, 'That is a good idea, for the hand of God, which holds the heart of kings,[12] has the power to guide all our actions towards the good.'

11 The Empress Serena[13] had long been keen to see Melania, having heard about her extraordinary and sudden change of lifestyle, which allowed her to attain such a state of humility after a life of worldly distinction. The empress had often asked many holy bishops to invite Melania to visit so that she could meet her. She was pleased by Melania's commitment to a life of austerity for she realized that this change had been brought about by the hand of the Most High. The empress also frequently sent the wives of senators to visit Melania. But Melania, who wished to have nothing to do with the admiration of the world, insisted that she was too unimportant to appear before the empress, and so she just gave a gentle and polite reply, excusing herself from going to the empress to be congratulated. But now she and Pinianus were forced by necessity to go to the palace to see the empress, in the bishops' presence. Many people thought that she should appear before the empress with her veil drawn back from her head, according to the custom of secular women presented to the empress. But Melania's view was that even if she had to lose all her possessions, she would not uncover her head, which she had covered up in the name of Christ, nor would she change any other garment apart from the one which she had put on in his name. For she considered it right that she should fulfil what was written in the Bible: 'I have put on my clothes – why should I take them off?'[14] She was well aware that there was a commandment that women should not pray to God without covering their heads.[15] Indeed every action and her whole way of life was a prayer. As Melania told us afterwards, she and Pinianus took with them the

richest and most precious luxury objects to present to the
empress, as well as crystal vases and many other things suitable
as royal gifts, together with expensive silken garments to offer
to the servants, eunuchs and chamberlains.

12 When we[16] entered, the empress immediately came to meet
us at the entrance to the colonnade and embraced Melania. Taking her by the hand, the empress went up to her golden throne
and sitting down she invited Melania to sit, too, and then
embracing her again she held her tight and kissed her face and
her eyelids. Then the empress summoned her whole entourage
to the palace and said to them, 'Come and see the woman whom
you saw four months ago resplendent in the finery of this world.
Now she scorns all luxury and grows old in wisdom for the sake
of Christ.' When Melania, the servant of Christ, heard this, it
did not make her proud; instead she showed that she thought
herself of no importance, being well aware that the glory of this
world fades as quickly as grass. So as we sat there, she began to
tell the empress of the problems they had experienced when they
wished to renounce their former way of life, explaining that her
father would not allow it on account of his attachment to empty
worldly attractions. But when he was close to death he had said
to Melania, 'Please forgive me, my dear children, for any wrongs
I have done you. Now I am going to the Lord and you have
complete power: so do what you want. Do not allow unscrupu-
lous people to snatch from you what Christ commanded should
be distributed to his poor.' And Melania told the empress of
how her husband's brother Severus plotted to get hold of all
their property, of which there was a great deal, while each of
their relatives who belonged to the senatorial class had instigated a number of court cases, hoping to become rich from her
wealth and that of Pinianus. Hearing all this, the empress said
to them, 'If you wish, I will now have them condemned and
their property confiscated, so that they dare not oppose you.'
But instead Melania and Pinianus entreated the empress on their
relatives' behalf, saying, 'No, my lady, for we have been told to
accept injustice but not to commit it and not to repay evil for
evil. That is why we are confident that thanks to your patronage
and good government the Lord will allow our modest fortune to

be well spent. It is not necessary to repay our enemies with evil, especially since they are our close relatives.' So the empress entrusted all this to her husband[17] Honorius Augustus, so that he might give orders to the leaders and governors and magistrates in every province to arrange for the sale of all Melania's and Pinianus' properties at their own risk or that of those in charge, and to give them the money collected from the sale after any debts had been paid. While we were still sitting there, the orders were immediately written out, confirmed and handed to us, together with executors. We were stunned by the great kindness of the emperor and empress.

13 Then Melania, in exchange for all their kindness, humbly took out the gifts she had brought with her and presented them, saying, 'Here you are, my lady, we offer you these as if they were two copper coins.[18] We hope you will be kind enough to accept them.' The empress laughed and said politely, 'Please believe that this is how it is in my heart and before Christ: anyone who takes anything of your wealth, apart from the poor of the saints to whom you have promised it, is no better than someone who steals something from the altar. In addition, anyone who tries to take what belongs to God, whether he has a good excuse or not, is heaping up for himself everlasting fire.' Then the empress ordered the eunuchs who were in attendance to go out of the palace with them and to take them to the place where they were staying. And she made the eunuchs swear by the health of her brother the emperor that none of them or any other of the eunuchs in the palace would take anything from Melania and Pinianus even if he were invited to do so, whether it was gold or clothing or anything else of the slightest value. 'If I find out that any of you have done this,' she said, 'he will be in serious trouble.' They obeyed the empress's order for fear of God for they were keen to protect Melania and Pinianus for the sake of Christ, and so they showed them to their lodgings, accompanying them joyfully.

14 Melania and Pinianus were overjoyed by this. They made generous arrangements to distribute all their possessions and to heap up for themselves in heaven a treasure that no one can steal,[19] for they had as a powerful guarantee the words of the

Lord who said that he would repay hundredfold in this world
and grant eternal life as a future reward. When they returned to
their cramped lodgings, they gave thanks to the heavenly God
and to the empress who had put such confidence in them. First
of all, they wished to sell the house they had in the city of
Rome, but since no purchaser dared to come forward to buy
such a large and magnificent building, it was abandoned. Later
it was partly destroyed by the enemy and then sold for nothing
after it had burnt down.[20]

15 I will now give an account of the income they derived from
their possessions, as I myself heard it partly from Melania's own
words. For she said that, apart from her movable possessions
(the value of which it was impossible to estimate), she had an
annual income of one hundred and twenty thousand gold pieces,
not counting what she held jointly with her husband. (Please do
not be irritated or blame me if I get these things in the wrong
order.) Melania believed in the one who said to Abraham, 'Listen to everything Sarah has to tell you',[21] and she trusted that he
would help her too in a similar situation. So she went to her
brother and said, 'Our burden in this world is very heavy:
weighed down by these possessions we cannot put on the yoke
of Christ. So let us get rid of our perishable possessions, so that
we may gain Christ who is everlasting.' Her husband, who was
always happy to go along with her advice, did what his spiritual
sister told him, for he was already prepared to agree with her so
as not to upset her in the slightest. So he began to sell his possessions and to receive gold for some of them, for others silver,
while for other things he accepted promissory notes, since his
possessions were many and the buyers were not able to pay for
them all at once, even though those who were buying them were
great and noble men. When they had collected a large sum of
money, they began to distribute it to the poor, using holy and
trustworthy men as intermediaries: by means of one group they
handed out forty-five thousand gold coins, by means of another
thirty thousand, and by means of yet another twenty thousand,
while they used one person to hand out ten thousand gold coins,
and so on, with God's assistance.

16 On one occasion when we were all begging Melania to tell us how she was able to go from the heights of worldly pride to the depths of humility, she replied in her usual manner, saying, 'When we started on the way of renunciation we were worried because everybody kept criticizing us – it was not so much a struggle against flesh and blood to lay aside such a large amount of worldly wealth, as against the rulers and powers of this world:[22] that is why we went to bed feeling depressed. It was as if we both saw ourselves anxiously trying to get through a breach in a wall; and when we had passed through that wall with difficulty, and our souls were weak with the effort, we were just about able to escape from that narrow space and so found a place of rest.' This was the outcome of those events after God revealed to them that they should work for him for the development of the faith.

17 One day Melania spoke to us for our edification so that we should learn not to pride ourselves on our achievements. She said that after they had sent a large amount of money (in fact, forty-five thousand gold pieces) through an intermediary to bring relief to saintly people and to the poor, they went into their bedroom, and there they saw something like a fire shining, either coming from a heap of gold or due to an illusion created by the devil. Melania said, 'The devil immediately caused this thought to occur to me: "What is this kingdom of heaven that is bought for such a high price?" But I confronted the adversary though I was inwardly terrified. I threw myself on the ground and prayed, "O devil, with these corruptible things you can buy what the eye does not see nor the ear hear and what does not ascend to the heart of man which God has prepared for all those who love him."'[23]

18 On another occasion Melania experienced the devil's attacks when he tried to instil doubt in her. She possessed an outstanding property, with baths and a swimming pool within it. On one side lay the sea and on the other some woodland containing a variety of animals and game, so that when she was bathing in the pool she could see ships passing by and game animals in the woods. The devil caused many different thoughts to spring to mind, reminding her of the precious marble, the various ornaments, large revenues and huge income (for in fact the

property included sixty large houses, each of them with four hundred agricultural slaves). But Melania pushed such thoughts away, saying that all this was nothing compared with what was promised to the servants of God. Her property could be destroyed by the barbarians and consumed by fire or broken up by the passage of time, but the things which were bought with them provided an everlasting banquet. By this means she threw the devil into confusion and from then on he did not trouble them any further.

19 So this was what happened when Melania and Pinianus began to sell their possessions and to distribute the proceeds to the saintly and poor, as I mentioned. Was there any country that was not given a share of their gifts? If you mention Mesopotamia or other parts of the east or west or north or south, I do not think there was a single island or town that did not receive a share of their gifts, as I myself learnt from many older people and from Tigridius, a priest from Constantinople, while I was on my way to that city. How many islands did they buy so as to provide settlements and land for monks! How many silken vestments did they donate for the altars and churches of God! They used their silver to make altars as well as lamps and other ornaments for churches, and they dedicated everything to God. They also began to make offerings to monasteries and they even bought monasteries and gave them to monks and virgins, donating to some of them a certain amount of gold as well. And so they sold everything they possessed around Rome, Campania and Italy, and after distributing it all they went to Africa. All the senators criticized them and accused them of being foolish and behaving irresponsibly in giving everything away. When they had sailed from Rome to Africa, Alaric immediately arrived at the properties they had sold in Rome. Then all their critics began to bless them and glorify the Lord, saying, 'They were truly blessed seeing that God has saved their property from the hands of the enemy.'

20 On arrival in Africa they set about also selling the properties they had in Numidia and Mauretania and in Africa itself, sending some of the proceeds to the east to be distributed to the saintly and the poor, and some to be used for ransoming slaves.

They were very pleased to distribute their wealth, saying cheerfully, 'He distributed freely and gave to the poor; his goodness endures for ever.'[24] When they had distributed everything, they were advised by the holy bishops who were in charge there, namely St Augustine and his brother Alypius[25] and Aurelius, bishop of Carthage, that what they were now giving to the monasteries would be used up within a short space of time. 'Do you wish to be remembered for ever? If so, donate buildings and income to each monastery.' When they heard this useful advice, they put it into practice and confirmed it by giving each monastery buildings, income and land. And so Melania, together with her spiritual brother, managed to continue to behave with all humility and obedience.

21 There was a small town called Thagaste where the saintly Alypius was bishop. They chose this town to live in because it was small and unpretentious, and particularly because they could be close to Bishop Alypius, who was not only a man of great virtue and saintliness but also had an outstanding knowledge of Holy Scripture and theology. This fact appealed particularly to Melania who always had a copy of the Bible in her hands. She adorned and enriched with her various gifts – whether with money or other ornaments – Bishop Alypius' church, which was extremely poor, so that he came to be envied by other bishops living in the larger towns of that province. For Melania donated tapestries decorated with gold or pearls as well as gold or silver discs, and indeed all the other decorations she made she gave to this same church. She also donated a property that provided a large revenue. This property was larger than the town itself, and included baths, many craftsmen (who worked in gold, silver and bronze) and two bishops, one belonging to our faith and the other to that of the heretics.

22 Melania and Pinianus also constructed two monasteries of their own in Africa, one for up to one hundred and thirty virgins of God and the other for up to eighty men, consisting of their own slaves and servant girls, and they provided each monastery with sufficient funds. In carrying out all these necessary tasks, Melania was following the example of the blessed Mary [sister of Lazarus and Martha]. Having got rid of her wealth

which she experienced as a burden, she began to practise abstinence. At first she used to eat in the evenings, using just a little
oil and drinking a lightly spiced drink: she said she could not
use wine seeing that even while living in the world she had
never been accustomed to drink it, for that was how the daughters of senators were brought up. A little while later she began
to eat every two days, without any oil, and then every five days,
and then only at weekends, once on Saturdays and once on
Sundays. In this way she surpassed everyone in her way of life.
She would talk to us about it for she trusted us particularly. She
was not interested in winning the admiration of others or in
being world-famous for her virtues – in fact, when she talked to
us she would use the Apostle's words, 'I know someone',[26] and
in this way she would talk of her own behaviour as if it were
that of someone else, saying for example, 'She began to fast for
a week at a time.'

23 She also used to write on parchment every day. While she
was writing, one of the sisters would read to her and so acutely
did she listen that she was able to correct the girl who was reading even if she only made a mistake of a single letter, while
Melania still managed to concentrate on writing. She had
decided how much she would write and how much she would
read from the canonical Scriptures and also from scriptural
commentaries. After this she would move on to read of the lives
of the monks as if she were eating honeycakes. It was at this
period that she slept a small amount during the first hours of
sleep. When she came to reading the lives of the saints, she
immediately woke up and roused the other virgins to worship
God, saying, 'Just as Abel presented the first fruits, so we too
ought to offer praises to God; we ought to stay awake the whole
time because we do not know when the Bridegroom will come,
whether late or early or in the middle of the night or at cock-
crow. We do not want him to come and find us asleep, not only
physically but also mentally.' When she had finished the divine
office as usual with her sisters, she would say part of the mass
to herself. With great care she instructed her sisters in the spiritual life, so that they should not utter a single useless word.
For the other sisters reported that she even checked on their

thoughts and did not allow the slightest wicked thought to reside in their hearts.

24 During Lent right up until holy Easter she fasted during the week, not eating until Saturday but without any oil. And those who knew her, witness to the fact that she always slept with a hairshirt and never ate before she had performed the set office on Saturdays and done her writing and reading tasks. In the evenings she would eat coarse bread with raw leek dipped in warm water. I trust no one will think I am telling a lie; God will destroy all who tell lies for it is written: 'The mouth that lies kills the soul.'[27] What good is it to me to die from something that will save others, if I tell things that are not true?

25 And so for many years she kept to the same degree of abstinence, persisting with the same way of life and the same fasting. At Easter she would eat every day because of the special nature of that period, but she was still content with her usual food. Her saintly mother was, however, upset by the fact that she refused to eat oil even at Easter. For her mother had adopted the way of life of certain women which I have not got time to describe at this point as I know nothing about it. Suffice it to say that a tree is known by its fruits and a good fruit is produced from a good root.[28] Then her mother together with Melania's brother and all the saintly men thought it a good opportunity to say that it was not right for a Christian not to rejoice or enjoy feasts for their body as well as for their soul at Easter. Then they persuaded her for three days to eat oil with her meals, though only as much as her stomach could take. Those who do practise extreme abstinence say that if they have not eaten oil for a long time, they can only manage a little. And so Melania obeyed these saintly people when they ordered her to eat, as if it were God ordering her, and for the three days of Easter she accepted it but then went back to her abstinence, like a good farmer returning to the cultivation of his fertile land.

26 She would read the Old and New Testaments four times a year and wrote out enough copies to distribute to saintly people, giving each of them a copy of the Psalms she had made herself. At the same time she lived according to a monastic rule with her sisters. With regard to works of exegesis there was no

book to be found that she did not know about and she would study each one carefully, whether it was her own or whether she was borrowing it from another source. She had such an expert knowledge of Latin and Greek that when she was reading in one of those languages, you would never think she knew the other one as well. She progressed as swiftly as a good runner: forgetting the things behind, she strained towards what lay before her, increasing in strength for the future. But the fact that she was so perfectly virtuous never made her arrogant. In fact, she always said in tears that 'We are useless servants for we have not done what we ought to have done.'[29] I also know that this blessed woman never ate enough bread to make her full and you would never see her eating anything except vegetables and pulses. In the heat of summer she would only eat ten figs every evening, not requiring any other food; and when she had perfected this degree of abstinence, she would move on to the next stage.

27 Words would not suffice to tell of the kindness she showed to those who lived an ascetic life. Was there anybody who possessed as much enthusiasm for the name of Christ, as much hatred of evil or such immutable faith? If she heard of any heretic, even if only by name, she refused to accept anything from him even to give to the poor.

28 I am now going to tell you something that you may find incredible. There was a married woman of noble family who was staying among the holy sites of Christ, although she was said to be a heretic. She used to take holy communion with us, pretending to share our faith. It happened that she died while holding these heretical beliefs, and when I was celebrating mass, I mentioned her name among the departed as I consecrated the host, for I was in the habit of reciting the names of the holy martyrs at that terrible hour, so that they might pray to the Lord on my behalf, as well as the names of sinners who had obtained mercy so that they could intercede for me. It happened that I named the woman I mentioned. Then Melania said to me angrily, 'Father, if you mention her name, as the Lord lives I will not receive communion from you.' Although I promised not to mention this woman again, she replied, 'Since

you have mentioned her even just the once, I will not receive communion.'

29 Melania loved chastity so much that she even managed to convert young men and women from their worldly way of life which was serving no useful purpose. She would entice some by means of encouraging words, others by means of money. To many worldly men and women she would say encouragingly, 'Our time is short.[30] Why should we corrupt our bodies when they are the temple of God?[31] Why should we allow filthy acts to contaminate the chastity in which Christ chose to live?' She told them that virginity is a very valuable thing, so much so that Christ chose to be born from a virgin. There were many who emulated her admirable way of life and adopted a similar degree of chastity. Who could say how many holy people's feet she washed? For he alone knows in whose name she used to do this. How many Samaritans, Gentiles and heretics did she offer to God, persuading them by means of her gifts and teaching? What monk or any other person known to her stumbled into sin without causing her suffering?

30 She loved alms-giving as much as the Lord himself, he who said, 'Sell all you have and give to the poor and you will have treasure in heaven',[32] and she hoped for mercy from him. So complete was her renunciation of money that before her death she claimed to possess nothing. She said that the small amount she kept to give away (about fifty solidi) was all she had left of her wealth, and in fact she sent this, too, to a bishop, saying, 'I do not want to possess even this when I die.' She not only gave her own things to God but she also encouraged other servants of God and secular people to give away their belongings. And in fact they did so, believing they could trust her to distribute wisely what they gave her. She accepted these things faithfully and handed them out with as much devotion as the person had donated them.

31 The hairshirt she wore during Lent she did not remove night or day until Easter. And because of her extreme abstinence and her love for God, all the clothes she wore which were specially for female use, whether outer or inner garments, were made of hairshirt material, not wool. In case anyone should think that

Melania could endure all this for God because she had become used to a harsher lifestyle and her body was strong, I will tell you what I heard from those who were close to her. As a result of her upbringing in a senatorial family, there was a time when she was not very robust – in fact, she was so physically delicate that when she wore a very expensive linen garment with embroidered motifs of purple and gold on top of another linen garment, it happened that one of the motifs touched her body and immediately brought out a bruise which did not disappear for many days. After this the amazing Melania was actually happier wearing a hairshirt than linen garments. But she received strength from him who said, 'Ask and it will be given to you',[33] for strength from above was also granted to her who made her requests out of faith.

32 And since all grace comes from above, from the father of light, even after such virtuous endurance, she was so overcome by love of God that she longed to demonstrate that she was prepared for even greater struggles. She wanted to live all the time enclosed within the confines of her cell without ever receiving any visitors, but her holy friends would not allow it for they considered it impossible due to the large number of people who came to her, seeking her helpful advice and the consolation she offered. As she was not allowed to do as she wished, she arranged that she would be available to see visitors at certain times, while at other times she would speak with God in holy meditation and do manual work. One day she had the idea of making a small wooden box for herself, so small that she could turn neither to right nor left and would not even have room to stretch out full length. But when she asked for permission she was not allowed to do it, and so she was content to obey the advice of those saintly people who wanted to prevent her from falling victim to pride.

33 It often happened that when she was sitting in silence or writing, her holy mother would come in, wishing to bring her comfort. But if Melania had not finished her work or her reading she would remain silent, neither answering nor asking any questions. When her mother realized this she was filled with admiration and deep respect and would go out, leaving her

daughter in silence; but when she thought that enough time had passed for Melania to have finished her task, she would humbly go back in, give her a hug and say, 'I consider myself lucky to have something in common with the mother of the children of the Maccabees. That fortunate woman witnessed the sufferings of her sons in the space of a single day and has everlasting joy. But I suffer more pain when, knowing how I brought you up, my daughter, I see you being tormented in this way, allowing your body no rest and enduring great martyrdom.' Then she added, 'I am very grateful to my Lord who arranged for me, unworthy though I am, to have such a daughter.'

34 When Melania and Pinianus had laid aside all the worldly possessions that weighed them down, they were seized by a desire to see the sites of the Holy Land where our Lord revealed the glory of his power. As I mentioned earlier I beg for indulgence not only from your holiness but also from future readers in the hope that they will be kind enough to forgive me and not be irritated if I get my facts in the wrong order. And so it happened that when they wanted to leave Rome, a prefect who was a pagan at the time, whose name I cannot remember, advised the senators of Rome to claim Melania's and Pinianus' wealth for the senate, saying that it was absurd for them to offer it to the Lord as the money ought rather to be under the control of the state and Senate. The prefect discussed these matters with the whole Senate at a sitting which went on until dawn, and when he went forward to the tribunal in the morning, wishing to announce this decision publicly, God's providence was active, for suddenly the people started rioting due to a bread shortage. To cut a long story short, within minutes the prefect was dragged from the tribunal and stoned to death in the city centre, and the senators were forced to admit openly that he had secretly set a trap for Melania and Pinianus: the sole cause of his death had been his vengeful treatment of them. Melania and Pinianus knew nothing of all this until they heard of his horrible death. When these good people learned of it, they gave thanks, though they were tormented by the thought of his gruesome death. In addition, some of their slaves who were of the same mind died a terrible death through the action

of divine providence. I would like to say how many thousands of slaves they set free, but I do not know the exact number, so I shall pass on to other matters to prevent myself becoming guilty of pride by giving too high or too low a figure: God and they themselves know the real figure.

While they were sailing to Sicily where the holy bishop Paulinus was staying, a terrible storm arose which put their lives at risk, for they did not even have any water to drink. They were sailing against a strong wind which even the sailors said was caused by God's anger. When they had lost all hope, Melania said, 'Perhaps God does not really want us to go where we decided to go. Let us go where the wind takes us.' So they immediately changed the sails and then came to land on an island which had been taken over by hostile forces who had rounded up all the important men with their wives and children and carried them off. They divided them up and demanded ransom money, threatening to kill those they had taken captive and to destroy the island by fire if people refused to pay the ransom. When the ship with Melania and Pinianus landed on the seashore and the local bishop heard that Melania had landed there (for her fame had spread everywhere), he came with the leaders of the town to beg them to help the poor creatures, if they could: about two thousand five hundred gold pieces were required as ransom for the hostages and there was no one to take pity on them. As soon as Melania heard this, she was as distraught as if she herself was being held, and she immediately offered the gold needed to pay the ransom for them all, from the oldest to the youngest. In addition she and Pinianus generously gave another five hundred gold pieces to be used for whatever the captives needed. She also gave them all the best she could from her food supplies, providing them with relief from their extreme need and hunger. There was a woman of a very noble family who was held captive by the barbarians: Melania and Pinianus sent five hundred gold pieces to her family to be paid as a ransom. When this was done they set off: setting sail they returned to Africa and stayed there for seven years, giving a lot of help to the captives there, too.

Then Melania sailed from Africa to the east with her mother

and spiritual brother. They reached Alexandria where they stayed with the holy bishop Cyril who offered them hospitality as befitted his saintly character. It happened that Nestor, a man of great prophetic grace, was also staying in the city at that time. He used to come in to the city occasionally to heal the sick – he possessed that ability, too. God's holy one went with her mother and brother to visit this man of God, who had a crowd of other visitors. When they tried to enter, the three of them got separated in the crowd, and it happened that Pinianus was the first to get in. Those who got in received some oil from the holy man. When Nestor looked round and saw Pinianus he realized who it was and summoning him out of the crowd he kept him by his side. Later Melania managed to get in along with the huge crowd, and noticing her in the same way, Nestor picked her out and placed her next to her spiritual brother. Thirdly, Melania's mother entered and when he noticed her he placed her with the other two. When the crowd had gone out, the holy man began to tell them what troubles they had endured, and he advised them as if they were his own children, saying, 'Do not be despondent for the end of suffering brings with it joy. "The sufferings of this present time are as nothing compared with the glory, as yet unrevealed, which awaits us."'[34]

35 They felt that they had received a great gift of blessing from him and were restored by his many encouraging words. Telling people of his virtues they then set sail for Jerusalem. Once they arrived they worshipped the Lord at the holy sites. They stayed in the church of the Holy Resurrection for they still had a bit of money to spend, which they gave to those intermediaries who were responsible for caring for the poor. They did not want to distribute the money themselves in case they should be seen to be doing something good: in this way they always maintained an attitude of humility. Melania said that they had come there as the result of a vow and a desire for humility, so that once they had distributed everything in Christ, they could be put on the church register and receive handouts with the other poor people. But it happened that while the excessive ardour of her faith and her desire for renunciation remained as strong as ever, she fell ill. As Melania never used anything but a hairshirt

because of her voluntary commitment to poverty and her ability to endure much, when many servants of God and young women came desiring to see her, one of the young women who was well known for her holiness, her way of life and her behaviour, with great reverence offered Melania a pillow for her head, but she had great difficulty in getting Melania to agree to accept it and place it under her head. Finally Melania accepted it and agreed to use it because of the great kindness involved and not because of the comfort it offered her.

36 And so Melania remained with her mother in the church of the Holy Resurrection. She stayed there secretly, performing the divine service every day and finding time for reading and learning the Holy Scriptures by heart. She did not show herself except when necessary nor did she go outside without a particular purpose, such as when important bishops or holy fathers who were well known for their saintly way of life came to visit: these she welcomed only for the sake of her salvation because she needed to question them about the secret mysteries of the Holy Scriptures and about theological matters. What is more, she would meet them, as always, with great reverence, kneeling before them and asking for a blessing. When they left, she would go back to her study of Scripture and her fasting. In the evenings when the caretakers locked up the church of the Holy Resurrection and everyone had duly left, Melania would come out of her cell to the gates of the Holy Resurrection and spend the whole night in prayer until the time when others gathered to sing the psalms. When the crowd gathered, she would slip away and allow herself to sleep for the short while that nature demanded. Then, at daybreak, she would get up again and devote herself to her normal routine, so that at all times she was doing what was pleasing to God.

37 When the barbarians overran Spain, a few of Melania's and Pinianus' properties remained which they could not sell because of the enemy invasion. But when peace returned to these areas, they sent their most reliable slave who had now been freed. On arriving in this area, he hastened to sell a proportion of the properties and then went back to hand over the considerable amount of money he had received. When Melania saw this

money, snatched as it were from the lion's jaws,[35] she gave thanks to God and decided immediately to hand all of it over to be distributed for the work of God. So she said to Pinianus, 'My lord, I want us to go to Egypt to see our masters, the holy servants of God who live in the desert, so that we can obtain their mercy through their visions and prayers.' When Pinianus heard this he was not opposed to the idea but happily supported her suggestion and agreed to go there immediately. So they set off for Egypt and while visiting the monasteries of the holy monks and virgins, they distributed everything to each person according to their need.

38 Since Melania was always concerned to take care of others and to try to make their lives more comfortable, they went to visit a very holy man, as she related to us, whose name was Hephaestion. When they met him, they first said a prayer and then Melania asked him to agree to accept a few gold coins from them to use for his own needs. But he firmly rejected what they offered, saying that he did not need any gold to spend on himself. They were unable to persuade him by any means to accept it so they asked him to say a prayer for them on their departure, as was the custom. When he knelt down with his face to the ground and prayed to the Lord for them, Melania walked round his cell looking for a place where she could secretly leave the money he had refused when they offered it to him. But it was utterly impossible because the holy man possessed nothing in his cell except a mat to lie on and a little basket in the corner containing a few rusks and a container with a little salt. Melania had just managed to find this and hide a few gold coins in it when the man finished his prayer, and they had to leave hurriedly so that the servant of the Lord would not have time to find the money and try to give it back. So they hastened to depart as quickly as they could. But when the man of God thought about the way Melania had begged him to accept the money, he got suspicious. He immediately looked round his cell and found hidden what he had rejected. Then he grabbed it and rushed out after them. But they had already crossed the river so when he reached the riverbank and shouted to them, 'I ask you, why have you left me something

that I have no need of in the desert? If I keep it, I may fall victim
to robbers.' Melania replied, 'If you so wish, arrange for it to
be given to the poor. For the Lord has been kind enough to
carry out my wishes.' The man then said, 'And where should I
go to find poor people, when I never leave the desert? Take this
back and give it to someone else.' But since she absolutely
refused to take back what she had given and he could not cross
the river, he threw the money he was holding into the river and
it dropped to the bottom. As there were many monks and virgins who refused to accept what she offered, she had to give it
secretly. So ardently did she desire to give that all those she
visited received something from her. For she knew that she
would receive a good deal of spiritual profit from doing this.

39 In their tour of Egypt they arrived in Alexandria where they
visited many holy people, among whom were those admirable
men, the archimandrites of the people of Tabennisis as well as
Victor Zeugites and Helias, those priests worthy of God, and a
certain holy priest, a native of Alexandria. Melania hastened to
collect from each of these men the fruits of their blessing. She
and Pinianus also went to Nitria and to the place known as
Cellia,[36] where she was given an amazing welcome by the holy
fathers who lived there, for they could see that she had a man's
spirit in her. She stayed with them for several days and all the
holy fathers gathered together to give her their blessing, treating her respectfully as a very holy woman, indeed, as if she
were their own mother.

40 And so Melania and Pinianus returned to Jerusalem where
they suffered much from the extreme climate. When she arrived
Melania found that her mother had made for her a cell out of
stones, on the Mount of Olives, just as she had asked her to do,
so that she could live there in silence. So after Epiphany she
went up the mountain, entered the cell and shut herself up in it,
staying there until Easter in hairshirt and ashes, living a life of
extreme abstinence. She had with her just one girl to help her
and she would only eat on Saturdays and Sundays, seeing no
one, receiving no visitors except her mother and spiritual
brother – and even those only on certain days. This was also
when she received her niece, the young girl Paula,[37] who came

to visit her from time to time. For Melania was the one who showed Paula the way to God, instructing her in all of God's commands and leading her to a life of great abstinence and humility. The girl who helped Melania told us that very often when Melania got up in the morning, as Easter approached, she would find enormous worms on the hairshirt on which Melania lay in the dust.

41 Melania spent fourteen years in Jerusalem leading this harsh life and training herself in every kind of holy and heavenly behaviour. During that time it happened that her holy mother passed away to the Lord. Melania buried her body on the Mount of Olives and she herself remained there for she did not want to live in the city any more. When she had spent a year in that dark little cell, devoting all her time to the Lord, and leading a life full of tears and devoid of any comfort, she built for herself a monastery on the holy mountain and asked Pinianus to find a few virgins to live with her there. In fact about ninety women joined her there. She taught them by her example and admonished them kindly, telling them to allow themselves to be seen by men as little as possible. In order that they should have no opportunity to go out she told them to construct a well inside the monastery. She said that she would cater fully for all their physical needs as long as they kept away from the gaze of men. As to how she brought them back to the way of the Lord when they were troubled by thoughts from the devil, by instructing them in theology and in prayer, it is not for us to say but for those who are wiser than us and who can correct our errors. But I shall give some account a little later. Because of the enthusiasm for chastity she engendered she was able to rescue women from degrading situations and dedicate them to God, for she knew the saying that 'Anyone who takes what is precious and not what is foul will serve as my mouth.'[38] Although they all wanted to submit to her authority, she refused to be put in charge of the monastery because of her great humility, but appointed another woman to rule them while she devoted all her time to prayer and serving the holy ones. And on those occasions when the woman who had been put in charge of them as their mother was a bit too hard on them, Melania, who

loved her sisters, took what each of them needed and gave it to them in secret, so that when they came in they found it ready there, without their mother's knowledge. The girls, however, knew that it was Melania who had done this. She even wrote to a certain person called Lausus,[39] a religious man who was one of the emperor's chamberlains, to ask him to help her by having a bath built for them in the holy monastery on the Mount of Olives so that when they needed to take a bath they would not risk being harassed in the city (which was about a mile away) or get into the habit of speaking to men.

42 Melania was always teaching the women about virtues and obedience. As for all the other things, as I said before I will leave them to some other person who is wiser than I am. She taught them about modesty and wisdom and how to resist the thoughts of the devil which threatened their well-being. She also taught them about humility and the need for constant prayer and for staying awake at night. She would say to them, 'My dear girls, you must learn to stay spiritually awake in psalm singing and prayer. And you must learn how to ask for forgiveness of your sins from the Lord, from whom you hope to receive the kingdom of heaven. For if you find yourself in the presence of some very noble or important person, does not great fear grip your soul? Do you not blush with embarrassment? Consider, my little ones, how neither angels nor archangels could worthily glorify his awe-inspiring majesty. Is that not so much more true of us, poor pathetic creatures that we are! Since it is the duty of the angels to sing psalms to his invisible power, we ought to sing psalms with even greater reverence, bearing in mind that he who sits with the angels in heaven on the throne of his glory watches us and sees into our hearts.'

43 Every day she used to encourage them very carefully to practise the love that they ought to have for each other, saying, 'You must read the Holy Scriptures each day and keep their commandments, knowing that love covers a multitude of sins.[40] For if any one of you practises every virtue, whether abstinence or fasting or staying awake or praying or chastity, but does not have love – listen to what St Paul said: "If I do everything but have not love, I am nothing and there is no use in what I do."'[41]

And since she herself practised and taught all these virtues, while always humbling herself as if she knew nothing, and since she listened to what other holy people taught, she said that 'the devil can imitate the servants of God in every way: for example when it comes to fasting, he has never eaten since he was created; and if you mention the virtue of staying awake, he has never slept; but he cannot imitate humility and love. So as far as you are able, love one another; hate pride which was what caused the devil to be thrown from heaven. Flee from the admiration of this world because it fades like the flower of the field. Recognize God in all things and keep a firm hold on your faith. For this is the foundation of all the virtues. Protect the holiness of your soul and body, for without them no one will see God.[42] For the Lord valued virginity so much that he was even born from a virgin to become the salvation of the world.' If she noticed that one of the women was practising excessive abstinence, she wished to prevent her from becoming too proud and so she would take the opportunity to say to her, 'The holy ones say that the monks' life and their abstinence should be like a bride in her wedding clothes: she should not wear black shoes in her wedding chamber, but should adorn her feet in some other way: in the same way fasting should be the least important of all the virtues.'

44 She also taught them a lot about obedience, saying that even those who lived in the world could not do without obedience. She gave them the following example: 'Consider the leaders and all the top positions where one person gives orders to another; in the homes of people living in the world, too, one person is more important than another. Remember also that in the holy church the bishops are under an archbishop and the archbishop is under the authority of the synod. So everybody and everything owes obedience and there is nothing good without obedience.' She then told us what one of the holy men said to his disciple when he wanted to teach him obedience and patience. 'He said, "Take a whip and go over there and whip that statue." The disciple went off in obedience to him and did as he was told. Then he came back and was asked by the man who had sent him, "What did the statue say to you or what

answer did it give?" The man replied, "It said nothing, sir." Then he sent him again, saying, "Go now and beat the statue again." And he went off and did this and came back. And again the holy man said to him, "What happened, my son? Did it not say anything in response?" And the man said, "No, nothing." Then he said to the disciple, "You must recognize, my son, that anyone who wants to be saved must put up with injuries and beatings without resistance, just like that statue." And so, my little daughters, you must practise obedience at all times. For obedience is a question of each person doing not what he or she wants to do but what he is told to do by the Lord. If he or she does what he wants to do, this is not obedience but the misguided will of one's own sinfulness. And those who want to please themselves rather than their neighbour in order to instruct him for good, will experience what the prophet described: "The Lord has scattered the bones of men who please themselves and those whom God has rejected will necessarily be thrown into confusion."[43]

45 With regard to fasting Melania advised them to act with restraint. She did not force them to extreme degrees of fasting, for she did not want them to be exhausted when it came to other virtues. But she did allow each of them to fast as much as her individual frailty allowed, saying that 'God knows the mind and will of each person and if someone can do something but does not do so, she must give an account to God; one can say to God, "I had a stomach ache" or an ache in another part of her body but it is inexcusable for her not to do good if she could. You must endure so that you will be judged righteous; strive to enter through the narrow gate; suffer a little so that you may receive much; treat the things of this world with scorn so that you may gain heavenly rewards.'

46 At night she would wake them for prayer, not when the others were getting up to gather in church but in accordance with the prophetic words of the holy David: 'In the night I remembered your name, Lord', and 'I rose before dawn and cried for help', but she also pointed out the time when she quoted, 'At midnight I rose to praise you.' [44] 'If churches do this it is not so that lay people might gather in church; it is we who ought to

get up earlier to glorify the Lord. For if we get up when we have had enough sleep, what is the virtue in that? We ought to take an aggressive attitude in this task because it is those who are violent who storm the kingdom of heaven. [45] If the farmer hurries to offer the first fruits to his earthly lord, should we not hasten all the more to offer them to our heavenly Lord!' After she had performed the regular office, she allowed them to catch up on sleep for a bit so that they could continue to perform this task, especially since they were of the weaker and more fragile sex.

47 For the night hours she had introduced the rule that three responsories should be said without a break, together with three readings and, during matins, fifteen antiphons. Then during the day she would pray at the third hour because that is the exact time when the Holy Spirit descended, and especially at the sixth hour, because it was at exactly that time that faithful Abraham welcomed the angels; and at the ninth hour because at that time the lame man was healed by the holy apostles but also because Daniel, the greatly beloved, used to pray three times a day, thereby teaching us long ago about the three times for daily prayer. Then one must pray at vespers because after the resurrection from the dead Christ went with the holy Cleopas and revealed himself at around sunset; and the Lord, speaking mystically in the holy Gospels, showed this when he said that the master of the household went out to call the workers to the vineyard at about the third hour, the sixth and the ninth hour and also at around the eleventh hour.[46] She told them to perform the services of prayer also on Saturdays, Sundays and feast days, saying, 'If prayer is good every day, how much more necessary is prayer on the day of our Lord's resurrection, because the prayers are heard more easily amidst the joy of the angels and heavenly beings.'

48 If it happened that the women occasionally became exhausted by the great effort of staying awake and Melania, taking pity on them, allowed them to rest a while, the girls themselves, because of her salutary teaching and the great kindness of the love she showed them, refused to be self-indulgent, saying to her, 'If you, although you are our mother and mistress, do not neglect to care for our material and spiritual needs, why should not we all the more obey God and your orders?' When Melania

heard this she was very pleased with them because she could see that they had listened to her words and understood them. She built for the women an oratory in the monastery and set up an altar there so that they could benefit from the holy sacraments. With the exception of feast days, one mass was celebrated for them on the day of the Passion which is the sixth day of the week (i.e. Fridays) and one on the day of the Resurrection (Sundays). She placed there the relics of some saints – of the prophet Zechariah, of Stephen the first martyr and of the forty saints from Sebaste, as well as others whose names it would take too long to record. Furthermore, she arranged for there to be three readings a day, so that the women's minds would always benefit from concentrating on the teaching and message of the church by means of set prayers. And she would say, 'Remember that the prescribed form of divine service should always be observed just as it is observed now.'

49 But let us return to the main theme. Her spiritual brother passed away eight years before her own death, in accordance with God's plan, and he now rests in the Lord. So Melania survived him, and forced herself to endure more severe fasts and more intense prayer, remaining for three or four years in the little Apostolium that she had constructed, where her mother and brother had been buried. When she saw that the church had no monks and that the services were being neglected, she was seized by a holy enthusiasm to create a home for holy men where they could live and pray and sing psalms day and night in the church of the Holy Ascension and in the cave where the Lord discussed the end of the world with his disciples. But on many occasions when she wanted to make a start on what she longed to do in hope and faith – a huge undertaking – she was prevented by a few people who said that even if she started it she would not be able to finish it because of a lack of funds. While she was considering this, it suddenly happened that not long afterwards a religious man who loved Christ offered her two hundred gold pieces. She accepted them, giving thanks to God, and then immediately called my humble self (for I continued to live by her side because she had taken me from the world and offered me to God, and Christ had led me, unworthy

though I was, to the rank of priest) and said to me, 'Take these two hundred gold pieces and quickly hire some workmen: they must deliver a load of stones and start to build a monastery for men, so that while I am still alive and present, I may see the service of God being performed soon. I also want the bones of my lord and brother and of my mother to lie here at rest, once these men are serving God.' So building work commenced immediately and as the Lord supported his servant's faith, this great and wonderful undertaking was finished that same year. All those who saw it were struck with amazement and asserted that it would not have been completed without the help of divine providence. The holy servants of the Lord lived there and performed the service of God wonderfully, either in the holy church of the Ascension or in the Apostolium where Melania's saintly mother and spiritual brother were buried.

50 While she was busy with these tasks, giving thanks to God in her great joy, a letter arrived from her uncle Volusianus, one of the prefects. He told her that he had gone to Constantinople to negotiate with the Empress Eudoxia[47] whom our Emperor Valentinian wanted to marry. On receiving the letter, she was pierced to the heart with a longing to see her uncle, primarily on account of the divine dispensation because she wanted his soul to be saved (for in fact he was still a pagan). She immediately put this plan into action and a week later she left Jerusalem, commending herself to all the holy men and asking them to pray that this plan had come to her from God (for she was always afraid of doing something contrary to God's will).

51 So Melania set off, but it would be impossible to describe the honour she was accorded by holy bishops and men in every place and town along the way. You could see people who spent long periods in the desert converging on each town to meet her for they were keen to see the woman whom they had heard about as a shining example of virtue. When the monks and virgins saw her they did not want to go back because they could not get enough of the sight of her and of her words which gave them so much pleasure. When the time came for them to leave, they were all overcome by tears because they would miss her so much.

52 But seeing that it is good to hide the mystery of the king but glorious and just to reveal the works of God, Melania went to Tripoli with her companions. There is a chapel there to the martyr Leontius where many miracles used to be performed through the power of the holy martyr, and Melania stayed there. As her entourage needed many beasts of burden to transport them, it happened that a certain municipal official, whose name was Messala, turned out to be very unhelpful and difficult when it came to providing transport and animals. Melania was upset by this and remained in prayer at the holy martyr's place from evening until the beasts finally arrived; she then left the shrine and set off immediately together with her entourage. But we had not gone more than six or seven miles when this official Messala came along the main road in pursuit. He caught up with us and asked, 'Where is the priest?' I was unfamiliar with the public charges we were supposed to pay and I was afraid that he would take the animals away because of the presence of an important person, so I got down and said, 'I am the priest; what do you want, my son?' He replied, 'I want to pay my respects to the holy woman and receive a blessing from her.' He approached Melania and took hold of her feet and said, 'Please look kindly on me, for I did not know who you were. That is why I dragged my heels over giving you the animals, and now I have hurried to make up for it, so that you will not be upset and God will not be angry with me.' Melania replied, 'May God bless you, my son, because you have let us go, even if a bit late.' He immediately offered me the gold pieces I had given him as a tip. When I saw them I refused to accept them, because I thought I had given him too little and I said to him, 'If it's not enough, I will give you twice as much, but I do not want that money back.' He replied, 'I do not want to keep this money nor do I want any more.' But I suspected he was afraid he would get into trouble in the palace, so I said to him, 'Do not be afraid, my son, for we are not the kind of people who go from country to country. We are making this journey out of necessity. Rest assured that we will not say anything bad about you, for that is not the right way for God's servants to behave.' At last he began to trust Melania and us.

He said, 'Believe me, you blessed people, and you, most holy woman: the martyr Leontius has been rebuking my wife and me all night and we both came out at the same time and ran to the martyr's shrine, hoping to find you there. As you had already set off, it was only with great difficulty that I managed to catch you up with the help of fast horses. My wife asked me to beg you because she could not come herself. And so we ask you to forgive us and to pray for us who are ignorant.' When we heard this we gave thanks to God and accepted those three pieces of gold. And the official went home very happy after receiving a blessing from Melania. Seeing that we were all amazed by this, Melania said to us, 'Rest assured, our journey has God's support.' We begged her to show us the cause of the mystery, for we suspected that she had had some kind of revelation. For several hours she refused to say anything in front of us all, but she was kind enough to tell me in private that she had spent the whole night awake praying to the Lord and to the holy martyr that they might show us a sign as to whether the journey had God's support; and this had indeed happened by means of the official who had delayed us. Then we went on our way with joy and it was with joy that we were welcomed by everyone we met, for many people said that they had had visions regarding Melania's arrival.

53 At last we arrived in Constantinople but before she entered the city Melania was very worried because she was a foreigner. When she reached the shrine of the martyr Euphemia, she was feeling low but she went in to worship the Lord. She immediately noticed a sweet smell and she felt better – it was as if she had found great consolation. Then, as befitted her faith, she found lodgings at the home of Lausus of blessed memory. She then found her uncle who was ill, which was in accordance with God's will. But when he saw her dressed like that and in such a humble condition, transformed from such great magnificence and the heights of worldly fame, he was shocked and began to cry. He said, 'Oh, if you only knew how this woman was brought up in our family – she was the apple of our eye and like the rose or lily when it begins to flower.' Then the holy Melania, seeing him lying ill, stayed by his side, teaching him and instructing

him in the faith of our Lord Jesus Christ and in the resurrection of eternal life. When she thought of suggesting to the emperor and the empress that they should convince him of this, he noticed this and said that he did not want it to be implied to anyone that he had given in to her will and sweet words. But Melania would not keep quiet. She then asked the holy bishop and some noble men to go and talk to her uncle about what she herself had asked. But since his mind was still sharp, he understood that they had come at her suggestion. He told her, as if he did not know, that 'If we had three men like the holy bishop Proclus, no one would still be a pagan in Rome.'

54 But while this went on for a few days, the devil grew envious, and as a result Melania experienced another temptation. When a number of married ladies and religious women eagerly came to visit her so that they could have the pleasure of seeing and hearing her, she spoke to them about her holy way of life and her firm faith; on hearing her delightful words, many married ladies of noble and distinguished families were strengthened in their faith and gave alms and decided to practise continence. As a result the devil was driven by jealousy to appear one day to Melania in the guise of a young Ethiopian of fearsome appearance who said to her, 'How do you have the audacity to come here and spend every day, from morning to night, teaching what comes from God? You are not aware that I have persuaded the hearts of the emperor and empress to turn against you, as well as that of Lausus with whom you are staying, and they will drive you away from here immediately. But if they do not do it or if you do not obey, I will inflict pain on your whole body and put your life in danger.' When the demon had said this he vanished like smoke from before her eyes. Straight away she called me and asked me to say a prayer, after telling me what the demon had said; while she was still speaking, an intense pain suddenly struck her in the kidneys and she lay for three hours as if she were dead. She had only just regained consciousness when she became a bit too confident and began to pray, saying, 'Lord, may your will be done in me, your servant.' But when she had endured five or six days in great pain and danger, and all of us who were with her were

overcome by despair and sadness, fully expecting her to die, someone came to her on the seventh day and said, 'Hurry and come, your uncle is asking for you. He wants to see you because he is at death's door, and if you do not hurry, he will die without baptism.'

55 As soon as Melania heard this she began to suffer even more and said to us, 'Take me to him.' But we were afraid and said, 'If we agree to take you, we fear you may die on the way, because you are in such great pain.' She replied, 'If you do not take me by some means or other, he will die there and I will die here. Take me, so that I can see him.' While she was being laid on the litter, as good as dead, so that she could go to him, the messenger returned and told Volusianus that she was very ill and unable to come. When he heard this, Volusianus immediately sent for the empress's nurse, a woman called Eleutheria, and dispatched a message to the empress to tell the bishop to come and give him holy baptism. The bishop hurried to Volusianus' home and baptized him in the name of the Father and of the Son and of the Holy Ghost. At once someone set off to tell Melania and met her in the forum of the Emperor Constantine as she was on her way, and said to her, 'I wanted to let you know that your uncle has been baptized. He sent me to tell you.' As soon as she heard this, Melania glorified God, and at once all the pain left her and the devil was thrown into confusion. Her feet, dry as wood, which she had been unable to move, recovered now that she was restored to health. As a result we knew that this attack had been caused by the devil who had made the saintly woman suffer and had begrudged her uncle his salvation, for fear that he might be saved as a result of her insistence. But God, who had seen his servant's faith and constancy, brought her good plan to fulfilment and brought her uncle enlightenment, thereby confounding the devil and his lackeys. So Melania reached her uncle's house and she, who had hardly been able to be carried in a litter, now walked unaided up the steps to the upper floor where the Empress Eudocia was visiting her uncle. When Melania got there she paid her respects to the empress, sat down next to her uncle and gave thanks to the Lord, overwhelmed with happi-

ness that he had received enlightenment and that she had recovered her health. When he had received the sacred body of the Lord, Melania said to him, 'Look, my lord, at what Christ has given you, so that you can lead a glorious life in this world and can enter the kingdom of heaven in the future, born again through holy baptism.' He replied, 'This gift of God is the result of your efforts.' Melania remained by his side, never ceasing to encourage him regarding God's promises. And so he joyfully passed away to the Lord just at Epiphany. We were so amazed and admiring of God's mercy and of the great goodness he shows to all, that we said, 'Look how God, with a view to the salvation of one man's soul, made him come from Rome and us from Jerusalem, so that this man might benefit from the work of his servant Melania.'

56 When all this was over, Melania felt that she had accomplished everything she had come for. As soon as she had celebrated the fortieth day after Volusianus' death and made an offering for him to the Lord, she hastened to leave Constantinople and return to her cell where she led her secret life of devotion to God. She was eager to leave because she had a long journey ahead of her and she wanted to see the holy places again. When the emperor and the empress, on account of the severe winter weather and because they very much wanted to enjoy her company a bit longer, refused to allow her to make the journey, she would not give up but instead asked and encouraged the emperor to tell the empress to come without delay to worship at the holy places. Then she said goodbye and set off. Although it was February and there was a threat of severe winter conditions (and in fact as we passed through the various places, the local bishops told us that there had never been a winter like it with such extreme cold), Melania did not have the worries usually experienced by women because of the fragility of their sex, for her faith gave her strength. Each day she would hurry on her journey for she was keen to celebrate Easter Day in Jerusalem. But as we travelled through different areas, a great amount of snow and rain fell from morning till night, with the result that for many days the stars were not visible at night, and because we were fasting (it being Lent), all of us men, whom you might

assume were stronger because of our sex and nature, were shattered by the hardships of the journey. When on the third or
fourth day we urged her to relax the fast a little on account of
the hardships we were experiencing, she replied that she was
not at all tired: 'I must not fast less, but more, because the Lord
has deigned to bestow such great gifts on me who am his
unworthy servant.' Comforting us with these and similarly kind
words, she strengthened our resolve so that neither she nor we
had any sense of danger. Finally, when we arrived at the mountain called Modicus we found that the animals were unable to
cross it on account of the severe weather. So Melania dismounted and set off on foot just as if she were a man – you had
to see it to believe it! We did not want to allow her to walk,
saying, 'Get up on your mule! You are exhausted by too much
fasting and your delicate limbs cannot bear the hardships of the
journey.' I am telling the truth when I say that she refused to
listen to anyone and she arrived in Malagurdolo with such
masculine determination, while continually talking to us
about scriptural matters, that we were all amazed to find that
we were weaker than she and that our faces were frozen by
the extreme cold, while she felt absolutely nothing. Those
who are familiar with that mountain would admit that it is
difficult for anyone to cross even in springtime, so you can
imagine how much more difficult it was when covered with all
that snow. Many holy bishops came to welcome her on her
arrival, showing her great respect. They tried to persuade her
to stay until the weather was more clement but she refused
and hurried on, determined – as I said – to celebrate Easter
Day in Jerusalem. And God granted her this, for he fulfils the
desire of those who fear him.[48]

57 And so we reached Jerusalem after forty-four days, on the
day before the Lord's Passion. Melania, restored by happiness,
celebrated the holy days of the Lord's Resurrection with her
young women on the Mount of Olives. After this she continued
with her customary routine of prayer and fasting, serving the
Lord, advising the women to remain firm in fear of the Lord,
and putting her efforts into managing the monastery for the
men. When she saw that the monks were performing the liturgy

of the holy church well, her spiritual ardour increased as did her love of God. As a result she had the idea of building a small martyr's shrine there. 'This is the place where the Lord's feet stood. I will make a small shrine so that after my death mass can be celebrated for my soul and for that of my husband.' In this way God fulfilled all her desires because her plans were in accordance with God. She also gathered together many monks there to praise Christ with hymns and songs in the monastery of God.

58 While she was building this she heard that the Empress Eudocia was on her way and in fact had already reached Antioch. Melania wondered whether she ought to go and meet her or not, and she pondered whether it was perhaps not right for her to wander through the towns dressed in this way. She also wondered whether she might seem arrogant and ungrateful if she did not go to meet the empress. Then she said, 'It is especially fitting for us as Christians not only to go to meet such a pious empress with humility, but even to carry her on our shoulders and to glorify God who in our times has appointed such a faithful empress who is so good to us.' So she went to meet her at Sidon, stopping at the shrine of the martyr St Phocas, where there was said to be a cell of the woman of Canaan who had said to the Lord: 'It is right, Lord, for dogs to eat the crumbs that fall from the table of their masters.'[49] For she was very careful that whatever she did or said, wherever she walked or stopped, it would be done in the name of the Lord. The empress welcomed Melania with great respect as befitted a loyal subject, showing her great affection. She said that Melania should know that she had come to venerate the holy places but also to see the saintly Melania, so that she could fulfil her desire to converse with her while she was still alive. Melania gave thanks to God and to the empress and encouraged her to spend more time in prayer and acts of compassion. Together they arrived in Jerusalem. The empress performed her vows of prayer to the Lord. The whole time that the empress spent there she did not leave Melania's side but was inseparable from her, every day enjoying conversation with the woman who was like a saintly mother to her. When the empress entered the monastery, she

invited all the young women and girls to come and kiss her as if they were her daughters. Then she went to the men's monastery and when she went in she saw that the martyr's shrine I mentioned was still being built, so she gave orders that the work be finished more quickly, asking Melania for the dedication to be celebrated while she was still there. This was done, with God's help.

59 But the enemy who is jealous of good people caused Melania to become dispirited. For the empress slipped on her way into the monastery and twisted her ankle which started to cause her pain that same day. Melania was very upset by this and so she went into the martyr's shrine with her young women and spent the whole night there in tears and prayer, begging the Lord to heal the empress. She would not leave the place until her request was granted. For she made her request confidently to him whom she had always tried to placate by means of her devoted service. The Lord was with his servant as she prayed and before she had finished praying, the empress was restored to health: all the pain disappeared and she returned safe and well to the church of the Holy Resurrection. She went into the martyr's shrine where the dedication had been made and worshipped the Lord, saying, 'I thank you, Lord, for being kind enough to visit me, not on account of my merit but in accordance with your kindness and the intervention of your saints and of your servant Melania.' Once the empress was feeling better, God's holy one rebuked the devil, saying, 'Devil, how long will you continue to upset me and to afflict me with so many different temptations? For the Lord will help me and he will utterly destroy your strength.' When everything had been duly accomplished, the empress returned to Constantinople at the proper time. Melania accompanied her as far as Caesarea and when she was about to say goodbye and return home, the empress burst into tears because she knew she would miss Melania. For a great and indissoluble affection filled her heart. On her return Melania spent the time praying that the empress should get back home to the emperor without any problems. A few days later she heard that she had got home safely, so she gave thanks to the Lord because he had performed many good works through her.

60 Melania was also granted the gift of healing, as was demonstrated by the case of a girl who was the daughter of a nobleman. She was a lovely young woman, as yet unmarried, but she had been stricken by a demon that left her mute so that she could not even move her lips or part her teeth. Her parents were very upset after watching her being tormented like this for three days and unable to eat any food. They appealed to the doctors to use various remedies to make her lips and teeth open at least a little bit, but their efforts were unsuccessful. Then Melania came to hear of it. Trusting in the Lord she asked that the girl be brought to her, saying, 'Bring her to me so that she can stay in the martyr's shrine for I believe that the Lord will help her and she will be cured by the saints' prayers.' So the girl came, accompanied by her parents, as well as by a group of neighbours. Melania began by praying, then took the oil of blessing and said to the girl, 'In the name of the Lord, open your mouth.' Her parents reminded her that the girl had not been able to open her mouth for three days now, but Melania replied, 'Have faith in the name of our Lord Jesus Christ that she will be able to open her mouth at once.' She touched the girl's lips with the oil and immediately she began to move her lips. Then pouring the oil in, she made her part her teeth. She gave the girl food which she accepted and ate, and everyone who was there was amazed and glorified the Lord. The girl returned home cured, with her parents, and gave thanks to the Lord who had taken pity on her by means of the woman who worshipped him.

61 Similarly the Lord made use of Melania to cure another woman who was affected in the same manner, and also healed a man who was horribly afflicted by a demon. While Melania's mother was still alive, there was a pregnant woman whose life was in danger when she went into labour. I hope no one will criticize me and say that this is one of those subjects that should not be mentioned because it is disgusting, even though this is another instance in which we saw Melania performing a miracle. God makes nothing unpleasant or foul in human beings, for he has created all the parts of the body with a purpose. Sin alone is foul and disgusting. No part of the human body can be

disgusting because God created it, and from it were born the patriarchs, the prophets, the apostles and the other saints. Anyway, this woman had been lying unconscious for three days and the midwives had tried every remedy in their attempts to save her, but without success. The only thing left was for the doctors to cut open her womb and take out the body of the stillborn baby, in the hope that this would save the mother. For it is very dangerous for a mother to give birth to a stillborn baby. When all hope of recovery was lost, the women told Melania all about it. They did not dare to ask her to come all the way to see this woman, so they just entreated her to pray for the woman's recovery, hoping that Melania could help her by her prayers, in the same way that she helped everyone. Melania replied, 'It is good to show compassion to every soul.' This is how she indicated that she was not ashamed to go and see the woman. Turning to her young women, she said, 'Let us go and visit her, my daughters', and then she got up and set off. On the way she started to instruct them, saying, 'My daughters, you ought to be so grateful to God for saving you from these labour pains.' When the woman saw that Melania had come to see her, she begged her in a tearful and faltering voice to have pity on her and to pray for her. When Melania heard this, she was deeply moved and very upset. She stood over her, praying. Then she took her leather belt and tied it round the woman: at once the baby was born and the woman recovered, to everyone's amazement. But Melania in her humility wished to conceal the gift granted to her and giving honour to God, she attributed it all to the merits of others, saying, 'This belt belonged to a servant of God, and it was his goodness which inspired the Lord to heal you.' For as has been said, she always tried to attribute to others anything that God had granted her. She then prepared some delicious food to restore the woman's strength.

62 We often questioned her, saying, 'Lady mother, how is it that arrogance and pride do not steal upon you, given that you practise such extremes of abstinence and have been granted such virtue?' But she would say (thereby instructing us by her humility), 'I am not aware of ever having done anything good, but if a proud thought regarding my fasting occurs to me, then

I say to the enemy, "Did you put this idea into my head, devil? Why do you put such thoughts into my head, as if I were doing anything special by fasting for a week? Do not other people continue to fast for forty days?" And if he suggests that I give up oil, I tell him that other people do not even drink their fill of water. If any thoughts occur to me about my rejection of wealth and the enormous amount of gold and silver or the huge number of gifts of different kinds, I say that many people captured by the enemy not only lose all their belongings, but also endure the slavery of cruel captivity. Many, too, are left in poverty by their parents and have to put up with the pressures of need and deprivation. Have I done more than these people if I endure a life of poverty for the sake of the Lord who has redeemed me? Again, when the devil tries to creep into my heart, saying, "Think of all those expensive linen clothes and silk garments you rejected! Look at you now, wearing that hairshirt! What a saint you are!" I say to him, "May Christ oppose you! Can you not see all those people lying on mats and on the bare earth?" Then I pray, saying, "Lord, you know that the thoughts of men are trivial. Blessed is the person taught by you, Lord, and instructed in your law."[50] That is how God drives away the enemy.' Again she said to us, 'It is clear that the enemy wages war on everyone, but particularly by means of those who wear the holy habit. For when he sees that we are hastening to carry out the precept of the Lord who says in the Gospel, "Sell all you have and give to the poor", and "Take up your cross, come and follow me",[51] he often sends people who say to us, "Is it not good to live in penury and poverty for God's sake, but in moderation? Is it not good to abstain for God's sake, but in moderation?" To such people I reply, "Do not people in the army strive to rise step by step to a higher rank? Like them we ought to reject the things of this world and try to win heavenly prizes, hastening towards heaven to reach heavenly status."' If it ever happened that someone upset her, she would say gently, 'I am sorry. I know I am a sinner and I do not dare to compare myself to the least of the women of the world.' To prevent the devil having any reason to accuse her, she would not take communion when she was angry with someone until she had made up with the person, even if it was the other one's fault. To be more accurate, did anyone ever perceive that she was angry without her having taken the first step to be reconciled, using great patience and gentleness to calm the feelings that were running high? She never ate any food until she had received the body of Christ: this she did especially to protect her soul, although it was also a custom among the Christians at Rome to receive the Eucharist once a day. For it was Peter, the most blessed of the apostles, who started this tradition while he was bishop of Rome, and he was then followed by St Paul who was put to death there.

63 At this point, I hope that despite my inelegant style I have produced a sufficiently full account of the life of our holy mother. However, we have been unable to give an account that truly represents her merits for neither my humble talents nor my pathetic memory are up to the task of recording for you, holy father, all her spiritual achievements or her longings in the love of Christ. But now that my account has brought me to the end and to her happy death, I will add just a few words. It happened that after she had endured many sufferings in this world, according to the words of Scripture: 'protecting the faith with the weapons of justice on the right hand and the left, she completed the race and waited for the crown of justice, set aside by Christ, to be given back to her, for she desired to depart and be with Christ, much more than to remain in the flesh.'[52] Then Christmas came, the birthday of our Saviour, our Lord Jesus Christ, and she said, 'I want to go to Bethlehem to celebrate the birthday of my Lord there. For I do not know whether I will live to see it next year.' So she went there, accompanied by her niece Paula, a virgin dedicated to the Lord, and celebrated the holy vigils and received holy communion. Then, as if she knew that she would soon leave this life, she said goodbye to her niece, saying, 'Pray for me, my darling. From now on you will celebrate Christmas on your own without me.' When those who were with her heard her say this, they began to cry. On her return, she went into the holy cave and prayed.

64 The following day when prayers were said for St Stephen the first martyr, she did not go to the vigils but went at dawn to

that martyr's shrine and asked for mass to be said at her monastery. For she was not in the habit of receiving holy communion unless she herself had made the offering. On her return
from the martyr's shrine, she stayed awake with her young
women whom she was now on the point of leaving as orphans,
physically if not yet spiritually, in accordance with the Lord's
will. For I was there with her and she said that I should be the
first to read the account of the discovery of St Stephen's relics.
Three of the sisters also gave a reading and then she herself
read the passion of St Stephen from the Acts of the Apostles,
because it was the custom for her to have five readings at the
saints' vigils. When she had finished matins, all the sisters said
to her, 'Give us a blessing so that we may deserve to have you
to celebrate many saints' vigils', to which she replied, 'May the
Lord bless you and keep you for you will not hear me reading
any more. The Lord is calling me now. Now I long to depart [53]
and be in peace. I advise you, dearest ones who are like holy
limbs to me, to live in Christ and perform the spiritual rule in
fear of God. For it is written, "Cursed is he who performs the
work of God carelessly."[54] Even if I am not here, God always
is.' Her words upset them all and they began to cry. She said to
me, 'Let us go so that I may pray at the martyrs' shrine in the
men's monastery, because the relics of St Stephen are also buried there.' While she was praying as if saying goodbye to the
holy martyrs, she began to feel a slight chill. On her return
home she found the sisters still singing matins. She then began
to feel worse. When the sisters realized this they begged her to
rest a little because, as she grew weaker, she was unable to
stand up. But she said, 'Leave me for a while, until we have
finished matins.'

65 Afterwards, having rested a while on her bed, she called all
the girls to her side and said to them, 'Above all, pray for me.
And if you have any affection for me, keep my commands and
rules. Please remember that I never reprimanded any of you
angrily: I always did so gently because I did not want to upset
anyone. I never allowed any of you to be angry with her sister
for a day or a night. Instead I urged you to be reconciled to one
another, because it is love that wins the heavenly crown. Avoid

the gaze of men for even if you do not consider yourself attractive, a man who looks at you may be seduced. It often happens that you can cause someone else to sin. Therefore I say to you, keep firmly to the rule. Respect the authority of the holy bishop in all obedience and humility. For he is concerned for you and keeps watch over you before the Lord, mindful that he will have to render an account.' Turning to the young girls she said, 'You must know, my daughters, that those who leave this world are aware of what is going on here; and so if one of you has an argument or disagreement with your sisters, I will come and tell you off.' And this is in fact what happened. After her death, if one of the sisters behaved in an arrogant manner towards another, Melania would appear to her in a dream and rebuke her and threaten her; or if one of them was overwhelmed by laziness and refused to get up for the night vigil, Melania would come to her at night and say to her sternly, 'Why are you not getting up to praise God?' or 'Be reconciled to your sisters, especially on the Lord's Day.' Perhaps what I am about to say may seem incredible but it is true, and many people know of it. The empress once sent for some of the young women from Melania's monastery and one of the girls, whose mother had handed her over to Melania at the altar, was told to go with the others. Melania appeared to her with a radiant face in the company of some men and began to rebuke the girl threateningly, saying, 'Did your mother not give you to me at the holy altar like a sheep for the sacrifice? And now you want to go to Constantinople? There will be trouble unless you promise me not to leave this place.' Then the terrified girl said, 'Even if I have to die, I will not go.' When she woke up she told all the others of this. But Melania also appeared to other sisters who were already on their way and rebuked them. And even the empress herself said that she had had a vision and that Melania had told her not to take the girls, so she sent a message while they were on their way, telling them to return to their own monastery. Melania would often appear to them, warning them and encouraging them to amend their ways for the better.

66 And so, as I promised a little earlier to relate, when she had been ill for five days and the doctors wanted to give her some

medicine to bring her a bit of relief, she said to them, 'If my days are at an end, the Lord is calling. For I have heard a voice in my heart, whether from God or from someone else – God knows – as if someone were saying to me, "Whatever they manage to do is of no use, for the summons has been sent." Why do you make these efforts to no purpose? You must not give the impression of resisting God.' But when we heard this, we could not stop ourselves crying. Then she said to me, 'Do not cry, father. Be brave, for we are not going to stay in this world for ever.' When the fifth day of her illness had passed, the sixth day arrived – it was a Sunday. As day dawned she told me to go into the martyrs' shrine next to which she was lying in her little cell, so that the offering could be celebrated. So I went in and offered the Eucharistic host to God. In my great sadness I poured forth a prayer in silence so she would not hear it in her cell, but she called to me, 'Please say that prayer a bit louder so that I can hear and receive encouragement.' And when the sacrifice of praise had been made, she took communion.

67 At dawn the next morning the bishop came to see her. She said to him, 'My lord bishop, I entrust to you this holy priest and the monasteries which, thanks to your prayers, God has been kind enough to assemble through my humility. And please pray for me, my holy friend.' Then she received communion again from the bishop. The monks came to visit her and she said to them, 'Pray for me, for I am already saying goodbye to you. I commend to you this priest and beg you not to cause him distress, for he has borne my burden for God's sake, even though he did not need to.' Next it was the turn of the young women to come in. Melania said goodbye to them, too, in the same words.

68 Then everyone came from the different monasteries and from the holy city. Melania said goodbye to them all as if she were setting off on a journey, commending herself to their prayers. When she had thoroughly instructed her own servants of God and given her niece Paula plenty of blessings, she said to me, 'I am entrusting the monasteries to your care. You took care of them while I was alive, and now you must do so even more carefully. Be aware that it is the Lord who will reward

you for your work. And please pray for me.' When she had said goodbye to everyone and cheerfully given the kiss of peace to her young girls, as if the time of departure was approaching, she said, 'Please say a prayer.' When the prayer was finished and they had all said, 'Amen', Melania added, 'Bestow a blessing on me, then go in peace, and leave me to rest now.' Around the ninth hour, when she fell into a deep sleep and we thought she was departing from her body, we tried in our sorrow to straighten out her feet, weeping as we did so. But she said, 'The time has not yet come', so I said to her, 'Well then, you tell us when it is time', and she replied, 'To be sure, I will let you know.' It was the custom among the Romans to place the Eucharistic host in the person's mouth when the soul was departing. There were also some who lived with the holy bishop and also the other holy anchorites from around Eleutheropolis who wanted to witness her blessed death. They said, 'We are sad but the angels will be happy', to which Melania's response was, 'It has happened as the Lord willed.' In that same hour she took communion from the bishop and at the end of the prayer she responded, 'Amen'. She kissed the bishop's hand and then lying down again she joyfully watched the angels, pointing them out to us, as it were, as she joined their throng and travelled peacefully towards heaven. Her death was as serene as her life had been gentle. After a hymn and a reading from the Gospel, in accordance with her wishes, the holy bishop and all those present commended her spirit in a period of silence. For she handed over her spirit to the Creator at the very hour when the Lord was conversing with Cleopas on their journey. Cleopas said to him, 'Stay with us, for it is evening and the day is coming to an end.'[55] In the same way Melania, on that Sunday, with the love which she always had for God, was told, 'Melania, our faithful servant, come and take your rest and stay with us. For I want those whom the Father has given to me to be in the same place as I am, with the Father and the Holy Spirit.'

69 I think it might be useful for the reader, and no trouble for me, if I describe what she was wearing at her burial. She wore a tunic belonging to some holy woman, of very poor quality but given as a gift. She also kept for herself a cloak, a monastic

garment and everything she had received from the other holy
servants acceptable to God. She had absolutely no linen garments apart from just one fine muslin one, with which she was
buried in the tomb. She gave orders that a little cushion belonging to a servant of God should be placed under her head, as
well as the hooded garment made of hairshirt material which
he had given her in the desert.

70 And so she ascended to heaven and in joy and exultation she
achieved her desire. She had fought a good fight[56] and the
enemy powers did not dismay her, seeing that they could find
nothing in her that belonged to them. For she heard from the
one whom she had loved with complete faith since her youth
speaking in Christ's words, 'Come, enter into the joy of your
master.'[57] When she wanted to please someone, she used to say,
'I wish that I could hear those words of the Gospel, "Good and
faithful servant, enter into the joy of your master"', and this is
in fact what happened to her, for she entered joyful and happy.
The angels praised her because they could see in her a reflection
of their own way of life, which she had lived to perfection while
she was still on earth. The prophets said, 'She did not pass over
a single word of our teaching without putting it into practice.'
The apostles said, 'Tell her to rest with us, for she has imitated
our way of life.' The holy martyrs said, 'She has honoured our
memories; glorify her with us.' For the labours which she had
endured and the virtues she had practised, she received what
the eye does not see and the ear does not hear and what has not
ascended to the heart of man, which God has prepared for
those who love him:[58] to whom be honour and glory for ever
and ever, Amen.

THE LIFE OF MELANIA
THE YOUNGER

by Palladius

Melania the younger

See headnote to Gerontius' *Life* (p. 181).

Palladius

See headnote to *The Life of Melania the Elder*.

Since I promised earlier in this book to give an account of Melania's granddaughter, I must carry out my promise, as is proper. It is not right to despise her for being young in the flesh and to let so much virtue lie hidden and uncommemorated – that great spiritual virtue in which she in fact far surpassed those who were advanced both in years and in devotion. Her parents forced her to marry one of the leading men in Rome but she was always influenced by descriptions of her grandmother and was so inspired by her that in the end she could no longer submit to the demands of marriage. After she had given birth to two sons, both of whom died, she developed so great an aversion to marriage that she said to her husband Pinianus, the son of Severianus, a man of prefectorial rank, 'If you choose to live an ascetic life with me, according to the principle of chastity, then I shall recognize you as my master and the lord of my life. If, however, this seems too difficult for you because you are still a young man, take all my goods and release my body, and allow me to fulfil my God-given desire to take on the mantle of my grandmother's spirit, after whom I was named. If God had wished us to have children, he would not have taken my babies from me prematurely.'

For a long time they argued, until finally God took pity on the young man and implanted in him too a desire to withdraw from the world, so that Scripture might be fulfilled, when it says: 'Wife, how do you know whether you will save your husband?'[1] Melania was married when she was thirteen years old[2] and lived with her husband for seven years but when she was twenty she renounced the world. First of all, she gave away

her short silk over-tunics for the altars, just as the holy Olympias[3] had done. She cut up her remaining silk garments and
made them into different kinds of church ornaments. She
entrusted her silver and gold to the priest Paul, a monk from
Dalmatia. She sent across the sea to the east ten thousand pieces
of gold to Egypt and the Thebaid, the same amount to Antioch
and the area around it, fifteen thousand to Palestine, and ten
thousand to the churches on the islands and those in exile
beyond the frontiers; she also personally allotted a similar sum
to the churches of the west. All these riches, and four times as
much again, her faith enabled her to snatch from the lion's
jaws[4] (if God will forgive the expression), in other words, from
Alaric. She set eight thousand slaves free who wished to be
given their freedom; the rest did not want to be set free, but
opted to become her brother's slaves. She allowed him to take
them for three denarii each. She sold her possessions in Spain,
Aquitaine and Gaul and kept for herself only those in Sicily,
Campania and Africa, using the income from them for the
upkeep of the monasteries. This was the wisdom she displayed
with regard to the burden of her wealth.

Her ascetic discipline was as follows: she ate every other day
– though at the beginning she ate every five days – and she
shared her daily routine with her serving women, whom she had
made her companions in the ascetic life. In addition, she had her
mother Albina living with her. Albina too had adopted the
ascetic life, first in Sicily and then in Campania, with fifteen
eunuchs and sixty virgins, both slaves and free women. Melania's husband Pinianus lived in a similar manner with thirty
monks, spending his time reading, gardening and having serious
discussions. When we went to Rome they received us with the
greatest possible respect on account of the holy bishop John,
even though we were a large party: their hospitality and their
most generous provision for our journey provided us with welcome refreshment. By means of the tasks that God had given
them to do and by the perfection of their way of life, they were
able to harvest the fruit of eternal life with great joy.

Notes

ECL Early Christian Lives (see Further Reading)
PL Patrologia Latina, ed. J. P. Migne (Paris, 1844–55), 221 volumes.
Contains editions of Christian ecclesiastical writings in Latin to 1216.

THE MARTYRDOM OF PERPETUA AND FELICITAS

1. *'in the last . . . dream dreams'*: Acts 2:17–18; Joel 2:28–9.
2. *the emperors' welfare*: The phrase 'for the welfare of the emperors' refers to the belief that sacrificing to the Roman gods, as each citizen was expected to do, meant that the gods protected the emperors and the Roman state. If specific emperors are being referred to here, they are Septimius Severus and his sons Caracalla and Geta.
3. *Emperor Geta's birthday*: Born on 7 March 189.
4. *love feast*: On this feast (for which the term *agape* is used), see also Jerome, *Letter* 22.32.
5. *'Ask . . . receive'*: John 16:24.
6. *'Keep . . . faith'*: 1 Corinthians 16:13; Acts 14:22.

THE LIFE OF MACRINA

1. *Thecla*: The cult of Thecla, who originated from what is now Konya in southern Turkey, seems to have been particularly popular in Asia Minor in the fourth and fifth centuries. See also Introduction, note 16.
2. *the philosophical ideal*: It was common for Christians in the fourth century to speak of the ascetic life focused on Christ as

'the philosophical life', for they believed that Christianity was the true philosophy. Gregory's portrayal of Macrina on her deathbed likens her somewhat to an ancient philosopher, lecturing those around her on the nature of the soul and dispensing wisdom and consolation. It is interesting, given the connection made between Macrina and Thecla, that in the early fourth-century *Symposium* by the Greek writer Methodius of Olympus, in which the discussion focuses on virginity, rather than on love as in Plato's *Symposium*, the prize for the best speech is awarded to a woman called Thecla.

3. *Basil*: (329–79) became bishop of Caesarea in 370 and is known to posterity as Basil the Great. He was one of the greatest church leaders and theologians, and the father of community monasticism in the Eastern church.

4. *the adversary's*: i.e. the devil, often referred to as 'the enemy' or 'the old enemy'.

5. *Peter*: He lived for many years as a solitary ascetic but in about 380 he was made bishop of Sebaste in Armenia. He died in 391.

6. *at Antioch*: The council took place in 379.

7. *a new one*: Gregory discusses the nature of the soul in his work *On the Soul and the Resurrection*.

8. *Apostle's words . . . the faith'*: 2 Timothy 4:8, 7.

9. *Valens*: Roman emperor, 364–78, supported the Arian Christians who had been condemned as heretical at the Council of Nicaea in 325 but who continued to flourish. Arians, named after the priest Arius (260–336), tried to safeguard the unity of God by stating that the Son was not an equal, independent being, but was created by God, though superior to other creatures. To non-Arians, whose views came to be accepted as orthodox, such doctrines seemed to make Christ less than God and this would have important theological implications. Although the Emperor Constantine condemned Arius, a number of later emperors, like Valens, supported Arianism. Valens persecuted the non-Arians, such as Basil and Gregory, and many other priests, bishops and monks. See also *Life of Marcella*, note 8.

10. *death*: Hebrews 2:15.

11. *trumpet*: 1 Corinthians 15:52.

12. *us*: Galatians 3:13 and 2 Corinthians 5:21.

13. *dragon*: Psalm 74:14.

14. *death*: Psalm 107:16, Matthew 16:18, Hebrews 2:14.

15. *womb*: Psalm 22:10.

16. *repose*: Psalm 23:2.
17. *sword*: Genesis 3:24.
18. *paradise*: Luke 23:43.
19. *judgements*: Psalm 119:120.
20. *sins*: Matthew 9:6.
21. *face*: Ephesians 5:27; Psalm 141:2.
22. *Tree of Life*: Refers to the cross on which Christ was crucified. Tiny pieces of wood believed to be from the cross (which had been discovered by Helena, mother of the Emperor Constantine, at the beginning of the fourth century, during the first excavations of the holy sites in Jerusalem associated with Christ's life), were used as amulets, to protect the owner. This is an early example of this practice. Although the cross was protected, supposed relics from it soon spread all over Europe and are still to be seen in many churches today.
23. *Song of the Three Children*: If this is the correct reading it is probably an allusion to Daniel 3:51 (or verse 28 of the apocryphal Song of the Three Holy Children, included in Bibles that adopt the text of the Greek Septuagint version), where the phrase 'as of one mouth' is picked up by the words 'in harmony' here.
24. *nakedness*: See Genesis 9:23.
25. *Noah . . . to do*: See Genesis 9:20–25.

THE LIFE OF MELANIA THE ELDER

1. *her son*: Publicola became the father of Melania the younger and did not look sympathetically on her attempts to live the same kind of life as his mother, as is clear from the *Life of Melania the Younger*: presumably he harboured some resentment at having been abandoned as a child. For Valens, see *Life of Macrina*, note 9.
2. *Rufinus*: Born near Aquileia in northern Italy in about 345 and died in Sicily around 410, but he spent nearly all his adult life in monasteries in Egypt and Palestine. He knew Jerome from his youth and at first they were close friends, united by their scholarly pursuits and interest in Origen, but they later became bitter enemies when Rufinus implied that Jerome was a supporter of Origen's doctrines: Jerome did not take kindly to being accused of heretical views. Rufinus was an important translator of Greek theological and monastic writings into Latin, including a number of works of Origen. Rufinus remained a close companion of Melania the elder till the end of his life.

3.   *Paulinus*: A bishop of Antioch at the same time as another anti-
     Arian bishop Meletius. Their supporters argued over the precise
     definition of the three persons of the Trinity. This situation is usu-
     ally referred to as the Meletian schism. Macrina's brothers, Basil
     and Gregory, supporters of Meletius, were among those who tried
     to heal the schism. Despite the fact that both Paulinus and Meletius
     were dead by 382, the schism rumbled on into the fifth century.

4.   *"the . . . Antichrist*: 1 John 2:18; the Antichrist was an unspeci-
     fied opponent of God whose imminent arrival had been proph-
     esied since biblical times. It is likely that the barbarian invaders
     of the Roman Empire, in the years leading up to the destruction
     of Rome in 410, were regarded as fulfilling that prophesy.

5.   *knowledge*: 1 Timothy 6:20.

THE LIFE OF MARCELLA

1.   *'And . . . day'*: Luke 2:36–7.
2.   *'Blessed . . . Lord'*: Psalm 119:1.
3.   *'Be . . . journey'*: Matthew 5:25.
4.   *'I treasure . . . day'*: Psalms 119:11, 1:2.
5.   *'So . . . God'*: 1 Corinthians 10:31.
6.   *'I gain . . . commands'*: Psalm 119:104.
7.   *'all . . . taught'*: Acts 1:1.
8.   *Athanasius . . . Arian heretics*: Athanasius, bishop of Alexandria,
     became entangled in the long-running dispute between the follow-
     ers of Arius (see *Life of Macrina*, note 9) and those who supported
     the doctrines regarding the person of Christ put forward at the
     Council of Nicaea in 325, a dispute which became as much to do
     with ecclesiastical politics as doctrine. Athanasius was sent into
     exile in the 340s to Rome where he stayed for several years.
9.   *at the time*: Antony died in Egypt in 356. See *Life of Paula the
     Elder*, note 8.
10. *Pachomian monasteries*: Pachomius (d. probably 346) had
     founded cenobitic monasteries for those who wanted to lead a
     life of communal austerity and prayer, in Egypt in the 320s.
     These settlements expanded greatly over the next half century.
     Jerome translated Pachomius' monastic rule into Latin.
11. *'Would . . . felled'*: A fragment from the play *Medea*, by the early
     Roman poet Ennius (239–169 BC), relating to the building of the
     unlucky ship *Argo* that brought Jason to Colchis in search of the
     Golden Fleece, ultimately causing Medea's tragedy.

12. 'Every day . . . disciple': 1 Corinthians 15:31 and Luke 14:27.
     The idea of philosophy as an exercise in dying can be traced back
     to Plato's dialogue, the *Phaedo* (67D–E).
13. 'For your . . . the past': Psalm 44:22, Ecclesiasticus 7:36, Persius,
     Satire 5.153.
14. 'in season . . . season': 2 Timothy 4:2. For Paulinus, see *Life of
     Melania the Elder*, note 3.
15. 'I do . . . teach': 1 Timothy 2:12.
16. *On First Principles*: By Origen, it was translated from Greek to
     Latin by Jerome's former friend Rufinus, to whom Jerome refers to
     as 'the scorpion' below. Jerome, having switched from being pro-
     Origen to believing Origen held heretical views, objected to this
     translation on the grounds that it had toned down some of Origen's
     doctrines, and so he prepared his own translation of it which is
     now lost. The work survives only in Rufinus' translation.
17. *Apostle*: Romans 1:8.
18. *himself*: Luke 16:8.
19. 'Do not . . . consume them': Jeremiah 14:11–12.
20. 'Do you . . . on earth': Luke 18:8.
21. *cold*: Matthew 24:12.
22. 'When you . . . belong to': Psalm 104:29, Psalm 146:4, Luke
     12:20.
23. *Jebus*: The ancient name for Jerusalem.
24. 'By night . . . fell down': Isaiah 15:1.
25. 'O God . . . bury them': Psalm 79:1–3.
26. *Who can . . . death*: Virgil, *Aeneid* 2:361–5, 369.
27. 'allow . . . heard': Virgil, *Aeneid* 6.266.
28. 'Naked . . . Lord': Job 1:21.

THE LIFE OF PAULA THE ELDER

1. 'Woe is . . . much': Psalm 120:5–6.
2. 'And its . . . overwhelm it': John 1:5.
3. 'I am . . . ancestors': Psalm 39:12.
4. 'I long . . . Christ': Philippians 1:23.
5. 'I punish . . . a thorn': 1 Corinthians 9:27, Romans 14.21, Psalms
    35:13, 41:3, 32:3.
6. 'Who will . . . peace': Psalm 55:6.
7. *the emperor . . . Cyprus*: The Council of Rome was convened in
    382 by the Emperor Theodosius and Pope Damasus to deal with
    the schism at Antioch and other matters. For Paulinus and the

Meletian schism, see *Life of Melania the Elder*, note 3. Epiphanius (310–403), bishop of Salamis, was an enthusiast for the monastic life, a supporter of Paulinus of Antioch and an opponent of Origenism and many other heresies of the time, which he documents in his work, the *Panarion*. Christians in the west tended to support Paulinus in the Meletian schism.

8. *Antony and Paul*: They were regarded as the men whose withdrawal into the Egyptian desert in the third century had sparked the desert monastic movement. Antony was the subject of a biography by Athanasius, and Jerome wrote a life of Paul of Egypt (both included in *ECL*).

9. *Flavia Domitilla*: She seems to have been related to Emperor Domitian and was accused of atheism (a charge often brought against Jews and Christians) and exiled to the island of Pandateria or Pontia. According to Jewish tradition she converted to their faith, but she is still venerated as a saint in the Greek Orthodox church.

10. *'stretched . . . islands'*: Virgil, *Aeneid* 1.173 and 3.126–7.

11. *knelt*: Acts 21:5.

12. *Josiah*: 2 Kings 23:29.

13. *house*: Acts 10:1.

14. *prophecy*: Acts 21:9.

15. *healed*: Acts 9:39–41, 32–4.

16. *from*: John 19:38.

17. *slain*: 1 Samuel 22:19.

18. *fled*: Jonah 1:3.

19. *church*: Luke 24:13–35.

20. *treaty*: Joshua 10:12–13, 9:27.

21. *Paul*: Judges 19:6–20:48.

22. *lain*: Matthew 28:2.

23. *rebuilt it*: 2 Samuel 5:6–10.

24. *'Woe . . . storm'*: Isaiah 29:1.

25. *'Its . . . Jacob'*: Psalm 87:1–2.

26. *fulfilled*: Acts 2:17–21, Joel 2:28–32.

27. *dying*: Genesis 35:18.

28. *'happy . . . tread'*: Isaiah 32:20; Isaiah also mentions the ox and the ass at 1:3. These passages, interpreted typologically, introduced the idea of the animals as essential elements in the Christian Christmas story, although they do not appear in the Gospel nativity accounts.

29. *'In . . . flesh'*: John 1:1.

30. *"And . . . Israel"*: Micah 5:2–3.

31. *"It . . . Gentiles"*: Acts 13:46.
32. *"I . . . Israel"*: Matthew 15:24.
33. *"The . . . peoples"*: Genesis 49:10.
34. *"I . . . Jacob"*: Psalm 132:3–5.
35. *"See . . . forest"*: Psalm 132:6.
36. *"We . . . rested"*: Psalm 132:7.
37. *"I . . . him"*: Psalms 132:17, 22:29–30.
38. *'Glory . . . will'*: Luke 2:14.
39. *dew*: Judges 6:37–8.
40. *doorposts*: Exodus 12:7.
41. *Gospel*: Acts 8:27–39.
42. *'bunch of grapes'*: Numbers 13:23–4.
43. *'I . . . me'*: Isaiah 63:3.
44. *glad*: Genesis 18:1, John 8:56.
45. *Joshua*: Joshua 14:15.
46. *life*: 2 Corinthians 3:6.
47. *estates*: Judges 1:13–15.
48. *debauchery*: Ephesians 5:18.
49. *brothers*: Genesis 43:34. In this section Jerome brings out the connections between the events and places in the Old Testament and the New, with their spiritual significance.
50. *Lord*: Ezekiel 11:22–5.
51. *on*: Matthew 21:5.
52. *church*: Luke 10:29–37.
53. *virtues*: Luke 19:4.
54. *water*: 2 Kings 2:19–22.
55. *race*: 2 Kings 2:8 for Elijah and Elisha; for Christ's baptism, see Matthew 3:13–15.
56. *condemned*: Joshua 7:24–5.
57. *head*: Genesis 28:11.
58. *cornerstone*: Zechariah 3:9, Isaiah 28:16.
59. *women*: Judges 21:23.
60. *faith*: John 4:5–42.
61. *water*: 1 Kings 18:4.
62. *transfigured*: Matthew 17:1–2.
63. *battle*: Judges 4.
64. *life*: Luke 7:11–17.
65. *jaw*: Judges 15:15–19.
66. *nitre*: A mineral that seems to have been used as a form of soap; Jerome here plays on the name Nitria, a place which derived its name from the collection of nitre there.
67. *'every . . . tears'*: Psalm 6:6.

68. *'I do not . . . none'*: 2 Corinthians 8:13–14, Luke 3:11.
69. *'Blessed are . . . money'*: Matthew 5:7, Ecclesiasticus 3:30, Luke 16:9, 11:41, Daniel 4:27.
70. *stones*: Revelation 21:18–21.
71. *'Skin . . . face'*: Job 2:4.
72. *tops*: Horace, *Odes* 2.10, 11–12.
73. *Edomite*: 1 Kings 11:14.
74. *Saul*: Genesis 27:41–5, 1 Samuel 21:10.
75. *"Overcome . . . good"*: Romans 12:21.
76. *"Do . . . just"*: Job 32:33.
77. *"Blessed . . . justice"*: Matthew 5:10.
78. *'When . . . lips'*: Psalms 39:1–2, 38:13.
79. *'The . . . soul'*: Deuteronomy 13:3.
80. *'You . . . tongue'*: Isaiah 28:9–11.
81. *us*: Romans 5:3–5.
82. *'if . . . eternal'*: 2 Corinthians 4:16–18.
83. *'I . . . you'*: Isaiah 49:8.
84. *'Through . . . us'*: Luke 21:19, Romans 8:18.
85. *'The . . . foolish'*: Proverbs 14:29.
86. *'when I am . . . consolation'*: 2 Corinthians 12:10, 4:7, 1 Corinthians 15:53, 2 Corinthians 1:5, 1:7.
87. *'Why . . . God'*: Psalm 42:11.
88. *'Anyone . . . save it'*: Matthew 16:24–5, Luke 9:23–4.
89. *'What . . . life'*: Matthew 16:26.
90. *'Naked . . . praised'*: Job 1:21.
91. *'Do . . . away'*: 1 John 2:15–17.
92. *'I . . . speak'*: Psalm 77:4.
93. *'Anyone . . . me'*: Matthew 10:37.
94. *'Possess . . . death'*: Psalm 79:11 (in the Latin translation from the Greek Septuagint version).
95. *'We . . . men'*: 1 Corinthians 4:9–10, 1:25.
96. *'You . . . weakness'*: Psalm 69:5.
97. *'He . . . Samaritan'*: John 8:48.
98. *'He . . . devils'*: Luke 11:15.
99. *'This is our . . . own'*: 2 Corinthians 1:12, John 15:18–19.
100. *'You know . . . me'*: Psalms 44:21, 44:17–18, Romans 8:36, Psalm 118:6.
101. *'My . . . him'*: Proverbs 3:9, Isaiah 35:4.
102. *'What . . . mildness'*: 1 Corinthians 4:21.
103. *'If . . . enough'*: 1 Timothy 6:8.
104. *'Do . . . burden'*: Ecclesiasticus 13:2.
105. *'My . . . my body'*: Psalm 63:1.

106. *'moderation . . . excess'*: Terence, *Andria* 61.
107. *'What . . . death'*: Romans 7:24.
108. *'As . . . God'*: Psalm 48:8.
109. *'You . . . happiness'*: Psalm 30:11.
110. *'My . . . night'*: Psalm 42:3.
111. *'Taste . . . king'*: Psalms 34:8, 45:1.
112. *'Behold . . . spirit'*: Isaiah 65:13–14.
113. *'As . . . God'*: Psalm 42:1–2.
114. *'the earthly . . . things'*: Wisdom 9:15.
115. *'it . . . body'*: 1 Corinthians 15:44.
116. *'Do not . . . reeds'*: Psalms 74:19, 68:30.
117. *"You . . . angels"*: Matthew 22:29–30.
118. *spear*: John 20:27.
119. *fish*: Luke 24:42.
120. *doors*: John 20:26.
121. *illusion*: Mark 5:35–43, John 11:43–4.
122. *surface*: Matthew 14:29.
123. *"Why . . . faith"*: Matthew 14:31.
124. *"Put . . . trusting"*: John 20:27.
125. *"Look . . . feet"*: Luke 24:39–40.
126. *"the Lord's . . . counsellor"*: Psalm 36:6, Romans 11:33–4.
127. *Christ*: Ephesians 4:13.
128. *'Be . . . listen'*: Deuteronomy 27:9.
129. *Paula*: The younger Paula who was only about four years old when her grandmother died: see *On the Education of Little Paula.*
130. *'Save . . . asleep'*: Luke 8:24, Psalm 44:23.
131. *'O Lord . . . wicked'*: Psalms 26:8, 84:1–2, 84:10.
132. *'Arise . . . living'*: Song of Songs 2:10–11, 12, Psalm 27:13.
133. *Dorcas*: Acts 9:39.
134. *man*: 1 Corinthians 2:9.
135. *'My . . . red'*: Song of Songs 5:10.
136. *'Flee . . . souls'*: Genesis 12:1, Jeremiah 51:6.
137. *'Your . . . God'*: Ruth 1:16.
138. *bronze*: Horace, *Odes* 3.30.1.

ON CHOOSING A LIFE OF VIRGINITY

1. *'Listen . . . beauty'*: Psalm 45:10–11.
2. *'I believe . . . living'*: Psalm 27:13.
3. *'Do . . . caught'*: Genesis 19:17.
4. *'Your . . . flesh'*: John 8:44; 1 John 3:8; Song of Songs 1:5; Psalm 45:11; Matthew 19:5.
5. *'Who . . . white'*: Song of Songs 8:5 (from the Latin version based not on the Hebrew text but on the Greek Septuagint version).
6. *'My . . . heaven'*: Isaiah 34:5.
7. *'Our . . . places'*: Ephesians 6:12.
8. *'You . . . you'*: Psalm 91:5–7.
9. *'What . . . theirs'*: 2 Kings 6:16.
10. *'Our . . . escaped'*: Psalm 124:7.
11. *jars*: 2 Corinthians 4:7.
12. *spirit*: Galatians 5:17.
13. *devour*: 1 Peter 5:8.
14. *'You . . . God'*: Psalm 104:20–21.
15. *kind*: Habakkuk 1:16.
16. *apostles*: Luke 22:31.
17. *sword*: Matthew 10:34.
18. *'If . . . Lord'*: Obadiah 1:4.
19. *'I will set . . . Almighty'*: Isaiah 14:13–14.
20. *I . . . princes'*: Psalm 82:6–7.
21. *'As . . . inclinations'*: 1 Corinthians 3:3.
22. *Christ*: Galatians 1:15.
23. *'Wretched . . . death'*: Romans 7:24.
24. *'The . . . up'*: Amos 5:2.
25. *fail*: Amos 8:13.
26. *'Anyone . . . heart'*: Matthew 5:28.
27. *'Come . . . evident'*: Isaiah 47:1–3.
28. *'The . . . colours'*: Psalm 45:9.
29. *toe*: Ezekiel 16:25.
30. *lived*: Isaiah 13:21–2.
31. *'God . . . me'*: Psalm 118:6.
32. *'Why . . . God'*: Psalm 42:11.
33. *'Unhappy . . . rock'*: Psalm 137:8–9.
34. *Christ*: 1 Corinthians 10:4.
35. *'We . . . perfumes'*: Song of Songs 1:3.
36. *'she . . . lives'*: 1 Timothy 5:6.

37. *'Do . . . ailments'*: 1 Timothy 5:23.
38. *'Wine . . . meat'*: Ephesians 5:18, Romans 14:21.
39. *self-indulgence*: Genesis 9:21–5.
40. *revel*: Exodus 32:6.
41. *God*: Genesis 19:35–8.
42. *water*: 1 Kings 19:5–6.
43. *Marah*: 2 Kings 4:40–41, Exodus 15:23–5.
44. *'Put . . . master'*: 2 Kings 6:22.
45. *Habakkuk*: Bel and the Dragon (= Daniel 14) 33–9.
46. *'greatly beloved'*: Daniel 9:23, 10:19.
47. *'Food . . . both'*: 1 Corinthians 6:13.
48. *'God . . . stomach'*: Philippians 3:19.
49. *'his strength . . . belly'*: Job 40:16.
50. *'Gird . . . man'*: Job 38:3.
51. *waist*: Matthew 3:4.
52. *Gospel*: Ephesians 6:14.
53. *'Your . . . cut'*: Ezekiel 16:4.
54. *'I . . . sight'*: Psalm 51:4.
55. *women*: 1 Kings 4:33, 11:4.
56. *sister*: 2 Samuel 13.
57. *pure*: Titus 1:15.
58. *Manichee*: Manichaeism was a popular religious movement at this time, to which Augustine, for a time, belonged. Manichees adopted a rigorously ascetic lifestyle which they believed would release the particles of cosmic light trapped in this world. See also section 38 for Mani, the originator of this dualistic movement that had spread from its beginnings in Persia in the middle of the third century.
59. *'You . . . shameless'*: Jeremiah 3:3.
60. *'Can . . . feet'*: Proverbs 6:27–8.
61. *chastity*: Matthew 13:8.
62. *'Where . . . noon'*: Song of Songs 1:7.
63. *'I . . . Christ'*: Philippians 1:23.
64. *'They . . . oven'*: Hosea 7:4.
65. *'Were . . . us'*: Luke 24:32.
66. *'Your . . . that'*: Psalm 119:140.
67. *'On . . . loves'*: Song of Songs 3:1.
68. *'Mortify . . . earth'*: Colossians 3:5.
69. *'I . . . me'*: Galatians 2:20.
70. *frost*: Psalm 119:83.
71. *'My . . . fasting'*: Psalm 109:24.
72. *'I . . . flesh'*: Psalm 102:4–5.

73. *'Bless . . . corruption'*: Psalm 103:2–4.
74. *'Because . . . tears'*: Psalm 102:9.
75. *die*: Genesis 3:16, 2:17.
76. *'Be . . . earth'*: Genesis 1:28.
77. *given*: Matthew 19:11.
78. *up*: Ecclesiastes 3:5.
79. *'Return . . . rest'*: Psalm 116:7.
80. *root*: Isaiah 11:1.
81. *'I . . . valleys'*: Song of Songs 2:1.
82. *hands*: Daniel 2:34.
83. *'His . . . me'*: Song of Songs 2:6.
84. *'Concerning . . . Lord'*: 1 Corinthians 7:25.
85. *'It . . . apostles'*: 1 Corinthians 7:7–8, 9:5.
86. *'Blessed . . . table'*: Isaiah 54:1, Psalm 128:3.
87. *'there . . . tribes'*: Psalm 105:37.
88. *'do . . . tree'*: Isaiah 56:3.
89. *'You . . . wife'*: Jeremiah 16:2.
90. *'I . . . are'*: 1 Corinthians 7:26.
91. *'The . . . not'*: 1 Corinthians 7:29.
92. *lair*: Jeremiah 4:7.
93. *'Thirst . . . them'*: Lamentations 4:4.
94. *shoulders*: Isaiah 9:6.
95. *'If . . . me'*: Matthew 16:24.
96. *so*: Matthew 8:21–2.
97. *head*: Matthew 8:20.
98. *'The . . . husband'*: 1 Corinthians 7:32–4.
99. *'If . . . life'*: 1 Corinthians 7:28.
100. *Tertullian's . . . sister*: Tertullian lived in North Africa around 200: his work, addressed to a philosophic friend, also referred to as *On Virginity*, is now lost. He also wrote *On the Veiling of Virgins*. Cyprian was martyred at Carthage in 258: he wrote a work on the appropriate dress for virgins. Pope Damasus died in 384, while Jerome was working for him on a translation of the Bible; no works on virginity by Damasus have survived, though a number of Latin verses are published in *PL* 13: 347–418. Ambrose (d. 397) wrote *Concerning Virginity, Concerning Virgins, Exhortation to a Virgin* and *Admonition to a Fallen Virgin*.
101. *'The . . . chosen'*: Matthew 10:22, 24:13, 22:14.
102. *dead*: 2 Samuel 6:6–7.
103. *covet*: 2 Kings 20:13–18.
104. *cups*: Daniel 5:2–3.
105. *'Your . . . desolate'*: Matthew 23:38.

106. 'Martha . . . her': Luke 10:41–2.

107. 'I . . . go': Song of Songs 3:4.

108. 'My . . . her': Song of Songs 6:9.

109. opening: Song of Songs 5:4.

110. 'A . . . fountain': Song of Songs 5:8, 4:12.

111. raped: Genesis 34:5.

112. 'I . . . love': Song of Songs 3:2.

113. 'Have . . . loves': Song of Songs 3:3.

114. 'Strait . . . life': Matthew 7:14.

115. 'I . . . me': Song of Songs 3:1.

116. city: Song of Songs 5:7.

117. 'I . . . awake': Song of Songs 5:2.

118. 'My . . . breasts': Song of Songs 1:13.

119. "Tell . . . companions": Song of Songs 1:7.

120. 'If . . . tents': Song of Songs 1:8.

121. 'My . . . passed': Isaiah 26:20.

122. precept: Matthew 6:6.

123. 'It . . . one': Song of Songs 5:2.

124. 'I . . . dirty': Song of Songs 5:3.

125. 'I . . . away': Song of Songs 5:6.

126. 'If . . . place': Ecclesiastes 10:4.

127. Jerusalem: Daniel 6:10.

128. 'Death . . . windows': Jeremiah 9:21.

129. 'How . . . another': John 5:44.

130. 'You . . . Lord': Psalm 3:3; 1 Corinthians 1:31.

131. 'If . . . servant': Galatians 1:10.

132. 'May . . . world': Galatians 6:14.

133. 'In . . . Lord': Psalm 44:8.

134. 'O . . . high': Psalm 131:1.

135. 'God . . . themselves': Psalm 53:5.

136. truth: 2 Timothy 3:6–7.

137. 'We . . . tricks': 2 Corinthians 2:11.

138. 'I . . . Christ': 2 Corinthians 11:2.

139. 'It . . . passion': 1 Corinthians 7:9.

140. 'Bad . . . morals': 1 Corinthians 15:33.

141. 'when . . . commitment': 1 Timothy 5:11–12.

142. Belial: 2 Corinthians 6:14–15.

143. gratitude: Titus 1:15, 1 Timothy 4:4.

144. also: Matthew 6:21.

145. 'Who . . . hell': Psalm 6:5.

146. 'Have . . . me': Psalm 57:1.

147. 'If . . . own': Luke 16:12.

148. 'The . . . wealth': Proverbs 13:8.
149. mammon: Matthew 6:24; Luke 16:13.
150. 'Do . . . them': Matthew 6:25–6.
151. 'This . . . arrogant': 2 Corinthians 12:10, 12:7.
152. Lord: Psalm 97:8.
153. 'Naked . . . it': Job 1:21, 1 Timothy 6:7.
154. evil: 1 Timothy 6:10.
155. you: Matthew 6:33.
156. 'I . . . bread': Psalm 37:25.
157. him: 1 Kings 17:6.
158. it: 1 Kings 17:10–15.
159. 'I . . . walk': Acts 3:6.
160. 'If . . . God': Genesis 28:20.
161. 'May . . . you': Acts 8:20.
162. 'Who . . . rest': Psalm 55:6.
163. Philo . . . Captivity: The early first-century writer Philo provides
     information about the Essenes in his treatise *That Every Good
     Man Is Free*. The work referred to by Josephus, writing in the
     second half of the first century, is usually known as *The Jewish
     War*: in 2.119–61 he discusses the Essenes.
164. ever: Lamentations 3:27–30.
165. 'The . . . portion': Psalm 73:26.
166. ceasing: 1 Thessalonians 5:17.
167. stand: Romans 14:4.
168. 'This . . . Lord': Isaiah 58:5.
169. 'For . . . me': Isaiah 58:3–4.
170. faith: This seems to be a conflation of 1 Timothy 1:19–20 and 2
     Timothy 1:15.
171. heart: 1 Samuel 16:7.
172. 'Let . . . spirit': 1 Corinthians 7:34.
173. 'Hail . . . you': Luke 1:28.
174. 'Take . . . brothers': Isaiah 8:1–3, Matthew 12:49.
175. innocent: Joshua 6:17, 25.
176. Christ: Philippians 1:23.
177. 'Who . . . sword': Romans 8:35.
178. 'For . . . Lord': Romans 8:38–9.
179. 'How . . . ones': Psalm 116:12, 13, 15.
180. 'For . . . accepts': Hebrews 12:6.
181. 'So . . . her': Genesis 29:20.
182. 'By . . . night': Genesis 31:40.
183. us: Romans 8:18.
184. us: Romans 5:3–5.

185. 'in . . . clothes': 2 Corinthians 11:23–7.
186. 'I . . . me': 2 Timothy 4:7–8.
187. 'The . . . force': Matthew 11:12.
188. sacrament: Matthew 7:7–9.
189. angels: 1 Corinthians 6:3.
190. conceived: 1 Corinthians 2:9.
191. 'Let . . . sea': Exodus 15:1.
192. 'Rise . . . gone': Song of Songs 2:10–11.
193. 'Who . . . sun': Song of Songs 6:10.
194. 'See . . . me': Isaiah 8:18.
195. 'Hosanna . . . highest': Matthew 21:9.
196. women: Revelation 14:4.
197. 'Set . . . it': Song of Songs 8:6–7.

ON THE EDUCATION OF LITTLE PAULA

1. 'If . . . holy': 1 Corinthians 7:13–14.
2. 'What . . . God': Luke 18:27.
3. paradise: Luke 23:43.
4. animals: Daniel 4:33.
5. overthrown: The temple of Serapis at Alexandria had been destroyed in 391 as part of the Christian emperors' plan to eradicate pagan worship. The temple of Marnas (the Hellenistic manifestation of the Semitic god Dagon) at Gaza was destroyed in 402, around the time that this letter was written.
6. flagon: Horace, Ars Poetica 21.
7. in: 1 Samuel 1:22, Judges 13:3–5, Luke 1:41.
8. purple: Horace, Epistles 1.2.70.
9. wishes: Both Praetextata and Hymetius, the brother of Eustochium's father Toxotius, seem to have died in 384, at about the time Jerome was writing Letter 22 to Eustochium to persuade her to adhere to a life of austerity (see On Choosing a Life of Virginity).
10. 'she . . . chastity': 1 Timothy 2:15.
11. says: Jonah 4:11.
12. die: Ezekiel 18:4.
13. 'He . . . himself': John 9:21.
14. 'All . . . within': Psalm 45:13.
15. 'The . . . bedroom': Song of Songs 1:4.
16. 'I . . . dirty': Song of Songs 8:10, 5:3.
17. 'You . . . habit': Publilius Syrus, Saying 180.
18. self-indulgence: Ephesians 5:18.

19. '*Go . . . multiply*': Genesis 35:11.
20. *embraces*: Ecclesiastes 3:5.
21. *children*: 1 Samuel 1:22.

ON VISITING JERUSALEM

1.   *Minerva*: The Latin proverb 'sus docet Minervam' (meaning 'a pig is teaching Minerva (goddess of wisdom)') implies that someone is trying to teach an expert something about which he or she knows nothing.
2.   '*Go . . . you*': Genesis 12:1.
3.   *Sion*: Psalm 137:1.
4.   *Jerusalem*: Ezekiel 8:3.
5.   *God*: Luke 1:26–31, 39.
6.   *Saviour*: Genesis 14:18.
7.   '*Order . . . me*': Song of Songs 2:4.
8.   '*Awake . . . light*': Ephesians 5:14.
9.   *mountains*: Psalm 87:1–2.
10. '*Your . . . you*': Matthew 23:37–8.
11. '*Let . . . place*': Josephus, *The Jewish War* 6.5.
12. *plentifully*: Romans 5:20.
13. '*Go . . . peoples*': Matthew 28:19.
14. '*It . . . Gentiles*': Acts 13:46.
15. '*His . . . glorious*': Isaiah 11:10.
16. "*The . . . crucified*": Revelation 11:7–8.
17. '*Rise . . . months*': Revelation 11:2.
18. '*The . . . gold*': Revelation 21:16–18.
19. '*Sodom . . . old*': Ezekiel 16:55.
20. '*I . . . believe*': Jude 5.
21. '*And . . . day*': Jude 6.
22. '*Sodom . . . fire*': Jude 7.
23. '*The . . . many*': Matthew 27:51–3.
24. *footstool*: Psalm 132:7.
25. *king*: Matthew 5:35.
26. '*What . . . Jesus*': Acts 21:13.
27. *world*: Virgil, *Aeneid* 1.67.
28. '*Wherever . . . gather*': Matthew 24:28.
29. *virtue*: In *Letter* 58.2 Jerome tells Paulinus that the important thing is not to have visited Jerusalem but to have lived a virtuous life while there.
30. *master*: Romans 14:4.

31. *Lord*: Matthew 7:1.
32. *Tarpeian rock*: A steep cliff overlooking the Forum in Rome, from the top of which criminals were hurled to their deaths.
33. *'Come . . . her'*: Revelation 18:4.
34. *'Flee . . . punishment'*: Jeremiah 51:6.
35. *'Babylon . . . spirit'*: Revelation 18:2.
36. *Lord*: John 11:43–4, Matthew 3:13.
37. *sheepfolds*: Luke 2:8.
38. *mausoleum*: 1 Kings 2:10.
39. *rock*: Amos 1:1.
40. *wives*: Sarah, Rebekah and Leah (Genesis 49:31).
41. *Philip*: Acts 8:36.
42. *persecution*: 1 Kings 18:4.
43. *wine*: John 2:1–11.
44. *people*: Matthew 14:15–21, 15:32–8.
45. *life*: Luke 7:11–16.
46. *beaten*: Psalm 83:9–10.
47. *'I . . . go'*: Song of Songs 3:4.

THE LIFE OF MELANIA THE YOUNGER
(GERONTIUS)

1.   *Scripture*: Proverbs 9:9.
2.   *jewels*: Wisdom 7:9.
3.   *man*: 1 Corinthians 2:9.
4.   *talents*: Reference to one of Christ's parables: Matthew 18:24.
5.   *'Let . . . doing'*: Matthew 6:3.
6.   *'Listen . . . own'*: Psalm 45:10–11, Lamentations 3:27–8.
7.   *'When . . . Olives'*: Luke 21:37.
8.   *'Love . . . yourself'*: Mark 12:31.
9.   *us*: Job 31:32.
10. *'If . . . me'*: Matthew 19:21.
11. *emperor*: Honorius, one of the sons of Theodosius the Great, was western Roman emperor from 395 until his death in 423.
12. *kings*: Proverbs 21:1.
13. *Serena*: Mother-in-law of Emperor Honorius. She was usually based in Ravenna, but visited Rome on occasion. She was put to death in 409 for suspected collaboration with Alaric, the barbarian leader.
14. *'I . . . off'*: Song of Songs 5:3.
15. *heads*: 1 Corinthians 11:13.
16. *we*: The use of the first person plural implies that Gerontius

himself was present at the meeting. This is the only indication
that he knew Melania before she moved to Jerusalem, at a time
when it is thought he would still have been very young.

17. *her husband*: Honorius was the empress' son-in-law, not her husband. The Greek text gives 'brother' rather than 'husband' at
this point, presumably meaning 'spiritual brother'.

18. *coins*: Luke 21:2.

19. *steal*: Matthew 6:20.

20. *down*: It was burnt in 410 during Alaric's attack on Rome.

21. *'Listen . . . you'*: Genesis 21:12.

22. *world*: Ephesians 6:12.

23. *him*: 1 Corinthians 2:9.

24. *'He . . . ever'*: Psalm 112:9.

25. *Alypius*: He appears frequently in the *Confessions* as Augustine's
closest friend from an early age, and his companion at the time
of his conversion experience (*Confessions* 8.12). Thagaste (in
present-day Algeria) was the native town of both Alypius and
Augustine.

26. *someone*: 2 Corinthians 12:2; in other words, Melania talks of
herself in the third person.

27. *'The . . . soul'*: Wisdom 1:11.

28. *root*: Matthew 7:17–20.

29. *'We . . . done'*: Luke 17:10.

30. *short*: 1 Corinthians 7:29.

31. *God*: 1 Corinthians 6:18–19.

32. *'Sell . . . heaven'*: Matthew 19:21.

33. *'Ask . . . you'*: Matthew 7:7.

34. *"The . . . us"*: Romans 8:18.

35. *jaws*: Amos 3:12, 2 Timothy 4:17.

36. *Cellia*: Kellia ('the Cells') and Nitria ('the place of nitre') lie a
day's walk from each other some forty miles south-east of Alexandria. Both were settled by large numbers of people, starting in
the 330s, who sought to lead a life of austerity, removed from
civilization.

37. *Paula*: This must have been Paula the younger, granddaughter of
Paula the elder: see *On the Education of Little Paula*. Paula was
not Melania's niece but her second cousin – Paula's maternal
grandfather Albinus (mentioned in *On the Education*) was the
uncle of Melania the younger's mother Albina. The use of 'niece'
is probably explained by the fact that Melania was about twenty
years older than Paula. It seems that Paula spent Christmas 439
with Melania; see also sections 63 and 68.

38. *'Anyone . . . mouth'*: Jeremiah 15:19.
39. *Lausus*: A high-ranking imperial official, the dedicatee of Palladius' *Lausiac History*, to which he gave his name.
40. *sins*: 1 Peter 4:8.
41. *do*: 1 Corinthians 13:2.
42. *God*: Hebrews 12:14.
43. *"The . . . confusion"*: Psalm 53:5.
44. *'In . . . you'*: Psalm 119:55, 147, 62.
45. *heaven*: Matthew 11:12.
46. *hour*: Matthew 20:1–7.
47. *Eudoxia*: She married the Emperor Valentinian III in 439. She is not to be confused with her mother, the Empress Eudocia, wife of Theodosius II and friend of Melania the younger. Eudocia made a pilgrimage to the Holy Land in 438–9 and was the author of poems and biblical paraphrases.
48. *him*: Psalm 145:19.
49. *'It . . . masters'*: Matthew 15:27.
50. *"Lord . . . law"*: Psalm 94:11–12.
51. *"Sell . . . me"*: Matthew 19:21, 16:24.
52. *'protecting . . . flesh'*: 2 Corinthians 6:7, 2 Timothy 4:7–8, Philippians 1:23–4.
53. *depart*: Philippians 1:23.
54. *"Cursed . . . carelessly"*: Jeremiah 48:10.
55. *'Stay . . . end'*: Luke 24:29.
56. *fight*: 2 Timothy 4:7.
57. *'Come . . . master'*: Matthew 25:21.
58. *him*: 1 Corinthians 2:9.

THE LIFE OF MELANIA THE YOUNGER
(PALLADIUS)

1. *'Wife . . . husband'*: 1 Corinthians 7:16.
2. *thirteen years old*: Gerontius says Melania was married 'at the age of about fourteen' (section 1).
3. *Olympias*: Became famous as a wealthy widow in Constantinople in the early fifth century. She, too, renounced her wealth, chose not to remarry and became the devoted friend of Bishop John Chrysostom; some of his letters to her, many written while he was in exile, survive.
4. *jaws*: Amos 3:12: see also Gerontius' *Life*, note 35.

Map

*The Roman Empire Around the Mediterranean
in Late Antiquity*

The Roman Empire Around the Mediterranean in Late Antiquity

CALEDONIA

Hibernia

York

BRITANNIA

London

Oceanus
Atlanticus

R. Rhine

R. Seine
Paris
Trier

R. Loire

Poitiers

R. Rhone

Lyons

Milan

Aquileia

R. Po

Ravenna

R. Danube

PANNONIA

Split

ITALIA

Adriatic Sea

CORSICA

Rome

Emerita

R. Guadalquivir

Cordoba

Seville

SARDINIA

Naples

Tyrrhenian
Sea

Lilybaeum

SICILIA

MAURETANIA

Hippo

Carthage

Syracuse

Thagaste

NUMIDIA

Mediterranean

N

AFRICA

1,000 mls

1,600 km

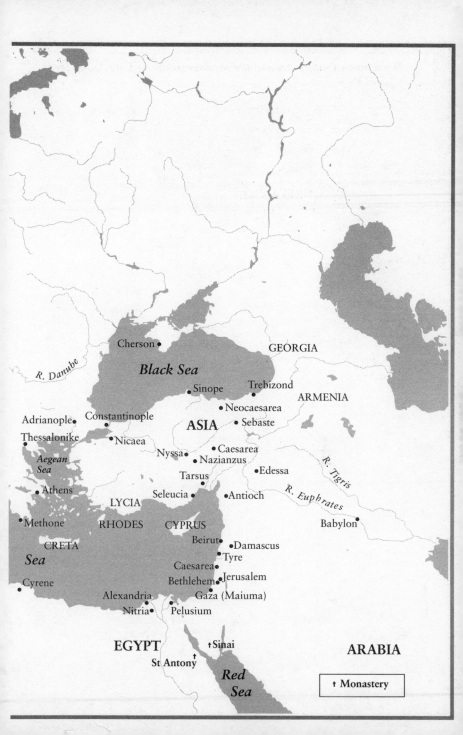

Family Tree

The family of Melania the elder, Melania the younger, Paula the elder, Marcella, Eustochium, Laeta and Paula the younger

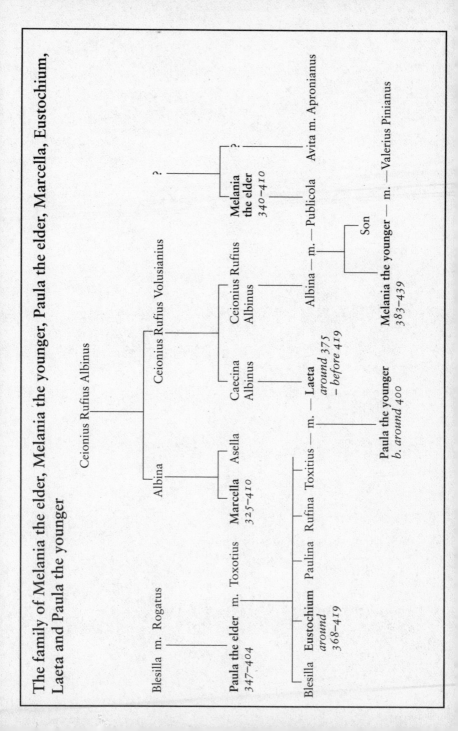

Index

Names of countries, cities and biblical sites have not been included; neither have references to Jerome because of their ubiquity.

THE STORY OF PENGUIN CLASSICS

Before 1946 ... 'Classics' are mainly the domain of academics and students; readable editions for everyone else are almost unheard of. This all changes when a little-known classicist, E. V. Rieu, presents Penguin founder Allen Lane with the translation of Homer's *Odyssey* that he has been working on in his spare time.

1946 Penguin Classics debuts with *The Odyssey*, which promptly sells three million copies. Suddenly, classics are no longer for the privileged few.

1950s Rieu, now series editor, turns to professional writers for the best modern, readable translations, including Dorothy L. Sayers's *Inferno* and Robert Graves's unexpurgated *Twelve Caesars*.

1960s The Classics are given the distinctive black covers that have remained a constant throughout the life of the series. Rieu retires in 1964, hailing the Penguin Classics list as 'the greatest educative force of the twentieth century.'

1970s A new generation of translators swells the Penguin Classics ranks, introducing readers of English to classics of world literature from more than twenty languages. The list grows to encompass more history, philosophy, science, religion and politics.

1980s The Penguin American Library launches with titles such as *Uncle Tom's Cabin*, and joins forces with Penguin Classics to provide the most comprehensive library of world literature available from any paperback publisher.

1990s The launch of Penguin Audiobooks brings the classics to a listening audience for the first time, and in 1999 the worldwide launch of the Penguin Classics website extends their reach to the global online community.

The 21st Century Penguin Classics are completely redesigned for the first time in nearly twenty years. This world-famous series now consists of more than 1300 titles, making the widest range of the best books ever written available to millions – and constantly redefining what makes a 'classic'.

The Odyssey continues ...

The best books ever written

PENGUIN (🐧) CLASSICS

SINCE 1946

Find out more at www.penguinclassics.com